MORAL

SENTIMENTALISM

MORAL

SENTIMENTALISM

Michael Slote

OXFORD

UNIVERSITY PRESS

OXFORD

UNIVERSITY PRESS

Oxford University Press is a department of the University of Oxford.
It furthers the University's objective of excellence in research, scholarship,
and education by publishing worldwide.

Oxford   New York
Auckland   Cape Town   Dar es Salaam   Hong Kong   Karachi
Kuala Lumpur   Madrid   Melbourne   Mexico City   Nairobi
New Delhi   Shanghai   Taipei   Toronto

With offices in
Argentina   Austria   Brazil   Chile   Czech Republic   France   Greece
Guatemala   Hungary   Italy   Japan   Poland   Portugal   Singapore
South Korea   Switzerland   Thailand   Turkey   Ukraine   Vietnam

Oxford is a registered trade mark of Oxford University Press
in the UK and certain other countries.

Published in the United States of America by
Oxford University Press
198 Madison Avenue, New York, NY 10016

Library of Congress Cataloging-in-Publication Data
Slote, Michael A.
Moral sentimentalism / Michael Slote.
   p. cm.
ISBN 978-0-19-539144-2 (hardcover); 978-0-19-997570-9 (paperback)
1. Ethics. 2. Caring. 3. Empathy. I. Title.
BJ1031.S585   2009
171'.2—dc22   2009011851

Printed in the United States of America
on acid-free paper

To
David Hume,
sine qua non

PREFACE

This book attempts to deal with both metaethical and normative moral issues in sentimentalist terms, and I believe it offers a more thoroughgoing, a more systematic, defense of moral sentimentalism than anything that has appeared since Hume's *Treatise of Human Nature*. What I am offering also seems to me to be more Humean than anything that has been written about sentimentalism since Hume's day. This explains why I have chosen to dedicate the book to Hume, but at this early stage, it is also open to misunderstanding. I am enormously indebted to Hume, but I also disagree with him in a number of very important ways.

For example, I think Hume's account of the artificial virtues is seriously inadequate, and I have given my reasons in an article "Hume on the Artificial Virtues" (appearing in my *Essays on the History of Ethics*, Oxford University Press, 2009). But I also think present-day sentimentalism should explain the morality of "justice" and "honesty" (and a lot more besides) in terms of what Hume would call "natural virtues." So rather than attempt to give a better account of the artificial virtues than Hume offered, I have circumvented the idea of such virtues altogether.

I also think that Hume got the phenomenology of approval and disapproval wrong, but I have sought, in what follows, to show how a better account of those phenomena (one actually suggested by Hume, later in the *Treatise*, in an almost offhand manner) can lead us to a viable explanation of the meaning of moral terms. Hume was, I believe, the first or one of the first to suggest such modern-day metaethical views as emotivism and subjectivism, but the present book—for reasons to be mentioned in just a moment—defends, instead, a semi-Kripkean reference-fixing account of moral terminology that allows moral utterances, moral claims, to have genuine objective validity, more validity than any semantic ideas suggested by Hume would allow for. However, *like* Hume, I shall be understanding moral meaning in relation to a theory of approval and disapproval that can be formulated in strictly sentimentalist terms and that, in particular, relies on what Hume called sympathy, but we now refer to as empathy.

The present book is also a lot more interested in feminist ideals and aspirations than Hume ever was (despite Annette Baier's compelling idea that Hume might be considered the "women's moral theorist"). And my politics are far to the left of anything Hume would have been comfortable with. The fact is that there has been a lot of water under the bridge since Hume's day, and it is now possible—probably even imperative—to deploy Humean and sentimentalist ideas in directions never anticipated by and quite possibly repugnant to earlier sentimentalists. Moreover, I am defending *just* sentimentalism, not the larger conceptual/metaphysical empiricism in which Hume's original moral sentimentalism was deeply embedded.

At the normative level, I am a care ethicist, but I don't think care ethicists have been hoping for or expecting a book like the present one. Most care ethicists haven't been terribly interested in metaethical or semantic issues, but I am hoping that this book will convince them that a sentimentalist approach to metaethical issues has something to offer them. I believe that such an approach helps to deepen, and gives additional support to, care ethics as a normative moral view.

And let me say something, finally, to those working in metaethics who have in recent years defended sentimentalist or neosentimentalist ideas in that area. Much of this work has been done by people coming out of cognitive science, and much of it has favored semantic views like emotivism and subjectivism. But what I think has been to some extent ignored in this process is how things look, and are reasonably understood, from a standpoint *within* moral theory and theorizing. Those who do such theorizing often have a sense of purpose: namely, to make good on the common or ordinary thought/intuition that moral utterances have, or at least claim to have, a certain objective validity. If one gives no weight or insufficient weight to that intuition, one skimps somewhat on one's own moral heritage (or inheritance), both as a member of the "folk" and as a potential contributor to the discipline known as moral philosophy. And my fear and suspicion is that many of those who do metaethics out of cognitive science and/or are satisfied with arguing against the objectivity of moral claims don't have enough of a stake in ordinary moral thought and in ongoing moral philosophy. They approach such thought and such philosophy so much from the outside that they miss the force and validity of what goes on *inside* these modes of human thinking and understanding. In other words, I believe it is a mistake to go at issues in metaethics on the basis of mainly scientific concepts and without according a certain presumptive force to ideas within the discipline of ethics itself—and if in this respect I sound like some sort of ethical rationalist, that is a comparison I welcome. Sentimentalists or this sentimentalist may disagree sharply with rationalists about a number of basic and less basic issues, but what we have in common, most of us, is a commitment to take ethics very, very seriously on its own terms. So it is my hope, in fact, that the present book, by offering rationalists a very systematic challenge to their own (various) views, will stir up a dialogue, or an argument, that the field of ethics itself can only, ultimately, benefit from.

ACKNOWLEDGMENTS

Many people have given me helpful suggestions during the writing of this book, among them: Jonathan Adler, Stephen Angle, Dennis Arjo, Larry Blum, Kristin Borgwald, Susan Brison, Claudia Card, Daniel Cohen, Brad Cokelet, Howard Curzer, Stephen Darwall, Raul de Velasco, Marilyn Friedman, Daniel Hampikian, James Harold, Seisuke Hayakawa, Eva Kittay, Keith Lehrer, Charles Pigden, Elizabeth Radcliffe, Philipp Schwind, Harvey Siegel, Christine Swanton, Mark Warren, and a reader for Oxford University Press.

I have a larger kind of debt to Nel Noddings and Carol Gilligan, whose advocacy of "care ethics" was what primarily influenced me to move away from Aristotelianism toward an ever more sentimentalist view of morality. (In addition, I am indebted to Noddings for specific advice about the present book.)

I would also like to thank Peter Ohlin for supporting this book project through two very separate incarnations, over a period of several years. And last, but very far from being least, I want to thank Jane, who has brought great joy into my life and who has been wonderfully supportive in intellectual ways as well.

CONTENTS

MORAL

SENTIMENTALISM

INTRODUCTION

Choosing the title I have chosen for this book is a serious business. We think of moral sentimentalism as an important moral-philosophical movement of the eighteenth century, associated with the great names of Hume, Hutcheson, and Adam Smith, and the idea of defending that sentimentalism in contemporary terms or on the contemporary scene is not all that familiar. People—philosophers—don't go around saying they are defending or trying to revive moral sentimentalism "across the board" or in a systematic and thoroughgoing manner, but that is precisely what I am going to attempt to do here.

To be sure, a certain amount of moral sentimentalism can be found in recent work in metaethics. What else, for example, is Simon Blackburn's projective theory of the meaning of moral terminology or moral utterances? Blackburn clearly and explicitly bases his metaethical views on ideas he and we associate with Hume more than we do with any other philosopher. But as far as I know, Blackburn doesn't offer any kind of general defense of normative sentimentalism (à la Hume or anyone else). Other recent work in metaethics—for example, by Allan Gibbard, Shaun Nichols, Jesse Prinz, Justin D'Arms—has sometimes attracted the label "(neo-)sentimentalist," but such approaches often mix sentimentalist with rationalist elements, as, for example, when rightness is conceived as what it is rational to have certain sorts of emotional reactions to. And in addition, these philosophers don't offer any sort of distinctive, sentimentalist account of normative ethics.

Where normative sentimentalism *is* being systematically revived nowadays is in the ethics of care and in some recent approaches to virtue ethics that look to Hume rather than to Aristotle or the Stoics for normative inspiration.

I have been and am such a virtue ethicist myself, but since that aspect of my thinking tends to blend in with my interest in and commitment to care ethics, let me focus here on the latter. Nel Noddings, the first person to explicitly formulate an ethics of care or caring, was also explicit about the influence of or similarity to Hume, and the connection with Hume and with Hume's emphasis on the sentiments—what we would nowadays speak of as emotions and feeling(s)—is certainly clear in care ethics as a normative approach to moral issues, that is, as giving us and defending substantive moral judgments. Some recent care ethicists have also investigated various important epistemological issues surrounding the justification of moral judgments, and to that extent, care ethics has engaged in metaethical thought and speculation. But this care-ethical interest in the metaethical has not, as far as I know, extended to issues about the meaning of moral terms, issues that Hume (in a somewhat vague and inconsistent, but often insightful fashion) addressed and dealt with in a distinctively sentimentalist way.

I think any complete revival of sentimentalism has to be interested in semantic/metaethical issues as much as normative ones, just as Hume was, and has to tie these together, too, though not necessarily in exactly the same way in which Hume attempted to do so. So I am using the title I have adopted for this book because I want to address semantic issues in a distinctively sentimentalist fashion and show how a sentimentalist metaethics of moral terms illuminates and supports—and is at the same time supported by—what a thoroughly sentimentalist normative care ethics has to say about individual and political morality.

More particularly, I shall approach both metaethics and normative ethics via the notion or phenomenon of empathy. Hume, of course, based much of his discussion of metaethical and normative issues on what he referred to as sympathy and we would probably call empathy. But we today know a lot more about empathy/sympathy (and how it develops) than was known in Hume's day, and I aim to make use of some of these new ideas/results in my discussions both of normative morality and of metaethical issues.

The fact that empathy arguably constitutes the basis for both metaethics and normative ethics will, I hope, make the overall sentimentalist picture we arrive at seem desirably unified. A sentimentalist theory that brings together and integrates its discussion of normative issues and its treatment of metaethical issues (and applies the result to questions of moral education as well) has obvious theoretical advantages over any form of sentimentalism that concentrates exclusively either on normative or on metaethical/semantic issues, and so I will try to deal systematically with both these areas of ethics in what follows, just as Hume attempted to do more than two hundred years ago. The answers I shall arrive at in normative ethics and in metaethics will in substantial ways differ from what Hume says about these topics—and this will also be true of what I say about moral education in the light of my overall metaethical and normative discussion. But rather than engage in a lengthy consideration of those forms of "neosentimentalism" that don't seek to extend themselves to the whole of ethics and don't seem in any clear way *capable* of such extension, I have been led by the advantages of taking a more systematic or general sentimentalist position to concentrate on those sentimentalist ideas that I think *can* be used for such more general purposes. In effect, my goal here is to try to defend moral sentimentalism on something like the scale one finds in Hume's moral philosophy—something that hasn't, I believe, been done since Hume's day.

This is a very tall order (even granting that I don't have Hume's more general epistemological and metaphysical aspirations), and I have over the years been in varying degrees unsure about how or even whether to proceed with the present project. At various points, I haven't seen how to make good on arguments or positions that are quite essential to anything like the present enterprise, and I have always been aware of the numerous trenchant or worrisome criticisms that have been leveled at moral sentimentalism over the past two and a half centuries. I am fairly contented with what I have now produced, but since I won't really be able to know how well my ideas and arguments work till I see how the philosophical community responds to them, that very fact has given me a strong motive to publish my thoughts, a motive that at this point has, obviously, been effective.

Since this book will be arguing that the idea or phenomenon of empathy forms the basis not only for acting morally but also for understanding what we are doing when we make moral judgments, I think our first task here must be to get a bit clearer about what empathy is and how it operates. As I suggested or hinted before, Hume was aware of the phenomenon of empathy—perhaps more so than any previous philosopher. But he in fact lacked a specific word for it. The term *empathy* wasn't invented till early in the twentieth century, but Hume could and did talk about what we refer to as empathy using the term *sympathy*—though things are complicated by the fact that he often (especially in the *Enquiry Concerning the Principles of Morals*) uses the term *sympathy* to refer to what we think of nowadays as sympathy rather than empathy. Roughly speaking (and I will have more to say about this in chapter 1), the difference between sympathy and empathy corresponds to the distinction between feeling (sorry) for someone who is in pain and (like Bill Clinton) *feeling their pain*. And I shall be arguing overall in this book that empathy is a motivating psychological mechanism that constitutes a key element both in ordinary moral motivation and in the making and understanding of moral claims. In chapter 1, I hope to say enough about empathy so that I can subsequently make use of the notion to explain the meaning of moral terms or utterances, and after having done that, I want to use the notion to explain (further) why we make the specific normative/moral judgments we commonsensically do make. I shall consider a large range of commonsense moral and political claims and issues and show how a metaethically backed normative sentimentalism can account for and clarify them. But at this point, I think it might be helpful if I summarized the book's argument chapter by chapter.

As I indicated, chapter 1 focuses on the nature of empathy. Hume had a lot to say about empathy, and there is much to be learned from him. (Some of his ideas are anticipated by Malebranche, whom he studied, and by various Chinese philosophers he presumably had never heard of. But it is worth noting that certain Chinese thinkers—such as Wang Yang-ming in the sixteenth century CE, Cheng Hao in the eleventh century CE, and even Mencius in the fourth century BCE—seem to be talking about empathy long before that ever occurred in Western philosophy.) However, there is a vast recent psychological literature on empathy that takes us well beyond Hume (or the Chinese philosophers) and that can be of great use to us in a project like the present one. Chapter 1 highlights certain important features of that literature and discusses their bearing on moral sentimentalism. In particular, it discusses two books— C. D. Batson's *The Altruism Question* and Martin Hoffman's *Empathy and Moral Development*—that summarize the recent psychological literature and argue that the development of different kinds of empathy plays a crucial role in the development of genuinely altruistic, caring motivation. Both books also maintain that the capacity for empathy increases as a child becomes cognitively more sophisticated about other people and what makes their lives go better or worse—and Hoffman's book in particular offers an account of moral education based on empathy that squares very well with sentimentalist ideas about the nature of morality. Hoffman and (to a lesser extent) Batson also point out certain "biases" that are built into empathy, like the preference for what one sees or perceives over what one merely hears about, and chapter 1 will say a good deal about these biases and the way they correspond to normative moral distinctions we intuitively and commonsensically want to make. (Given this latter fact or assumption, it is perhaps better to speak of "partiality" rather than of "bias.")

Chapter 1 will also take up some important issues about moral education in the light of Martin Hoffman's recent work in that area. Hume said much too little on this topic, but Hoffman's discussion of the empathic mechanisms/ processes of what he calls "inductive discipline" offers moral sentimentalism a chance to say more about how altruistic caring and moral dispositions more generally develop and can be made to develop in children (or adults). However, a full-blown sentimentalist account of moral education needs to take Hoffman's views much further than Hoffman himself has taken them, and chapter 1 will have a good deal to say about how this can be accomplished.

Chapter 2 makes use of the previous discussion of empathy to begin a discussion of the meaning of moral terms or utterances. What is distinctive of—and perhaps most suspect about—sentimentalist theories of moral language is the idea that certain affective psychological states form the basis for moral judgment, the idea, in other words, that we can ultimately account for or understand the meaning of moral terms and utterances in terms of certain affective psychological states and the ways we operate upon (or work with) them. In particular, the psychological states that sentimentalism paradigmatically considers to be the basis of moral judgment are states of approval and disapproval, and that means that sentimentalism has to regard approval and disapproval as affective states that don't presuppose the very moral utterances or judgments they are supposed to ground and (be used to) clarify. This has seemed implausible or ridiculous to many philosophers over the centuries because it has seemed to them obvious that one can't, say, disapprove of someone's conduct unless one thinks it is wrong or less good than it should be. But if disapproval presupposes or involves explicitly moral thinking, it can't be used to ground and account for such thinking.

A full sentimentalist metaethics needs to be able to answer this objection in clear and plausible terms, and chapter 2 seeks to do so. It discusses Hume's, Hutcheson's, and (to a lesser extent) Smith's views of the nature of moral approval, and the criticisms it makes of these views lead toward a conception of moral approval and disapproval that borrows from the earlier sentimentalists but crucially differs from them. Chapter 2 attempts to show that approval and disapproval can best be conceived in sentimentalist terms if they are viewed as involving certain kinds of empathic reactions to moral agents and what they do (rather than to the results of what they do). And it makes clear that what it calls approval doesn't involve or presuppose any sort of moral judgment (though, as with most adult empathy, it certainly has cognitive aspects).

Chapter 3 continues the argument and attempts to show how the new theory or conception of moral approval and disapproval helps to explain various key features of moral judgment or utterances: for example, that they typically motivate, that they can be positive and negative, and that they are self-other asymmetric. Many rationalists have held that the action-guiding or motivating character of moral judgments doesn't preclude their having an objective or cognitive status, and chapter 3 uses the present account of approval and moral judgment to show how metaethical sentimentalism can also make that claim.

But it is possible to use our empathy-based notion of approval (or disapproval) and the assumption that moral judgment requires attitudes of approval (or disapproval) not only to account for various *important features* of moral judgment but also to offer a specific explication of the meaning of moral judgments and terms. Chapter 4 argues that we can accomplish this if we borrow from Saul Kripke's account of "natural kind" terms and use the notion or phenomenon of empathy to fix the reference of moral terms. But this has to be done carefully, because if we assume that the reference-fixing of moral words is exactly parallel to that of natural kind words, we end up having to say that it is a posteriori that cruelty is wrong, and that doesn't seem acceptable. However, chapter 4 develops a way of fixing references that isn't exactly parallel to the reference-fixing that occurs with respect to natural kind terms, and this new mode of reference-fixing actually allows moral claims to be a priori—*and objective.* That enables us to give a fairly precise and plausible reference-fixing account or explication of the meaning of moral terms along strictly sentimentalist lines.

Chapter 5 picks up on chapter 4's explanation of the a priori character of (motivating) moral claims or judgments and offers an argument to the effect that sentimentalist metaethics actually permits us to deduce an "ought" from an "is." Hume, of course, famously queried the possibility of doing this, but as others before me have noted, Hume can be interpreted as offering metaethical theories that allow such a deduction. For example, if the ideal observer theory of moral terms is correct, then we can derive claims of right and wrong and, presumably, ought as well from descriptions of what an empirically specified observer would approve or disapprove, and Hume sometimes seems to hold an ideal observer view of moral language. Perhaps (as others have argued) that is a good reason to deny that the Hume who worried about going from *is* to *ought* could really have held an ideal observer theory, but in chapter 5, I shall argue that—whatever Hume himself might or should have held—there is no reason to fear the idea of deriving or deducing an *ought* from an *is*. What seems implausible or even preposterous about this notion can be shown, step by step, though perhaps quite surprisingly, to involve nothing untoward or unacceptable.

In chapter 6, I take up some important implications of the previous account of moral judgment. Recent sentimentalists have held that it is morally preferable if we don't have to consult or follow moral principles or injunctions in our dealings with others—for example, in our attempts to help them. (Both Hutcheson and Hume appear to agree.) But there are times when sentimentalistically understood moral principles/injunctions can be morally very helpful, perhaps even necessary, and chapter 6 offers an account of how and when this is so. (It also and at the same time expands on what was said in chapter 1 about moral education and moves it in the direction of certain explicitly Humean ideas.)

Chapter 7 takes up a criticism that Kantians have directed at sentimentalism, namely, that the sentiments, feelings, are unreliable as a basis for morally acceptable action, because they sometimes point us toward the wrong actions and because, even when they point in the right direction, their force often fades before they can efficaciously ensure that we do what is right. I shall be arguing that feeling and motivation based on empathy are a more reliable guide to acting morally than has been thought. The connection between caring motivation and right action is not *accidental* and *intermittent* in the way Kant and contemporary Kantians have supposed. However, the sentimentalist account of the meaning of moral terms I will have offered earlier on does imply that actual consequences are less important to right action than non-Kantians, at least, have tended to believe, and chapter 7 goes on to argue that the moral irrelevance of actual consequences is in fact commonsensically plausible. When bad results occur and someone has acted wrongly, we can always discover some motivational moral inadequacy in the way the agent approached a given practical issue, and whenever it turns out that we can't do that, we intuitively reject the idea that a given act deserves moral criticism. So our moral sentimentalism emphasizes the inner or internal as the target or basis of all moral criticism, and in this one respect it—ironically—resembles Kant's views more than those of Hume (in some of his moods) and of the utilitarians who took some of their inspiration from (that) Hume.

Chapters 5, 6, and 7 in effect make a slow transition from metaethics to normative ethics, and in the last part of this book, starting in chapter 8, the focus will mainly be on care ethics and the plausibility of what it has to say about normative issues. But since, in the earlier chapters of the book, I will already have examined various issues of individual or personal morality in the course of offering a full-scale sentimentalist metaethics, I want to concentrate on social issues in chapters 8 and 9. Chapter 8 approaches issues having to do with paternalism and patriarchy in terms of care ethics and argues that (despite what one might initially think) respect and autonomy can both be understood in purely sentimentalist terms. Chapter 9 goes on to discuss issues of social justice, again in purely sentimentalist terms. If these discussions seem as full and plausible as what other traditions tell us about these topics, that will show sentimentalism to be capable of functioning as a total approach to morality, something that has been doubted for a long time now. And I am talking here not (just) of the doubts about sentimentalist metaethics that I mentioned earlier but as well of doubts that naturally arise regarding whether social justice or respect for autonomy can be adequately conceived in sentimental terms. After all, if we think there are human rights, we tend to think that those rights have a source in something other than human feeling or emotion—in fact, rights are supposed to morally protect us from bad emotions (like hatred and prejudice) and even from typically good emotions like benevolence, whose paternalistic "reach" can threaten or seem to threaten our ability to insist on and make use of those rights. So if justice and respect require honoring various rights, it would seem that justice involves more than certain feelingful motives, however benign.

In addition, there is the historical example of Hume, the inadequacies of whose account of justice and of social morality more generally have been pointed out ad nauseam. But as chapters 8 and 9 will make clear, a sentimentalist account of social/political morality doesn't have to operate with Hume's problematic assumptions about the "artificial virtues" and can in fact make use of the notion of empathy to accomplish what the rationalist tradition seeks to accomplish by using (traditional) notions of rights and justice. Normative sentimentalism can build a conception of justice, respect, autonomy, and rights via the notion of empathy (and of empathic caring), and that conception yields the same sort of intuitive conclusions that rationalism and common sense find plausible in this area—plus some others than the latter views actually don't seem capable of delivering or accounting for. A sentimentalist ethics of empathic caring can explain, for example, why substantial humanitarian foreign aid can be required in the name of justice, and it can also (and perhaps surprisingly) explain why the Inquisition's use of torture "for the sake of the souls" of heretics and nonbelievers was unjust and wrong and lacking in respect. And chapters 8 and 9 will deal directly with these topics and others related to them.

Chapter 10 will broaden our discussion to take in philosophical questions that are not strictly ethical. There has been a great deal of talk in recent years about the (possibility that there is an) inextricable link between reason and emotion—some of this talk (especially outside of philosophy) having been very vague and not well reasoned. But I think we can make good on the idea that reason or rationality, even outside of ethics, constitutively involves emotion or feeling, if, having seen what a significant role empathy plays inside the moral life, we consider the role it may also play in our intellectual life (including the work of scientists). Chapter 10 will take sentimentalism outside the moral and the ethical by arguing that intellectual or scientific objectivity and rationality require empathy with the points of view of those who disagree or might disagree with one—and are thus in an important sense relational. Following to some extent the work of Michael Stocker, I shall argue that this requirement is intrinsic to intellectual reason or rationality rather than (just) a matter of contingent physiological fact. This is reminiscent of the way in which Hume treats episte-mological issues (outside morality proper) as involving feelings, ideas or impres-sions with certain kinds of phenomenologically felt charge. But I don't intend to make feeling as central as Hume arguably does to the whole of philosophy. By our present lights, that would seem a crazy excess of empiricism, and (for reasons I shall say a bit more about in a moment) I am not in general any sort of empiricist, even if I do accept one important thesis that many empiricists have accepted, the idea that morality is based in sentiment. Still, sentimentalism has some interesting uses outside of ethics, and the idea that intellectual objectivity involves certain empathic/emotional reactions will constitute a (further?) vindi-cation of the more limited, but nonetheless very important, recently advocated thesis that reason, reasoning, and rationality involve nonrational, feelingful elements. And once again, the argument will depend on paying more attention to empathy than philosophers have tended to do.

Care ethics is, furthermore, the most widespread and influential form of normative sentimentalism visible on the current philosophical scene, but its lack of attention to empathy has meant that it has, at least till recently, lacked as full an account of moral education as what Kantians and liberals (following Lawr-ence Kohlberg) have been able to offer. That lack of attention has also prevented care ethics from offering any sort of account of the meaning of moral terms—though most care ethicists haven't been all that interested in semantic issues. Care ethicists have also tended to focus on issues of personal or individual morality rather than on questions of social or international justice (or rights), though this one-sidedness has to a certain extent been corrected in recent years (and in ways that support feminist ideals and aspirations). But if it turns out, as I shall be arguing here, that care ethics can treat the full range of individual and political issues that Kantianism and utilitarianism have addressed, and if it turns out, further, that care ethics can speak substantially and plausibly to issues of semantics and moral education, I think care ethicists might welcome those developments. For better or worse, care ethics has been moving toward a place in the sun of philosophical attention and (yes) prestige. Its importance is recognized in encyclopedias and anthologies in a way that it wasn't twenty years ago, and it is today (considered) more "mainstream" than it has ever previously been. Nor should it be particularly surprising that the present book defends a care ethics committed to feminism at the same time that it seeks a fuller revival of eighteenth-century sentimentalism than anyone else has advocated. Hume was, after all, the greatest of the sentimentalists, and it is by no means an accident that Annette Baier has suggested (though with certain caveats) that Hume might appropriately be called "the women's moral theorist." If we can embed care ethics within the larger movement known as moral sentimentalism, that can only serve to make it seem more, rather than less, philosophically important.

But let's be very clear about one thing from the start. In defending and espousing sentimentalism, I will not follow Hume in assuming empiricism as some kind of overall philosophy. Some of our concepts may not be acquired from or by (sense) experience, and I want to leave room for the possibility (or fact) of innate knowledge defended either à la Chomsky or in other ways. Empiricism naturally takes some sort of moral sentimentalism on board, but empiricism doesn't in any way have to be part of the bargain when one's main purpose is to argue for sentimentalism with respect to morality.

It is time, however, to launch the metaethical portion of this book with some discussion of the nature and implications of empathy.

EMPATHY

Cement of the Moral Universe

As I indicated in the introduction, the notion of empathy will be the main tool of this book. I believe it is central to understanding normative issues along contemporarily plausible sentimentalist lines but also crucial to a sentimentalist metaethical understanding of what moral judgments or utterances *mean*. Since this book will treat the normative and the metaethical sides of moral sentimentalism and their interrelations, one could say that empathy is the cement of the present project, the cement, arguably, of sentimentalism as a total, present-day, theoretical approach to moral issues. But the title of this chapter is supposed to—indeed, has to—mean more than this. In our moral lives (i.e., if we are leading morally good or decent lives), we are concerned about and act on behalf of other people—not just people we know intimately, but others, more distant or at least personally unknown to us, whose distress, misery, or tragic circumstances cry out for our compassion and our help. We also try to avoid hurting or harming people or making their condition worse than it was previously (or might otherwise have been). And we sometimes make moral judgments and follow moral precepts or principles that (to some extent) help us and others live harmoniously, justly, and well. Empathy is arguably crucial to all these aspects of living morally, and that is what I mainly mean in speaking of it as the cement of the moral universe. It is not only the cement of the present sentimentalist theory but also, if the theory is correct, the cement of the moral life or morality that the theory seeks to understand and do justice to.

When Hume called causality the cement of the universe, I believe (though I can't textually prove this) that he was in substantial measure thinking of the fact that, as he understood it, causality works via spatial and temporal contiguity. Cement (or glue) works that way, too: it works by spatial contact and depends for its success on the timing of its hardening or drying, and these facts make the cement metaphor seem quite apt in application to causality. But it is also apt in application to empathy and its role in the moral life. The moral(ly good or decent) life depends on our being altruistically concerned with others and on refraining from harming them and treating them unjustly, and I shall be arguing that empathy makes all of this possible. But empathy is also partialistic: we normally feel more empathic concern for potential or actual harm or pain that we notice in our vicinity than for what we merely know about or have heard of, and when we hear of a contemporaneous threat to human life (say, if coal miners are trapped underground), our empathy is more sharply aroused than if a(n even larger scale) threat arises concerning future loss of life. As I shall indicate in somewhat greater detail in what follows (and as the psychology literature on empathy and moral development makes very clear), we tend to feel more empathic concern when threats or suffering is spatially and temporally nearer.[1] But if empathy, like causality, is more easily nailed down and efficacious when there is more, rather than less, spatial and temporal contiguity, then the cement metaphor can plausibly be applied to it, too, and that is what the title of this chapter, in anticipation of its contents, does. And none of this should be surprising. Empathy is conceived by Hume as a causal mechanism, so it is no wonder that it can be regarded as operating via the same factors or principles as (Hume ascribed to) causation generally.

Hume was certainly aware, since he explicitly says so, that empathy (which he called "sympathy") works more strongly when there is greater spatiotemporal contiguity. He also says that we empathize more readily with those who are similar to us, and this finds its parallel in the Humean idea that it is easier to believe in a relation of cause and effect when there is some common element or resemblance between cause and effect. This strengthens the analogy between empathy and causation, but at the same time, it attenuates some of the force of the metaphor of cement, since I don't believe that cement tends to work better between similar items than between dissimilar ones. Still, if empathy is a causal mechanism, and causation works via factors like space-time contiguity and resemblance, it is no wonder that empathy, too, works via these factors. But empathy is a form of causation that seems specifically or distinctively relevant to the moral life, and that is why we can say that it is the cement of the moral universe.

The fact that Hume was able to bring both morality and metaphysics under the same associationist ideas is part of the initial appeal of his overall philosophical approach. But in the present book, I don't want to do any metaphysics, and I am by no means committed to thinking that what we shall be saying about empathy and morality along sentimentalist lines can somehow be generalized to

---

1. This holds only *other things being equal*: I will be more empathically responsive to my distant daughter than to most people I see nearby. I am indebted for this point to a reader for Oxford University Press.

apply universally outside the sphere of the ethical.[2] I actually make one outside application in chapter 10, but chapter 10 also makes it clear that the moral sentimentalism of the present book is really no more (or not *much* more) than that: sentimentalism applied to the moral sphere, and I have no desire to defend empiricism as a general thesis over rationalism or innatism. I'm in fact very much inclined, on the basis of Chomsky's work and a host of other relevant considerations, to doubt or deny empiricism as a general thesis or approach. But our emphasis on empathy will be similar to and partly derive from what Hume, pushing his empiricist ideas into moral philosophy, said about the role of empathy/sympathy in morality, and the challenge (and opportunity) that that represents is more than sufficient for the present book. It is time now, however, for me to be a little more specific about what empathy is and how it works.

1. Introducing Empathy

Before I introduce some of the recent psychological literature on empathy, let me just make a few preliminary remarks about what the term *empathy* means. The word didn't exist in English till the early twentieth century, when it was introduced as a translation of the German word *Einfuehlung*. But that doesn't mean that the concept of empathy was previously absent from our culture or from philosophy. Hume in *A Treatise of Human Nature* says important, groundbreaking things about what we would nowadays call empathy. (This is also true of Adam Smith in *The Theory of Moral Sentiments*.) But Hume used the term *sympathy* to refer to empathy, and the picture is further muddied or obscured by the fact that he (naturally enough) also used the term to refer to what we would call sympathy (especially in *An Enquiry Concerning the Principles of Morals*). However, we today have both terms and are constantly talking about empathy, and I think I should say something about how we now understand the distinction between sympathy and empathy.

In colloquial terms, we can perhaps most easily do this by considering the difference between (Bill Clinton's) feeling someone's pain and feeling *for* someone who is in pain. Any adult speaker of English will recognize that *empathy* refers to the former phenomenon and *sympathy* to the latter. Thus empathy involves having the feelings of another (involuntarily) aroused in ourselves, as when we see another person in pain. It is as if their pain invades us, and Hume speaks, in this connection, of the *contagion* between what one person feels and what another person feels. He also talks of one person's feelings being *infused* into another person. However, we can also simply feel sorry for, bad for, the person who is in pain and positively wish them well, and that is what we mean by sympathy. Stephen Darwall gives us another good illustration of the distinction between sympathy and empathy when

---

2. Moreover, I won't be assuming Humean views about causation when I discuss the role of causality in moral contexts. (Thanks, again, to the reader for Oxford University Press.)

he points out that one can sympathize with someone who is depressed without at all (via empathy) becoming depressed oneself.[3] (The same point also applies to cases where we see someone else being humiliated.)

The recent psychological literature contains many empirical studies of empathy and various discussions of the difference between empathy and sympathy (a small number of which run counter to what I have just been saying). That literature takes us far beyond what was known or available to Hume, but I don't propose to survey it here. Nonetheless, I do want to speak a bit about two books that do survey the recent psychological literature on empathy. C. D. Batson's *The Altruism Question* and Martin Hoffman's *Empathy and Moral Development* both argue that various studies and experiments show that empathy plays a crucial enabling role in the development of genuinely altruistic concern or caring for others.[4]

Batson considers what he calls the "empathy-altruism hypothesis" in relation to a large literature that discusses whether (genuine) altruism is possible. The hypothesis says, in effect, that empathy is a crucial factor in determining whether someone will feel and act altruistically toward someone in distress or in need, and one thing that seems to favor it is the fact that where people feel empathic distress in the presence of another person's distress, they very often act to relieve the other's distress rather than simply removing themselves from the scene and thus from the source of their own distress. Doing the latter would clearly indicate selfish or egoistic motivation, but Batson (much more than Hoffman) thinks that acting on behalf of the person originally in distress, rather than leaving the scene, might also be explainable in subtly egoistic terms. He spends a great deal of his book considering various studies and various ways of conceptualizing what goes on in the kind of situation just described in order to see whether altruism is the most plausible explanation of the results that have been obtained in different studies and experiments, and in the end, he concludes that the existence of genuine altruism and the empathy-altruism hypothesis are the most plausible hypotheses in this area. These conclusions are helpful, even indispensable, to a sentimentalist ethics of care that assumes there is such a thing as genuine caring and that seeks to understand both the development of caring and various intuitive moral distinctions in terms of empathy. But it is Hoffman's book that offers us the clearer picture of how empathy actually develops and influences our capacity for caring, and his work also distinctively points the way toward a conclusion that sentimentalist care ethics needs and I believe can deliver: namely, that distinctions of empathy and of empathic caring correspond very well to the commonsense normative moral distinctions that most of us subscribe to.

---

3. See his *Welfare and Rational Care* (Princeton, N.J.: Princeton University Press, 2002).

4. C. D. Batson, *The Altruism Question: Toward a Social-Psychological Answer* (Hillsdale, N.J.: Lawrence Erlbaum Associates, 1991); and Martin Hoffman, *Empathy and Moral Development: Implications for Caring and Justice* (Cambridge: Cambridge University Press, 2000).

Hoffman argues that individual empathy develops through several stages and that its connection with prosocial, altruistic, or moral motivations is more ambiguous or inchoate in the earlier stages of that development. A very young child (or even a newborn baby) can feel distress and start crying at the distress and crying of another child within hearing distance, and this operates via a kind of mimicry and seems like a form of "contagion." But as the child develops conceptual/linguistic skills, a richer history of personal experiences, and a fuller sense of the reality of others, a more "mediated" form of empathy can be involuntarily aroused in response to situations or experiences that are not immediately present and are merely heard of, remembered, or read about. It also becomes possible for the normal child to deliberately adopt the point of view of other people and see and feel things from their perspective. Although we sometimes speak of both these forms of later-developing empathy (and especially of the latter *projective* type of empathy) as involving identification with the other, Hoffman and others insist that the identification isn't a total merging with or melting into the other: genuine and mature empathy doesn't deprive the empathic individual of her sense of being a different person from the person she empathizes with.[5]

Empathic identification, then, doesn't involve a felt loss of identity, but according to Hoffman, it does involve feelings or thoughts that are in some sense more "appropriate" to the situation of the person(s) empathized with than to the situation of the person empathizing. And as an individual's cognitive sophistication and general experience increase, she becomes capable of more and more impressive "feats" of empathy. Thus, at a certain point, we may, for example, feel an acute empathic sadness on seeing a person we know to have terminal cancer boisterously enjoy himself in seeming or actual ignorance of his own fatal condition. In general, as we become more aware of the future or hypothetical results of actions and events in the world, we learn to empathize not just with what people are actually feeling but with what they will feel or what they would feel, if we did certain things or if certain things happened. It seems we even learn to empathize with their (situated) condition and not just with their

5. See Hoffman, *Empathy and Moral Development*, esp. pp. 276ff. Hoffman calls the kind of empathy that is (involuntarily) *aroused* by others' situations, rather than deliberately adopted, associative empathy. Where such empathy depends on acquired concepts or knowledge, he speaks of *mediated* associative empathy, and it should be clear that such empathy is more like the sympathy/ empathy by infusion and contagion that Hume wrote of than like the kind of "projective" empathy (or simulation) that involves deliberately putting oneself into another's shoes/position. (Note that Hoffman's views undercut the frequently heard complaint that a sentimentalist care ethics has to be based on pure feeling and for that reason cannot account for the cognitive demands of the moral life.) In *Caring: A Feminine Approach to Ethics and Moral Education* (Berkeley: University of California Press, 1984), Nel Noddings stresses the importance, for care ethics, of (what, following Hoffman, I am calling) the associative kind of empathy. But she was reluctant to use the specific word *empathy* there because some dictionaries tend to focus exclusively on the projective side or kind of empathy. However, she has indicated to me that she is nowadays much more comfortable with the term, and we certainly both agree as to the importance of involuntarily aroused empathy.

hypothetical or actual reactions to it. Moreover, as children become adolescents, they become aware of the existence of groups or classes of people and the common goals or interests that may unite them, and this makes empathy with, say, the plight of the homeless or the challenged or various oppressed or unfortunate races, nations, or ethnicities possible and real for adolescents in a way that would not have been possible earlier in their lives.[6]

Finally, Hoffman holds that the development of full moral motivation and behavior requires the intervention of parents and others making use of what he calls "inductive discipline" or, simply, "induction." Induction contrasts with the "power-asserting" attempt to discipline, train, or influence a child through sheer threats (carried out if the child doesn't comply) and with attempts to inculcate moral thought, motivation, and behavior (merely) by citing, or admonishing with, explicit moral precepts or injunctions. Inductive training depends, rather, on the child's capacity for empathy with others and involves someone's (a parent's) noticing when a child hurts others and then (in a nonthreatening but firm manner) making the child vividly aware of the harm that he or she has done—most notably by making the child imagine how it would feel to experience similar harm. This leads the child (with a normal capacity for empathy) to feel bad (a kind of rudimentary guilt) about what he or she has done.

Hoffman believes that if such training is applied consistently over time,[7] children will come to associate bad feelings (guilt) with situations in which the harm they can do is not yet done, an association that is functionally autonomous of parents' or others' actual intervention and constitutes or supports altruistic motivation.[8] He calls such habitual associations scripts and holds, roughly, that

---

6. The fact that human beings are capable of empathy and of altruism is an empirical claim. But it is a priori, I think, that morality depends on altruism, and I shall be arguing that anyone well acquainted with empathy in their own case and that of others can also see a priori that altruism and morality involve empathy (among other things). The psychological studies (cited by Hoffman) that show that, and when, empathy for groups emerges in the course of empathy's overall development are likewise empirical. But anyone with full-blown empathy can recognize that full empathy involves a capacity for empathy with groups (or with an unaware cancer victim) without having to cite or do specific psychological studies. As in many other cases (and in line with what Kant points out in the first *Critique*), it may take empirical experience to acquire the full-blown concept of and capacity for empathy, but what we know on the basis of having the full concept can be a priori. I shall have some more specific things to say in this direction when (in chapter 4) I offer a reference-fixing account of moral terms that treats certain aspects of empathy as involved in the very meaning of such terms.

7. Hoffman thinks power assertion invariably plays some role in parental discipline but holds that a preponderant use of inductive discipline is more likely to bring about individuals with moral, altruistic, caring motivation: after all, induction engages and stimulates a child's capacity for empathy in a way that power assertion clearly does not. For discussion of some of the evidence that favors this view, see Mark Davis, *Empathy: A Social Psychological Approach* (Madison, Wisc.: Brown and Benchmark, 1994, pp. 70ff.); and Nancy Eisenberg, *The Caring Child* (Cambridge: Harvard University Press, 1992).

8. What we have just said points to the source of the desire to act and be morally better in the future. If, as a result of inductive discipline, children associate feeling bad (a kind of guilt) with various kinds of harming, then, as Hoffman says, children are going to start associating feeling bad with situations in which the harm they can do is not yet done, and this will tend to inhibit the doing of

they underlie and power (the use of) moral principles or rules that objectify (my term) that association in claims/rules like "hurting people is wrong." (I shall be arguing later in this book that empathy-laden moral rules or injunctions have a significant and distinctive role in the moral life.)

Now Hoffman indicates that (previous) induction within the family plays a role in leading adolescents to develop empathic concern for disadvantaged groups, but he also points out that educative techniques similar to induction can reinforce or strengthen (and certainly help to sustain) such empathic concern. For example, inductive techniques can be, and often are, extended so as to bring about or enhance an older child or adolescent's concern for (groups of) people in other countries. Both parents and schools can and often (though not often enough) do expose students to literature, films, or television programs that make the troubles and tragedies of distant or otherwise unknown (groups of) people vivid to them, and they can encourage their sensitivity to such people by asking students to imagine—and getting them into the habit of imagining—how they or some family member(s) would feel if such things were happening to them.

In addition, families, schools, and countries could provide for more international student exchanges than now exist, with visiting students living with local families and attending local schools—thus bringing home to both visitors and those visited the reality and real humanity and distinctiveness of those who might otherwise just be names or descriptions. (I have read somewhere that various government-sponsored and nongovernmentally sponsored programs involving exchanges between Palestinian and Israeli students have been going on for some years now in the Middle East.) Finally, parents and schools could inculcate in students the habit of thinking about, and being concerned with, the

---

such harm. So children build up a *resistance* to harming, and that is equivalent to desiring not to harm as they have done in the past. This is less morally self-conscious than the desire to be or act morally better, but once children are making explicit moral judgments, the desire not to harm people again can be expressed as the desire not to do the kind of wrong actions one has done in the past, and this is, in effect, the desire to be or become a morally better person. More needs to be said, but what has just been said at least gives one the sense of how the desire to be better takes root in the inductive process and can be explained in fundamentally sentimentalist terms if, as I shall be arguing, we can explain moral judgment in fully sentimentalist terms. (I am assuming here that the desire to become morally better can't just come out of the blue. Some ways of raising/treating children, for example, leave them without any psychological access to such a desire.)

The desire to emulate or model oneself on some morally admired figure can also be seen from the perspective of the inductive process. If one seeks (for nonegoistic reasons) to be like some such person, one does so because one feels that that person is superior to oneself, doesn't do the kinds of things that one feels bad about having done oneself. So I want to say that the sentimentalist can make the most psychological sense of the spirit of moral emulation by thinking of it as involving a desire not to do various things that one has done in the past or recently, that one feels bad about having done, and that one sees the person one admires and wants to emulate as *not* doing. Such emulation/modeling can occur either consciously or subliminally, but later in this chapter I shall also discuss a kind of modeling that typically occurs without the knowledge or deliberate efforts of those modeling themselves on another individual.

effects of their own actions and inactions (and those of their family, neighbors, and government) on the lives of people in other countries.[9]

Now the complete implementation of all these forms of moral education would require substantial resources, great commitment, and less jingoism than one finds in most countries or communities, but what I have just said should at least indicate how strong empathic concern for groups one doesn't personally know *can* be instilled and strengthened. Of course, I have been assuming—what almost every moral philosopher would assume—that being moral involves some sort of substantial concern for those *beyond* one's immediate family or circle of friends. And in what follows, I shall also assume what Batson and Hoffman have argued for on the basis of recent studies and experiments, namely, that empathy is a crucial source and sustainer of altruistic concern or caring about (the well-being or welfare of) others. But I would like at this point to mention and discuss *another aspect* of the role empathy plays in moral development and moral education, something that takes us beyond anything Hoffman tells us about the uses and usefulness of inductive discipline.

When parents use induction, they demonstrate an empathic concern for the child (let us assume) who has been hurt by their own child, and there is in fact no reason why a child can't take in such an attitude, such motivation, directly from a parent. Hume held that people's basic feelings can spread to others by contagion or infusion, but he also believed that (moral) opinions and attitudes can spread in that way.[10] So in most cases, induction will involve not only a parent's deliberately making a child more empathically sensitive to the welfare or feelings of others but also the child's directly taking in, by a kind of empathic osmosis, the parent's own empathic concern for others. And such taking in will not, presumably, be limited to occasions where induction is used but will occur at other times when the child notices how empathic and caring a parent is.

It is often said that moral education takes place to a large degree through modeling, through children's modeling themselves on parents or others. But the kind of modeling I am now speaking of isn't deliberate or necessarily even conscious. Still, it can, and it does, occur, and so a deeper understanding of what is involved in induction can lead us to see that there are at least two major modes of moral education that don't directly involve any appeal to moral principles.[11]

9. Hoffman, *Empathy and Moral Development*, p. 297.

10. For Hume's views about the way others' (moral) opinions and attitudes influence our own, see the *Treatise of Human Nature*, ed. Selby-Bigge (New York: Oxford University Press, 1978), pp. 320–324, 346, 499, 589, 592, and 605. Similar but more rudimentary or inchoate ideas about interpersonal influence can also be found in Malebranche, whose work Hume is known to have been acquainted with. (See Nicolas Malebranche, *Search after Truth* [Cambridge: Cambridge University Press, 1997], Book V.)

11. On the idea that moral education often occurs through modeling, see Nancy Eisenberg, *The Caring Child*, chapters 7 and 8. And remember that we now have spoken of two different kinds of moral modeling: one that can occur in conjunction with inductive discipline and that can be either

Children who undergo inductive discipline are made to pay attention to the harm they have done, and if this has been done right, it makes children more empathically sensitive to the feelings and welfare of others (and to how their own actions can have an effect on these). But in addition, the child who learns to be more empathic via inductive discipline can and presumably will directly imbibe the attitude/motive of empathic concern for others that the parent who uses such discipline also demonstrates. And this (unconscious or nondeliberate) process of modeling oneself on one's parent—and of course this can also occur with people other than parents—can take place in situations where inductive discipline isn't being applied. So on sentimentalist assumptions, there are at least two important ways—induction and modeling—in which empathic concern for others can be strengthened and the aim(s) of moral education furthered or fulfilled.

Note, though, that induction-using parents are likely to care more in general about the well-being of their own child than about that of some child outside the family who has been hurt by their child. Empathy comes in degrees, and that is a pervasive feature of our moral psychology. And just as the presence or operation of empathy is necessary to caring (or concern) for others generally, the literature of moral development indicates that differences in the strength or force of empathy make a difference in *how much* we care about the fate of others in various different situations. This is something that Hume's genius was capable of understanding even in the absence of empirical social-scientific research. But I need now to be more specific about how differences of or in empathic responses can be brought to bear on normative moral issues and shown to be relevant, in particular, to a sentimentalist ethics of care.

2. Empathy, Partiality, and Morality

I believe that empathy and the notion of empathic caring for or about others in fact offer us a plausible criterion of moral evaluation. Much of this book will be devoted to arguing for this point, but to begin with, it is worth noting that differences in (the strength of) our empathic reactions (or tendencies to react) to various situations correspond pretty well to differences in the (normative) moral evaluations we tend to make about those situations.

For example, Hoffman (along with a good many other psychologists) points out that we empathically react to nearby and visible suffering or need more than to suffering or need we merely hear or know about.[12] But, as I mentioned earlier

---

deliberate or unconscious, and another that takes place in a relatively automatic and nondeliberate fashion via a kind of empathic osmosis.

12. Hoffman, *Empathy and Moral Development*, pp. 209ff. For other sources of this idea, see my *The Ethics of Care and Empathy* (New York: Routledge, 2007), but of course Hume was well aware of this phenomenon and seems to have been the first to offer anything like an explanation of it.

and as Hoffman, too, points out, we are empathically partial not only to what we perceive (and what is therefore, given the way things are in the actual world, in our vicinity) but also to what is contemporaneous with our concern. Thus, if miners are trapped underground, we have a reaction to their plight that impels us to help them and affects us more than the consideration that we could spend the same money we use to rescue them to instead install safety devices in the mine that would save more lives in the long run. The temporal immediacy of the need, the clear and present danger, evokes a stronger empathic reaction than we would have in regard to dangers and lives to be lost at some time in the future.

But both these kinds of greater empathic reaction correspond to common-sense moral judgment(s). When miners are trapped in a mine, we feel more empathy for them than for the greater number of future miners we might save by installing safety devices, and we also think it morally better to save those miners than to invest in safety devices. (The suggestion that we should invest in safety equipment *rather than* saving the miners would actually *horrify* most of us.) Similarly, it goes more against the grain of empathy to ignore a child drowning right in front of one than to not give money to Oxfam that one believes will save a single child in a distant country, and we tend to think that it is morally worse to ignore the drowning child than to not give to Oxfam. Of course, in "Famine, Affluence, and Morality," Peter Singer famously questioned our commonsense judgments here, and he argues elsewhere that the kind of partialism that is implicit in holding onto commonsense views in this area needs a better defense than it has ever been given.[13] But the main point of the present book is to give such a defense, in sentimentalist terms, so we shall just have to see if Singer's challenge is met in these pages.

For the moment, however, let us stick with commonsense moral thinking. Its distinctions correspond to distinctions in empathy or empathic reaction/ sensitivity, and I propose to use that fact to support common sense. But the correlation between empathy and commonsense morality also holds in an area where it hasn't been much anticipated or expected, in the area of deontology. Most philosophers think of deontology and deontological agential reactions/ dispositions as arising from something other than feeling/emotion (usually as derived from reason in some way or other, depending, for example, on whether one is an intuitionist or Kantian)—and also as required to stop feeling from running away with us in morally suspect (or worse) ways. But, as I argued at great length in *The Ethics of Care and Empathy*, I think the disposition to honor commonsense deontological restrictions or act in accordance with them can be seen as coming from empathy in something like the way our tendency to prefer what is perceived or contemporaneous does. Much of what is central to

---

13. See "Famine, Affluence, and Morality," *Philosophy and Public Affairs* 1 (1972): 229–243. On the need for a better defense of moral partialism, see Singer's "A Response [to Critics]" in Dale Jamieson, ed., *Singer and His Critics* (Oxford: Blackwell, 1999), 308.

deontology depends on the distinction between doing and allowing harm (e.g., killing vs. letting die), but I think that we empathically *flinch* from harming more than from allowing harm (and the same goes for causing vs. allowing pain in another person), and some recent studies in neuroscience nicely illustrate this point.[14] Thus causal distinctions are in fact just one *modality* of the way empathy engages and affects our concern for and actions toward others—perceivability and contemporaneity being two others.

Don't, then, say that the cases are different because our (greater) aversion to killing is based on prior moral notions and assumptions, whereas the influences of contemporaneity and perceivability are independent of (and ground) such moral considerations. As our earlier discussion of inductive discipline indicates, one can feel bad and guilty about what one has done, say, to another child independently of any introduction of moral concepts or precepts and on the main basis, therefore, of one's empathic tendencies (and knowledge of the world around one). And I am saying that one tends to feel more such empathic guilt if one is made to recognize the harm one has done than if one is made to recognize harm that one has (merely) allowed to happen. These empathic tendencies don't require one to be thinking of right and wrong; rather, as I argued in *The Ethics of Care and Empathy* and am arguing here in this book, they constitute the grounds and justification for such thinking. If (because of prior inductive training) we flinch more from harming than from allowing harm, that can be the result of our empathic tendencies and need in no way reflect or presuppose any prior moral thinking—which is just what sentimentalism needs to show about the grounding basis or bases of deontology.

It has long been thought that Hume's discussion of promising, honesty, and other topics generally considered deontological is a total failure and that something like a Kantian appeal to rationality/practical reason is therefore needed to get full-scale deontology off the ground. I myself have doubts about how successful Kantian ethics has been and can be with (justifying) deontology, but my main point here is that, surprising as it may be, sentimentalism does have the resources to explain and support deontology—and not just that part of it that deals most explicitly with questions of doing and allowing harm or pain. As I argued in *The Ethics of Care and Empathy* (chapter 3), our ordinary deontological views about the morality of promise keeping and truth telling also correspond very closely to how empathically responsive we are to differences in the strength or directness of agential causality. So even if Hume's artificial virtues approach to deontology and to his notorious "circle" isn't at all promising, moral

14. See, e.g., Michael Koenigs et al., "Damage to the Prefrontal Cortex Increases Utilitarian Moral Judgments," *Nature*, online version, 21 March 2007. This empirical study nicely illustrates the possibility of empathic sensitivity to differences in the strength or immediacy of causal connection for those to whom that possibility may not have occurred. But the idea of such sensitivity makes inherent (a priori) sense to us, just as our greater empathic responsiveness to what is contemporaneous or actually perceived is inherently (a priori) understandable to us.

sentimentalism has a *second chance* to justify and understand deontology based on a more systematic and wider appeal to empathy than Hume's deontology ever encompassed.[15]

Now we are not absolutists about deontology. Most of us think there is some number such that one can be morally justified in killing one innocent person (say) to save that number of innocent lives. (Of course, this isn't going to be very exact and will vary with circumstances, and I also won't worry about sorites issues here.) But considerations of empathy can help account for this too, because we are empathically sensitive to the sheer size or (as we say) enormity of some potential losses of life or well-being. In cases where we have to choose between our aversion to killing and our desire to save a great number of lives, empathy (in different ways) weighs in on both sides of the scale, and it seems plausible to suppose that where the number of lives that are likely to be lost is great enough, empathic concern with those lives can or may overwhelm the empathic dismay one feels at *killing* another person. I don't propose to try to be more precise about that number, but the considerations I have mentioned do correlate well with our actual moral opinions about these matters.

As Hume and Hoffman point out (and *The Ethics of Care and Empathy* also discusses in detail), empathy also helps account for the greater concern we feel for the welfare of people who are near and dear to us. And here, once again, the difference between our empathic reactions vis-à-vis problems for those we know or are related to and our reactions vis-à-vis problems for people we don't personally know (well) corresponds pretty well to common moral opinion. We think of our moral obligations to (help) near and dear as stronger than our obligations to (help) strangers, mere acquaintances, and unknown others.

---

15. In *The Ethics of Care and Empathy*, I also argued that the moral distinctions we are inclined to make regarding (variants on) trolley cases correspond very well to distinctions in the immediacy, strength, or directness of causal agency, distinctions that empathy is sensitive to in the same way (though not, perhaps, to the same degree) that it is sensitive to the general distinction between doing and allowing. One might wonder, however, whether relying on differences of empathic tendency might not in some cases yield invidious moral distinctions. After all, and as psychological studies indicate, we have an initial tendency to be more empathically concerned with or for people who resemble us, who have the same skin color, or who belong to the same gender or ethnic group. *The Ethics of Care and Empathy* (see pp. 34–38, 41) argued at length, however, that these initial empathic differences don't yield anything morally invidious and can be comfortably fitted within the overall moral picture that a normative sentimentalism based on empathy arrives at.

However, one issue that Claudia Card has mentioned to me and that wasn't discussed in *The Ethics of Care and Empathy* concerns our differing reactions to (supposedly) beautiful and ugly people. Doesn't the presumed fact that we tend to be less empathically concerned about the ugly mean that empathy sometimes is a poor guide and doesn't correspond to considered commonsense moral judgment? Well, if someone is ugly, we may well react with shock or repugnance at seeing them for the first time, and that might at least initially prevent us from helping them. But someone who is really empathic is likely to recognize that supposedly ugly people have been (and often show signs of having been) buffeted with such negative reactions for much or all of their lives, and if anything, this is likely to make an empathic individual feel *more* concern or compassion for such a person than for someone who is more attractive. And that actually makes some moral sense. (See the discussion of compassion and of what it is like to be badly off "in absolute terms" in chapter 9.)

But all this needs (more) justification. It is certainly very interesting—something that hasn't been pointed out previously—that moral distinctions correspond so well with distinctions in our empathic (reactive) tendencies. That very fact can't plausibly be treated as a mere accident, and it therefore supports the idea that empathy has something to do with morality, that it is or may well be relevant to moral thinking and moral justification. But it would greatly help if we could show that empathy has something important to do with our *understanding* of moral claims and moral distinctions. I made a substantial move in that direction in the concluding chapter of *The Ethics of Care and Empathy*, but I have thought of more to say now, and the next four chapters will be where I say it.

2

MORAL APPROVAL AND DISAPPROVAL

In this chapter, I am going to argue that empathy helps to create or constitute (something like) moral approval and disapproval. Then, in chapter 3, I shall defend the idea that empathy-derived approval and disapproval are a/the major element in our understanding and making of moral claims. I shall go on to argue in chapter 4 that a strictly sentimentalist approach to the semantics of moral discourse can account for the meaning of terms like *right* and *wrong* by making use of a new kind of reference-fixing, one that involves empathy and that is based on the phenomena of approval and disapproval. In all, the three chapters represent both a defense of sentimentalist metaethics and a reply to critics who have thought the whole sentimentalist approach to be hopelessly circular (or otherwise inadequate). I shall be referring to Hume and also to Saul Kripke, but the views I defend will differ from theirs. Hume had a theory of approval and disapproval and used it to give various (mutually inconsistent and not terribly explicit) accounts of the meaning of moral terms. But the theory of approval and disapproval I shall offer will differ from Hume's (while at the same time being strictly sentimentalist), and the theory of the meaning of moral terms I shall defend will also differ from—and be much more explicit than—anything Hume said. It will in fact borrow from what Kripke has said about reference-fixing but, at the same time and in disanalogy with what Kripke claimed about natural kind terms, will argue that moral judgments like "cruelty is wrong" are a priori true (and so unlike "water is H_2O").

In the present chapter, I am going to be talking about Hume's sentimentalist view of approval and disapproval but arguing that sentimentalism can and should offer us a more plausible theory of approval (and disapproval) than Hume did. Still, Hume was, I think, the first to identify the mechanisms that *any* sentimentalist theory of approval must operate by, and I shall be attempting to show—and this is no easy matter—that Hume's views about approval may at least have been on the right track. Most philosophers nowadays, and not just rationalists, would find it implausible to suppose, with Hume, that moral approval and disapproval can occur prior to, and form the basis of, moral judgment.[1] But this (or something very close to this) is what a sentimentalist in metaethics has to say, and though I shall be rejecting Hume's particular theory of approval and disapproval and his varying, mutually incompatible accounts of—or suggestions about—the way (moral) approval enters into moral judgment(s), I *will* be defending an account of approval and disapproval that doesn't presuppose moral judgment. And if we can use this account to help us toward a better understanding of the nature of moral claims or judgments, that would be some sort of vindication of (a major part of) what Hume was trying to accomplish in Book III of the *Treatise*.

As sentimentalists, Francis Hutcheson, David Hume, and Adam Smith all offered theories of approval that didn't rest on or presuppose (the making of) moral judgments and that didn't treat approval as primarily based in rationality or reason. I am not going to talk much about Smith here because, although his ideas are very interesting in themselves, I don't think they are particularly useful in helping us develop a plausible contemporary form of sentimentalism vis-à-vis approval and moral judgment. At least, they don't help *me* to go in the direction *I* find most plausible.[2] But a brief consideration of Hutcheson will help us, I think, to see how Hume's discussion of approval represents an advance over what Hutcheson said about it, and the particular nature of that advance—namely, that it specifies a mechanism of approval in a way that Hutcheson never did—is very helpful in moving us toward the kind of view that I do want to defend and that I believe is more plausible than what Hume tells us about approval. The kind of approach I want to argue for relies on a mechanism or mechanisms of approval and disapproval—just not the particular ones that Hume relies on in his account of moral judgment. And the view of approval and its mechanisms that I shall be advocating naturally leads toward a certain interesting, and I hope plausible, way of understanding moral judgments.

---

1. I realize that the term *judgment*, or even the term *claim*, doesn't fit very well with what are frequently or even standardly thought to be Hume's views about what is happening when we make use of moral language. But it is easier to use such terms than to employ the circumlocutions that turn out to be necessary if one wants to speak in ways that are strictly neutral regarding the meaning of moral epithets and of moral utterances, and my discussion in fact won't depend on any particular view of moral language at any point when it isn't *supposed* to depend on such views.

2. Although (the Third Earl of) Shaftesbury is usually regarded as the first of the moral sentimentalists, the first in a line that proceeds through Hutcheson and on to Hume and Smith, he is a very incomplete or imperfect exemplar of the tradition he is thought of as inaugurating. In particular, his conception of moral sense is rather rationalistic, so I prefer to begin my discussion with Hutcheson, who has a genuinely sentimentalist notion of moral sense.

Francis Hutcheson regards the most extensive, that is, universal, benevolence as the morally best of motives and treats that status as independent of the consequences of that motive.[3] Utilitarianism à la Bentham evaluates all motives (and of course all acts) by reference to their consequences, and Bentham leaves open the possibility that universal benevolence might turn out to be a less than morally good motive if it led to overall less good results than (acting from) other motives did. But Hutcheson is not a utilitarian or consequentialist about motives, even if he was the first, at least in English, to introduce a version of the principle of utility with regard to human *actions*. He considers motives to carry their moral value intrinsically and is to that extent a virtue ethicist.

In addition, however, he holds that we apprehend the value of motives via a moral sense analogous to the senses of sight, smell, and so forth. Benevolence is morally good, and we know or detect that goodness via a moral sense. So just as sensations of red are the way our sense of sight allows us to apprehend or register the redness of objects outside us, the moral sense allows us to apprehend the moral goodness of benevolent motives via pleasurable feelings of approval—and the moral badness of other motives via disagreeable feelings of disapproval.

Now the Hutchesonian idea of a distinct moral sense was rejected by subsequent sentimentalists and, for reasons that are or soon will be perhaps too obvious to need restating, has never (again) had much appeal for ethical theorists. To be sure, Hume sometimes speaks of a moral sense or sense of morals, but he also makes it clear that he doesn't understand this, in literal Hutchesonian terms, as a distinct mode of perception on all fives with the other human senses. Because there is no distinct organ or psychological mechanism for moral sense, Hutcheson's idea has widely been regarded as a nonstarter. The idea of a moral sense clearly does rule out reason/rationality as the basis for moral approval and judgment, but it is difficult to take it literally, and it is certainly also vague, because the metaphor involved here doesn't tell us (enough about) how moral knowledge actually occurs. But at the very least, the concept of a moral sense can function as a placeholder for a fuller sentimentalist account of the mechanisms of moral knowledge, and Hume certainly rises to this challenge. So however implausible it may be in itself as an account of what approval is, Hutcheson's theory (if that is the right word for it) performs the useful, the important, task of staking out a claim for further sentimentalist exploration and elaboration.

Hume, responding immediately to Hutcheson's view, sought precisely to supply what Hutcheson's theory seems mainly to lack, namely, a theory of the mechanism or mechanisms of moral approval and judgment—rather than relying on the metaphor/hypothesis of a moral sense. Hume held that our

3. For fuller discussion of both Hutcheson and Shaftesbury, see Stephen Darwall, *The British Moralists and the Internal "Ought": 1640–1740* (Cambridge: Cambridge University Press, 1995), chapters 7 and 8. The present discussion of Hutcheson draws on his *An Essay on the Nature and Conduct of the Passions, with Illustrations on the Moral Sense* (ed. Paul McReynolds, Gainesville, Fla.: Scholars' Facsimiles & Reprints, 1969).

capacity for moral approbation/approval and moral judgment depends on our "propensity" or tendency to sympathize with others, but the sympathy at issue here is not the kind of sympathetic concern for others that we nowadays readily designate by using the term *sympathy* but is rather, for Hume, a mechanism of psychological influence.[4] Sympathy is involved when the passion or feeling of another is mirrored in us, when we receive "by communication" the passions and feelings of others and thus feel something analogous to what those others feel. Hume says a good deal about how such communication or psychological "contagion" works, but we don't, I think, need to go into all the details of his account here. However, it is at this point probably worth repeating something I pointed out earlier: namely, that the sort of "sympathy" Hume is talking about is or involves what we nowadays usually refer to as empathy (rather than as sympathy)—the kind of phenomenon Bill Clinton was invoking or referring to when he said, "I feel your pain."[5]

In any event, what is most important at this point is the fact that Hume views moral approval and disapproval as based in or involving the mechanism(s) of "sympathy"—what I am going from now on to refer to as empathy. For Hume (as, essentially, for Hutcheson) approval is a feeling, not a judgment to the effect that something or someone is morally right or good. (That is one reason why Hume says that morality is "more properly felt than judg'd of.")[6] And Hume holds that that feeling can be aroused via mechanisms of empathy: when we become aware of the pleasures that other people have experienced as a result of their own or others' prudence or benevolence, for example, we feel pleasure at their having been given pleasures in that way, and that received, mirroring, or (as Hume himself sometimes puts it) "infused" pleasure, roughly, constitutes our approval of the prudence or benevolence that caused the pleasures. (Notice that no moral *judgment* or *concept* is involved here.) In similar fashion, the disapproval of malice, selfishness, or indolence results through pained empathic awareness of (i.e., awareness that reflects) the pains that people (both those who have the traits and others) have experienced as a result of such traits.[7]

---

4. See especially the *Treatise of Human Nature* (ed. L. A. Selby-Bigge, Oxford: Clarendon, 1958), 473. The present discussion of Hume draws mainly on the *Treatise*, Book II, Part I, Section XI, and Part II; and Book III, Part III, Sections I and III. Note that I shall for the most part be ignoring Hume's *Enquiry Concerning the Principles of Morals*, where the term *sympathy* is more often used in the present-day sense that is equivalent to sympathetic concern for (the welfare of) others. (See Selby-Bigge, ed., *Hume's Enquiries*, 2nd ed. [Oxford: Clarendon Press, 1961], e. g., 298 n., 303.)

5. Again, for a fairly comprehensive contemporary treatment of (the mechanisms of) empathy, see Martin Hoffman, *Empathy and Moral Development: Implications for Caring and Justice* (Cambridge: Cambridge University Press, 2000).

6. See Hume, *Treatise*, 470. On the next page, Hume says: "To have the sense of virtue, is nothing but to *feel* a satisfaction of a particular kind from the contemplation of a character. The very *feeling* constitutes our praise or admiration.... Our approbation is imply'd in the immediate pleasure [character traits] convey to us."

7. I am stating Hume's view very roughly at this point, but the criticisms I shall be making of his view don't, I think, depend on any finer discriminations. For a more nuanced account of Hume on

However, apart from such considerations of traits' utility, Hume also thinks that moral approval and disapproval occur when (we believe that) a trait or motive is "immediately agreeable or disagreeable" to ourselves or others, but here, too, he seems to want to say that the approval and disapproval occur via some sort of empathic mechanism.[8] In addition, according to Hume, our pain and pleasure at the pain and pleasure of others varies with and is influenced by how closely we are related to them by space, time, consanguinity, and other factors. Thus, and as I mentioned earlier, Hume thinks that some of the same associative mechanisms that influence our willingness to ascribe causal influence also mediate how much empathic pleasure (and approval) we feel at or because of the pleasures others feel. But according to Hume, moral judgment seeks or is supposed to abstract from such differences. We judge—or are supposed to judge—the murder of a spatially and temporally distant person with whom we are personally unacquainted to be no less blameworthy than the murder of one of our kin. And Hume certainly attempts to explain this phenomenon.

In order to arrive at a general and stable basis for communicating with one another, Hume argues, we need to "correct" our tendencies toward greater empathy with those best known to us, and for that reason, we set up a more impartial standard or rule for making moral judgments that depends not on our variable and often mutually contradictory empathetic relations to those affected by different actions or motives, but rather on the point of view of those "who have any immediate connexion or intercourse" with the person we are judging.[9] So (at least in "calm" moments) we are equally critical of child abuse involving people we don't know and of child abuse involving a person or people we do know and even love. But Hume also thinks that the actual consequences of various traits or kinds of action are more variable and irregular than their causal tendencies, so he goes on to argue that moral judgment is reasonably grounded in the *tendency* to cause harm (or good) rather than in actually caused harm (or good).

Thus according to Hume, moral judgments are or should be made in a (relatively) impartial way that abstracts from the judger's relation to those who are or tend to be benefited or harmed by given traits or actions, and the same point can be made regarding those who are or tend to be immediately pleased or displeased by certain traits or actions. But judgment is not the same thing as approval or disapproval, and Hume never says that the latter requires, or exists only when subjected to, the previously mentioned corrections. He does, however,

---

approval and disapproval, see, e. g., Stephen Darwall, "Hume and the invention of utilitarianism," in M. A. Stewart and J. P. Wright, eds., *Hume and Hume's Connexions* (University Park: Pennsylvania State University Press, 1994), 58–82.

8. See, e. g., Hume, *Treatise*, 590.

9. See Hume, *Treatise*, 602f. For interesting discussion of the need to "regularize" moral judgment in the way Hume suggests, see Geoffrey Sayre-McCord, "On Why Hume's 'General Point of View' Isn't Ideal—and Shouldn't Be," *Social Philosophy and Policy* 11 (*Cultural Pluralism and Moral Knowledge*) (1994): 202–228.

seem to think (though he isn't very clear about the point) that approval and disapproval only count as *moral* approval and disapproval, when the particular relationships of the person registering approval or disapproval have been substantially discounted or set aside in the process of arriving at the approval and disapproval. So although Hume thinks that both moral approval and moral judgment can involve mechanisms of empathy, that empathy is or is supposed to be corrected or regularized in the direction of an impartiality that, according to Hume, natural virtues like benevolence don't require and even preclude.

However, if we for the moment set aside the differences between approval and judgment and the question of partiality versus impartiality, we can see that Hume allows two different routes to virtue status and to moral approval and judgment as well: what immediately pleases and what is useful (in Hume's empiricist hedonic terms). But there is a problem with this view that Adam Smith (and others) early on pointed out.[10] If moral approval and judgment can be based on how certain traits or actions affect or tend to affect (certain) people's welfare, it is unclear why inanimate objects or events cannot be the subject of moral approval and disapproval: for example, why we shouldn't and don't morally criticize hurricanes for tending to cause harm and misery. And if approval and judgment can be based on whether something immediately pleases or displeases, there likewise seems to be no reason we can't morally disapprove of an ugly sunset or unpleasant nonhuman noise(maker).

Hume seeks to answer that objection (which it is thought he originally received directly from Smith himself) in a long footnote in *An Enquiry Concerning the Principles of Morals*.[11] That reply appeals to the (assumed) fact that the pleasure we feel regarding inanimate things is simply (phenomenologically) different from that we feel in respect to human beings. Even if the mechanism of empathy/sympathy can operate to make us feel pain at the pain caused by a hurricane, that second-order pain is not of the right kind to qualify our attitude toward its cause as one of disapproval, and similarly when we feel pleasure at the pleasure (that we know or see) inanimate things or entities cause.

This reply seems rather tendentious or question begging (a point that Hume comes very close to making against his future self near the end of the *Treatise*, p. 617). Aside from the desire to shore up a particular account of human approval

---

10. See Smith's *The Theory of Moral Sentiments*, ed. D. D. Raphael and A. L. Macfie (Oxford: Oxford University Press, 1976), Part IV, Ch. II. For discussion of similar early criticisms of Hume, see James Fieser, "Hume's Wide View of the Virtues: An Analysis of His Early Critics," *Hume Studies* 24 (1998): 295–311.

11. Hume, *An Enquiry Concerning the Principles of Morals*, Section V, p. 213n. See also the *Treatise*, 471–473. Hume's view also allows for approval and disapproval of animals, and for animals to possess certain virtues and vices, but Hume doesn't seem to have thought this would be problematic. See, e. g., Tom Beauchamp, "Hume on the Nonhuman Animal," *Journal of Medicine and Philosophy* 24 (1999): 322–335. I won't take up this issue in its own right here.

and disapproval, is there really any reason to think that the pleasure we feel at the pleasure caused by humans is phenomenologically different from what we feel in regard to pleasure caused by inanimate entities? And more generally, is Hume really right to assume moral approval is (always) pleasant and disapproval unpleasant or disagreeable?

On the face of it, there are many occasions when approval doesn't seem pleasant and can even seem unpleasant. Thus, as Pall Ardal has pointed out, one can feel *begrudging* approval of the decent or noble acts of someone one strongly dislikes; similarly, it can sometimes feel good and even be enjoyable to disapprove (and criticize) other people.[12] And surely such an appeal to phenomenology is a dialectically fair form of criticism to direct at someone like Hume who places such importance on phenomenological considerations. Still, one might hold that approval and disapproval have a distinctive feel, even if that feel isn't apparent or realized on every occasion when they occur, and so I prefer to argue against Hume's account at least partly on the grounds that the difference in phenomenology between approval and disapproval (and between those phenomena and other phenomena) is *better* captured in terms other than pleasure and pain. But in order to see why, I believe we need an account of approval and disapproval that focuses on agential traits and the standpoint of those who possess them, rather than on (empathy with) the effects such traits have on the welfare of others.[13]

That is precisely what Hutcheson does in holding that the moral sense of approval or disapproval is primarily directed toward the greater or lesser benevolence of moral agents, rather than toward any results of such motivation. (This is also true of Adam Smith's account of approval and disapproval.) But we also want a theory that goes beyond the implausible (or purely metaphorical) idea of a distinct moral sense, one that spells out an understandable *mechanism* for moral approval and disapproval but that also, as I have just been suggesting, allows our approval and disapproval to focus on moral agents rather than on the consequences of their actions. And what I want now to argue is that we may be able to find what we are looking for in a certain way of using or understanding the notion of empathy. Empathy focused on agents will not only offer us

---

12. See Pall Ardal, *Passion and Value in Hume's Treatise* (Edinburgh: Edinburgh University Press, 1966), 114ff. A reader for Oxford University Press has pointed out that Hume can allow for the unpleasantness of contemplating, say, the courage of an enemy by insisting that if one takes an impartial point of view, that courage will then be pleasing to one. But even if one is impartial enough to approve the courage, will the original unpleasantness really go away? Is it realistic to suppose that one could actually come to feel *pleasure* at the courage of one's enemy (rather than simply recognizing that less-involved others will tend to be pleased by that courage)? These issues seem to me to represent problems for Hume.

13. Elizabeth Radcliffe has pointed out to me that Hume himself moves to some extent in this direction when he allows that we can sometimes evaluate actions and settled traits favorably even when they don't produce their usual good effects. But even here Hume thinks our approval depends on our *imagining* the usual effects, and this seems to me to place too much emphasis on effects rather than agents. See the *Treatise*, pp. 584f.

a mechanism for approval and disapproval but also allow us to understand the phenomenology of approval and disapproval more accurately and intuitively than Hume's theory enables us to do. (Unlike Hutcheson, Adam Smith in fact makes use of what we would call empathy in his account of agent-directed approval, but as I indicated earlier, I believe a reliance on his views would take us in an ultimately less satisfactory and in fact less *sentimentalist* direction than I and other sentimentalists would like. So I will not discuss his views further.)

Now the most familiar form or instance of empathy is not directed at agents but felt *by* agents for those who need help or are suffering. Empathically sensitive and caring agents will act on behalf of (some of) those who need or could use their help, and in chapter 1, I discussed some of the ways in which our helpfulness toward those in pain or need is mediated by empathic mechanisms— mechanisms, for example, and as I mentioned earlier, that make us more concerned about our intimates and about people we see than about people we only casually know or merely hear *about*. But agential empathy or empathic concern for others is itself a psychological state that may be the subject or object of empathy. We sometimes see that someone else feels empathic concern for another and/or see that empathy reflected or expressed in their actions toward that other person, but our ability to see or notice such things may itself partly or wholly depend on our ability to empathize with such an empathic agential point of view, with the empathy of agents.

When we empathize with agential empathy, what we are doing is very different from what the agent is doing. The empathically concerned agent wants and seeks to do what is helpful to some person or persons (leaving aside animals for simplicity's sake). Empathic agents feel empathy, for example, *with* (the point of view of) certain people their actions may affect and are concerned *for* or *about* (the welfare or wishes of) those people. But when we feel empathy with empathically concerned agents (as agents), we empathize with *them*, not with the people they are empathizing with or focused on. We empathize, in other words, *with what they as (potential) agents are feeling and/or desiring*, and such empathy is, I believe, the core or basis of moral approval and disapproval. If (as I have been suggesting here and as I argued at great length in *The Ethics of Care and Empathy*) moral goodness consists or is embodied in certain sorts (or a certain pattern) of empathic concern for or about (the well-being of) those who may be *affected* by given actions or traits, then, I believe, moral approval may involve a different sort or direction of empathy, empathy with (the standpoint of) *agents*.

People whose capacity for empathy is fully developed will, I believe, have a different empathic reaction to (the characteristic actions of) agents whose empathy is also fully developed from that which they will have to (the characteristic actions of) agents who have less-developed empathy. In particular, if agents' actions reflect empathic concern for (the well-being or wishes of) others, empathic beings will feel warmly or tenderly toward them, and such warmth and tenderness empathically reflect the empathic warmth or tenderness of the agents. I want to say that such (in one sense) reflective feeling, such *empathy with empathy*, also constitutes moral approval, and possibly admiration as well, for agents and/or their actions.

This view is interestingly similar to some things that Hume and Shaftesbury say about approval. (We will be speaking about disapproval in just a moment.) On pages 604 and 605 of the *Treatise*, for example, Hume points out that our approval of love has an origin different from the prospect of utility to oneself or others and depends, rather, on our being moved to tears or "infinitely touched" by tender sentiments and those who have or exhibit them. This at the very least implies that we feel tenderly toward those who themselves are tender, and Hume then goes on to say: "Where friendship appears in very signal instances, my heart catches the same passion, and is warm'd by those warm sentiments, that display themselves before me."

If one were to regard *all* approval as having such a basis (and so deny that approval can be grounded in the utility of motives or traits), one would be very close to my suggestion that we empathically warm to empathic agential warmth toward others and that approval consists in our having such a reaction. And notice, too, how Hume's image of our being moved to tears by tender sentiments (his actual words are "[t]he tears naturally start in our eyes") works against his general view that (all) approval is phenomenologically pleasant or pleasurable in a univocal or unambiguous way.

What I am saying about approval (and disapproval) also bears some resemblance to Shaftesbury's views on that topic. Shaftesbury explicitly treats moral approval as involving a kind of affection and liking for certain agential affections (and disapproval as involving an aversion to negative feelings and actions on the part of agents), and this is quite similar to the view I want to defend here.[14]

Disapproval can then be understood on analogy with approval. If a person's actions toward others exhibit a basic lack of empathy, then empathic people will tend to be chilled (or at least "left cold") by those actions, and I want to say that those (reflective) feelings toward the agent constitute moral disapproval. Thus empathy with an agent's lack of empathy or empathic concern for others, with an agent's cold indifference (or worse) toward others, yields a similar feeling in the person who *has* empathy, and that feeling, which I have just said amounts to a feeling of disapproval, is very different from the warmth or tenderness that is characteristically expressed in what an empathic person does as an agent.

We are clearly, then, talking about two different points of view here: that of agents and that of someone who approves or disapproves of a given agent or agents. The latter is not exactly the point of view of a judge, because we are

---

14. See Shaftesbury's *Characteristicks of Men, Manners, Opinions, and Times*, 2 vols., ed. J. Robertson (Indianapolis, Ind.: Bobbs-Merrill, 1964), vol. I, p. 251. I am indebted here to Darwall's discussion in *The British Moralists*, pp. 233f.

speaking here only of moral approval and disapproval and are understanding these as feelings that aren't as such tantamount to any kind of moral claim or judgment. Perhaps the point of view of approval and disapproval is best characterized at this point as *third-personal*, since, like the notion of a judge, this allows us to draw the contrast between the first-person standpoint of agents deciding what to do or choose and what happens when we react to agents and their actions with approval or disapproval without ourselves being (immediately or as such) in the position of having to decide what to do or choose.

These distinctions are very important, if we are not to slip into the mistaken belief that a theory like the one we are proposing regards empathic concern for others and the moral approval or disapproval of an empathic person as the very same thing—which we could simply call empathy. First of all, and most obviously, I am not treating approval as being the same as disapproval, because the latter involves feeling some kind of chill in contemplating (the actions of) some agent, whereas approval involves the/an *opposed* or *contrary* feeling of warmth or tenderness.[15] To be sure, it takes empathy for someone to arrive at either or both of these opposed feelings, but the empathy and/or the capacity for it isn't the feelings and isn't the approval or disapproval. But then, too, and as I indicated earlier, the empathic warmth that constitutes approval most immediately reflects what is going on in some agent as an agent, and this clearly differentiates it from the warmth that an agent concerned about (the welfare or wishes of) others feels about or toward those others. The feelings of warmth may or may not be phenomenologically similar, but (as we shall soon see more clearly) they are in any case different with respect to their source.

But note that our account also explains why (or yields the conclusion that) people incapable of empathy are not only lacking in virtue but also incapable of genuinely approving or disapproving the virtues and vices of others. (They may be able to use language that is typically used to express approval and disapproval, but as we have known at least since Hare's discussion of "inverted commas" value judgments, this may be compatible with saying they aren't really capable of moral approval and disapproval.)[16] So the unvirtuous or immoral agent who is coldly indifferent or unempathic toward others doesn't have the empathic capacity to *feel* the indifference or cold that *other* immoral agents feel and manifest in the direction of others, and to that extent, ironically but not implausibly, a morally good person can momentarily, through empathy, take in (or "pick up") something from a bad person that another bad person will not be able to take in (or "pick up") despite his or her *similarity* to the first bad person.

---

15. It may well be possible to feel a *mixture* of approval and disapproval, warmth and chill, in regard to a given action or character trait.

16. Someone who is partly or occasionally immoral may be capable of empathy and thus, according to the present view, of moral approval and disapproval (of self and others). Note too that Hume allows that some people are more capable of empathy and warm feeling than others.

But I think we need to say a bit more at this point about some of the feelings that I have said are involved in moral disapproval. We can presumably understand the way in which virtuously feeling empathic concern for other people involves feeling warmly toward them, and the idea that empathy with such warmth involves warm feeling makes a good deal of sense. But what about the idea that disapproval involves empathically reflecting the coldly indifferent attitudes of those we consider unvirtuous and lacking in empathy? Do unvirtuous unempathic people really have such attitudes?

What the unvirtuous, morally bad, unempathic person feels toward others may be indifference or may be malice, but both of those feelings contrast with warmth and show a lack or absence of warmth. Comparatively speaking, then, such people are cold (or cold-hearted or very cool) in their attitudes or feelings toward other people, and someone who empathically registers that coldness will thus be *chilled* by the attitudes or desires of a morally bad person (as expressed in certain actions). Such a person will, in effect, "catch (or pick up) a chill" from "cold-hearted" agents who lack a warm concern for others, and the chill thus caught will constitute disapproval of such agents (or their actions).[17] On the present theory, then, the familiar phrase "the chill of disapproval" applies much more literally than (I suspect) philosophers and others who use that phrase ever imagine.[18]

17. One can be chilled by one's own previous actions, but such feeling typically has to *compete* with the bad or guilty feelings any agent who has received inductive training will feel at having, say, hurt another person. Since we don't feel such guilt about others' actions, we are more likely to feel chilled by what others have done than by what we ourselves have done, even when we see the harm and/or immorality of our own actions. Spinoza tells us that one (strong) feeling tends to drive out another, and what I have just said about chilly disapproval and guilty bad feelings illustrates (and depends on) this idea. But given my theory of what disapproval is, this also constitutes an argument for the surprising conclusion that when we feel bad or guilty about what we have done, we aren't feeling disapproval of ourselves. Surprising or not, however, this last idea isn't, when one thinks of it, all that counterintuitive. Disapproval as a notion seems intuitively to involve strictness, coldness, and tightness in one's feelings, whereas the idea of feeling bad or guilty about one's actions conveys notions of free-flowing feeling and even something like warmth. That is, in disapproval, our warmth is somehow suppressed and feeling isn't loosened or flowing, whereas just the opposite seems to be true for or of feeling bad or guilty about something; these thoughts may help us see that feeling bad about what one has done *simply isn't the same psychological phenomenon* as self-disapproval, just as the present sentimentalist account of moral emotions wants to claim.

18. However, one must be careful in saying this, because the phrase "the chill of disapproval" typically applies to how someone feels when *disapproved of* rather than to how the disapprover feels. But if one feels the chill of someone's disapproval (of oneself or possibly of another), there presumably has to be something chilly in (and emanating from) the attitude of the disapprover, and *that* chill, according to the present theory, both reflects the cold-hearted or chilling attitudes/motives/actions of the person disapproved of and constitutes disapproval of them. So the chill or cold at issue here can go full circle: the agential coldness or lack of warmth of certain individuals can be reflected, as disapproval, in those who behold or learn about it, but that chilly disapproval can in turn be felt as "the chill of disapproval" by someone—possibly the agent who is disapproved of—who comes into contact with the disapprover (though that person has to be capable of some empathy and not be a psychopath, for this to happen).

Furthermore, the present approach also avoids the difficulties that Adam Smith attributed to the Humean approach to moral approval and disapproval.[19] If approval and disapproval involve empathy with (the point of view of) agents, then there is no danger that we will morally approve or disapprove of boulders, houses, storms, or other things that can be useful or harmful to people. If we feel chilled or, possibly, repelled by certain people and that constitutes a disapproval of them, that is because those people are cold-hearted toward others and our being chilled or repelled empathically reflects that (immoral) attitude/motivation on their part.[20] But inanimate objects don't harm or hurt us as a result of having such motives or attitudes. So there is nothing for empathy to latch on to in what inanimate objects do in their (quasi-)agential capacity, and our theory therefore makes it understandable, as indeed it ought to be, that inanimate objects are not the targets of moral approval and disapproval.[21]

At this point, however, some further issues need to be considered. I have said that approval involves feeling warmth in empathic response to the agential warmth involved in morally good or approvable action and that disapproval involves a similar relation to the (relative) coldness or cold-heartedness underlying immoral behavior. But if these feelings are similar or analogous to what they reflect, then they may seem to lack the right intentionality to count as approval or disapproval. Warm agential concern for others focuses on those others, for example, and empathy with such concern might focus on the same people, rather than being (exclusively) directed toward the agents themselves. But approval is primarily an attitude toward an agent, not toward those the agent is concerned about, so it may be wondered how empathically feeling (some of) the warmth the agent feels toward others can constitute approval *of the agent*, and the same point can, of course, be made about coldness and disapproval as well.

But here we must remember an important distinction we drew earlier between the empathy felt by an agent concerned with other people and the empathy felt by someone who empathically reacts to and approves of such empathy. The two kinds of empathy differ with respect to their *source*, and

---

19. Emotivism is sometimes criticized for making facts only causally, rather than logically, relevant to evaluative attitudes and utterances. (See, for example, Richard Brandt, "The Emotive Theory of Ethics," *Philosophical Review* 59 [1950]: 305–318.) But the present account of approval and disapproval and, eventually, of moral judgment asserts precisely such a tighter connection.

20. I take it that feeling repelled is (like) feeling a kind of chill. But I won't attempt to be more fine-grained about this here.

21. Disapproval may be an empathic response to the indifference to others of an immoral person, but indifference is a real (cold-hearted) attitude that disapproval conceived as empathy can latch on to. The so-called indifference of the universe or of inanimate objects is not literally a (cold-hearted) psychological attitude, so our theory is not committed to (making sense of) disapproval of inanimate objects. The trouble with Hume's view that disapproval embodies a (corrected) sympathy with the point of view of those who receive certain benefits and harms is that it doesn't in and of itself rule out disapproval of inanimate causes of such harm. But if disapproval embodies empathy with something, and in particular with cold or cold-hearted attitudes/motives, there is no way that we can disapprove of mere things. And similar points can be made about approval as well.

this not only distinguishes them but also allows us, I think, to understand approval (and disapproval) in the terms sketched previously. The source of agential empathy (or empathic concern) is the plight or state of certain individuals seen as potentially affected by her or his actions and not (in that respect) as agents themselves. But empathy felt in response to agential empathy has a somewhat different causal history, a different kind of source overall, precisely because it is responsive to what an agent (as an agent) feels. The source(s), in turn, of that agential feeling may also be included among the sources of empathy with empathy, but the difference between the empathy involved in approval and the empathy involved in agential concern is that the former has an agential source that the latter lacks.

I want to say that this difference in source helps to constitute empathy about or with empathy as approval of an agent. Even if the empathic warmth the approver feels for the warmth of someone concerned about others takes in that very concern and is to that extent focused on those others, its immediate source is the agent, not those the agent is concerned about, and what approval is approval *of* depends to a substantial extent, I think, on such causal matters rather than on pure phenomenology or seeming intentionality. After all, we have causal theories of reference and of memory that tell us that what we refer to or are remembering at a given time is more dependent on the causal source or origin of a putative reference or memory than on the phenomenology or seeming intentionality of what we are doing.[22] And although I think some such theories don't sufficiently acknowledge intentional or phenomenological factors that may also be involved in the phenomena they theorize about, they at least helped us (for the first time) see how important a role causality plays in our mentalistic vocabulary. There may be (and indeed I believe there are) limits to what, on grounds of intentionality or phenomenology, can constitute reference to an object, memory of an event, or empathic (dis)approval, but it is important to see how causality plays a role in constituting these psychological phenomena. Thus even if the empathic warmth felt third-personally in response to agential concern for others may be phenomenologically similar to that concern and share some of its focus and origins, its causal origin is different because that origin includes agential empathy itself, and so, on the theory I have been describing, moral approval is a kind of second-order empathy and to that extent differs from the empathy of agents concerned simply with how other people may be affected by their actions.[23]

22. On causal theories of reference, see especially Saul Kripke, *Naming and Necessity* (Oxford: Blackwell, 1980). On causal theories of memory, see C. B. Martin and Max Deutscher, "Remembering," *Philosophical Review* 75 (1966): 161–196.

23. I have spoken of approval and disapproval as causally reflecting the actual warm or cold attitudes of agents. But one can also approve or disapprove of actions and individuals that one merely hears about and that may not actually exist or have existed (in the way they are depicted to one). But just as one may have empathic concern for a group that one merely hears about and that may not, in fact, exist, so, too, may one empathically respond to what, on the basis of false accounts or misleading perceptions, one takes to be the warm concern (or cold indifference) embodied in the actions or

Now the present sentimentalist approach also treats moral disapproval as *discordant* in a way that approval isn't. For those it regards as empathic enough to be capable of approval and disapproval, generally feel warmly toward other people. Yet when they disapprove of someone's motives, character, or actions, they empathically register that agent's coldness or coolness, and this at the very least will be disharmonious with their general warmth or tenderness (though it is not obvious that such disharmony has to be felt as unpleasant or disagreeable). By contrast, approval is a matter of warm feeling that harmonizes with an empathic person's overall warm agential concern about others (though, again, such harmony may not need to be felt as positively pleasant or agreeable).

Hume typically speaks of moral disapproval as involving a feeling of uneasiness, rather than of unpleasantness, and the use of that term at the very least suggests, though it doesn't actually say, that disapproval is discordant or inharmonious with the usual feelings of the person who disapproves. But in any event, I think there is nothing implausible in the idea that disapproval involves disharmony in a way that approval does not. (People who are totally inhumane and unempathic in their actions toward others presumably lack the empathy that is necessary to register either approval or disapproval of other agents. So such people won't experience or exemplify either the harmony or the disharmony I have just been speaking of.)

In addition, however, both Hume and Hutcheson hold that approval is a pleasant and agreeable feeling, and although we have seen how an empiricist/ associationist psychology operating via pleasure/pain mechanisms might want to say such things, present-day sentimentalism needn't rely on such a narrowly empiricist psychology. The present theory of approval and disapproval doesn't have to say that approval is (automatically) pleasant or disapproval (automatically) unpleasant, and this seems truer to experience than what Hume says about approval and disapproval. Phenomenologically speaking, the difference between approval and disapproval seems more a matter of warmth versus coldness than of pleasantness versus unpleasantness,[24] but at the same time, our

---

character of some supposed agent. In such cases, there is a causal connection between what one thinks one knows about an agent and one's own empathic *response to it*, so although the causal picture is more complicated for situations where one is misinformed or even hallucinating, I don't think this casts doubt on our account of approval and disapproval. However, it does show that that account is somewhat different from causal theories of reference, memory, and knowledge. But even if empathy/ (dis)approval doesn't work entirely the way memory and the like do, many mental phenomena work very similarly to the way I have said it works. Thus anger doesn't require the existence of what one is angry with or at, but causal factors are involved in determining what one is angry with/at, and there may also be phenomenological/intentional limits on what such causal factors can qualify as anger. If this seems plausible for anger, the present view that things work similarly for empathic (dis)approval is given some plausibility as well. (Compare Hoffman, *Empathy and Moral Development*, 8.)

24. In "Toward *Fin de Siècle* Ethics: Some Trends" (in a volume they edited titled *Moral Discourse and Practice: Some Philosophical Approaches* [New York: Oxford University Press, 1997, p. 22]), Stephen Darwall, Allan Gibbard, and Peter Railton say that moral approbation doesn't seem to have a distinctive phenomenology. But the present theory is seeking to show that (despite what it

account doesn't want or have to say that all warmth constitutes approval and all feelings of chill or coldness disapproval. Differences of causation can distinguish phenomenologically similar feelings, and we now need to consider some important further issues about the causation of approval and disapproval.

As we have described them, approval and disapproval are feelings, roughly, of warm tenderness and coldness or chill that are part of an empathic, but to that extent also a causal, response to the motives/attitudes/feelings of agents.[25] But feelings can be disrupted or prevented by other factors, and especially by other feelings, and Hume famously noted the various ways in which our personal relations to a given person may alter or affect our approval or disapproval of what they have done. Thus a mother whose son is on death row for murdering a baby may be so concerned about saving him from death that she fails to experience the feelings of disapproval she would feel about another killer, but by the same token, the baby's parents may be too angry as a result of their personal loss for their disapproval of the killer to register as a distinct or separate phenomenon. Such facts fit well with Hume's contention that we need a more neutral or impartial perspective from which to make open and public moral judgments, but they are also consonant with what I have been saying, and they have interesting implications worth dwelling on.

We can get angry when someone frustrates our purposes or the purposes of those we love, but if we keep our moral heads about us, we can sometimes recognize the difference between the targets of such anger and those we morally disapprove of. We may become angry with a person who gets a job we would have liked for ourselves or for someone in our family, but there may be nothing immoral, cold, or lacking in empathy in that other person's actions, and we may know both that our frustrated anger isn't an empathic response to the coldness and anger of an agent and that it isn't tantamount to disapproval. On the other hand, there are times when we or others may *not* be able to tell whether our feeling of chill toward another represents genuine disapproval or a phenomenologically similar feeling that has arisen in reaction to, say, the frustration of personal desires and purposes. This is a familiar fact of the moral life (though it tends to be obscured when one is oneself angry with another person), and our present approach has no problem accommodating it, because it understands disapproval (and approval, too) in substantially (though not exclusively) causal terms and because it is often so difficult to know the origins of a feeling like being chilled.

---

takes—and these authors presumably would take—to be Hume's failed efforts in that direction) there *is* such a phenomenology and that this phenomenology makes possible the kind of reference-fixing approach to moral language we will be defending here. (I don't want to speculate on why the moral phenomenology of warmth and chill has largely gone unnoticed by philosophers.)

25. Note how *idiomatic* or *natural* it is to think of someone who warms to another's attitudes or actions as approving of them and to think of someone who is chilled by another's attitudes or actions as disapproving of them. The present complex theory of moral approval and disapproval rests on some very intuitive ideas, and that very fact stands somewhat in its favor.

So certain personal feelings, desires, or reactions can interfere with approval or disapproval and/or make it unclear whether someone's feelings really are feelings of approval or disapproval, but the influence can also work in the reverse direction. Seeing someone one is concerned to help do something hurtful to a third party may arouse feelings of disapproval that disrupt or weaken one's original desire to help. In any event, what seems to follow from our prior discussion is that disapproval and approval are more likely to occur and to be recognizable as such in cases where we are not closely involved with the people whose motives or actions are being considered or with those whose lives they are likely to influence. Hutcheson says that the human tendency to approve and disapprove of actions in the remote past that we have nothing to gain or lose from is a very good argument for the nonselfish character of (some) human motivation, but in the terms of the present discussion, we can also say that such cases are (among) the ones in which it is easiest to know that any seeming approval/disapproval that has been elicited really is approval/disapproval. Moreover, it may be easier for empathy to glom on to what is morally bad or good and for it to produce a state of approval or disapproval, if that process doesn't have to compete with a person's other concerns and emotions. And this is perhaps most likely to happen when we are told in some evocative way about the motives and actions of some person in the remote past, since what this person has done or failed to do will have presumably had no practical bearing on ourselves or those we love (or dislike). (I am indebted here to discussion with Elizabeth Radcliffe.)

As I mentioned earlier, Hume can be interpreted as saying that it is desirable for moral judgment and moral approval and disapproval to be anchored in a disinterested or impartial standpoint, and he cites the *social usefulness* of having common terms of communication as the basis for that desideratum. However, leaving aside issues of moral judgment till later, the present account of approval and disapproval lays stress on impartiality for somewhat different reasons. The present causal-sentimentalist theory of approval and disapproval treats conditions of impartiality, rather, as helping to (epistemically) *clarify* whether given warmth or coldness really constitutes approval or disapproval and (whether this is a desirable thing or not) as *facilitating* the actual occurrence of these moral reactions.[26] So the present theory treats impartiality as importantly relevant to moral approval and disapproval (and moral judgment), but the importance it places on impartiality is to some extent independent of the considerations that the eighteenth-century sentimentalists treat as favoring or requiring impartiality.

Let me also say something, finally, about the difference between approval and admiration. As we have been describing it, approval doesn't have to be as positive or laudatory an attitude as admiration clearly is, for when we approve of some action of our own or others, we may simply be viewing it as morally acceptable or all right, rather than as positively good—or admirable. But then, too,

---

26. However, compare Hume, *Treatise*, e.g., p. 472.

admirability is a characteristic that is exemplified outside the moral realm—we admire sheer intelligence, great beauty, and great art. But our discussion of approval has been implicitly confined to the sphere of the moral. We don't "approve" of intelligence, beauty, and art precisely because, or when, these subject matters don't touch on moral issues. And the account I have offered of approval and disapproval is specifically geared toward the moral through its central focus on empathy concerning others. Someone who wants to prove a theorem needn't feel any such empathy, but the concern to help others and the concern not to break promises or kill the innocent *are* moral, and the fact that they involve a responsive empathic concern for others helps to characterize them as moral. And similarly, for empathic approval of other people's agential concern for third parties or ourselves.

To be sure, empathy is sometimes said to be necessary to understanding and properly responding to works of art, but the kind of empathy involved here doesn't seem to entail any empathic concern for anyone, and that is why it is natural not to regard it as particularly moral. So the theory of approval I have offered is ipso facto a theory of moral approval, and that makes it appropriate to use it, as I now propose to do, in understanding and explaining the character of explicit moral judgments.

3

EMPATHY IN MORAL JUDGMENT

Sentimentalist accounts of moral approval and disapproval have often been criticized for failing to allow for a judgmental aspect to or basis for these attitudes. The sentimentalists regard moral judgments as grounded in feelings of approval and disapproval, but numerous critics—starting with Richard Price in *A Review of the Principal Questions in Morals* (1758) and Thomas Reid in *Essays on the Active Powers of* Man (1788), but including many others up to the present day—have argued that such an approach misses an essential element of approval and disapproval: the fact that they involve or are constituted by judgments about the rightness or wrongness (or goodness or badness) of certain (kinds of) acts, motives, or traits of character. In that case, the sentimentalist metaethical enterprise is doomed to a kind of circularity. Far from having the potential to help us understand the character of (or even define) moral judgments or moral "sentences," approval and disapproval presuppose, involve, or are equivalent to such judgments or sentences, and the sentimentalist attempt to base moral attitudes in judgment-free feelings of approval/disapproval (or more generally in nonrational elements in human psychology) is therefore doomed to failure.

The last chapter, however, offered an account of moral approval and disapproval that seems truer to the emotional quality or phenomenology of those attitudes than anything rationalists have to say about them. And the account was genuinely sentimentalist, because nothing that was said about empathy as the constituting basis of approval and disapproval presupposed the making of, or a commitment to, specific or general moral judgments. The idea that moral approval doesn't require a moral judgment about rightness may seem odd and implausible at first, but the empathic reaction of being warmed by someone's helpfulness toward others doesn't appear to involve any judgment and *does* seem to involve a positive emotional attitude toward the person('s helpfulness), one that contrasts with the empathic "chill" we take from seeing (learning about) someone else's cruelty or indifference toward others, a chill that it is natural to describe as constituting or involving a negative feeling toward the cruel or indifferent person('s behavior).

However, things are a little more complicated than I have just implied. If, as I argued earlier, warm approval isn't always (unambiguously) pleasant, we might wonder what actually marks it as positive and cold disapproval as negative and what therefore marks particular moral judgments or properties as either positive or negative. This problem is raised in a slightly different form by Simon Blackburn in his article "Circles, Finks, Smells, and Biconditionals," and we need to say something about it because a sentimentalist account of moral judgment needs to be able to make the distinction between positive and negative in sentimentalist terms. And that means being able somehow to say *why* the empathic chill of disapproval is negative and the (not necessarily pleasurable) empathic warmth of approval is positive.[1]

Now as I indicated earlier, someone whose empathy in regard to others is well developed will (as an agent) empathize with and have some desire to help those who need or could benefit from help, but such a person will also (as an observer of the actions of others or even of self) empathize with other agents. It follows that someone with well-developed empathy who disapproves of the action of another person because it displays selfish indifference or malice toward some third party will have some motive/desire not to do that kind of action (similarly, if the disapproved action is a merely potential action of the agent). But if to disapprove of some action is to be motivated *away* from doing actions of that kind, that gives us a sense in which chilly disapproval counts as a negative attitude; and if, as we could analogously show, warm approval of an action motivates us *toward* doing actions of that kind, that means that approval is a positive attitude. This explanation doesn't presuppose or make use of moral judgments, but it does allow us to use our account of approval and disapproval to explain why judgments of rightness and moral goodness based in approval count as positive, and judgments of wrongness or moral badness based in disapproval count as negative. And it also helps us understand why both classes of judgments motivate as they do.[2]

---

1. *Philosophical Perspectives* 7 (1993): esp. p. 275. In this article, Blackburn argues that metaethical accounts of moral terms that analogize such terms with color terms will have to explain and have a hard time explaining why moral terms are positive or negative, but color terms aren't. This is a powerful challenge to (the) metaethical sentimentalism (defended here), which at various points and in various ways *does* invoke an analogy with color terms.

2. The present discussion can be reinforced by the consideration that empathy with the presence or absence of empathic warm concern in agents is clearly second-order. It is hard to imagine such empathy existing in the absence of a capacity for first-order (warm) empathic concern for others, and in that case, again, disapproval will involve a tendency to *resist* doing a certain kind of thing and thus be naturally viewed as a *negative* attitude toward what is disapproved. To the extent, then, too, that

Moreover, the fact that certain nonjudgmental empathy-derived attitudes or feelings toward (the ways) agents (treat others) can be characterized as positive and negative lends definite support to the view that they *are*, respectively, attitudes of approval and disapproval. If what we are talking about here isn't full-blown moral approval or disapproval, then at the very least it can be plausibly viewed as the ur-phenomenon of moral approval and disapproval, and if we can now use what we have said about these (ur-)attitudes to clarify moral judgments and any sort of (full-blown) moral approval and disapproval that springs from or requires moral judgment, then the sentimentalist approach will be largely vindicated or at least made to seem somewhat plausible as a way of doing metaethics.

Now Hume attempts to clarify—some would even say that he suggests some possible ways of *defining*—moral judgments/claims/sentences on the basis of his views about approval and disapproval as nonjudgment-presupposing attitudes or feelings, but we earlier rejected the Humean consequence-oriented account of these attitudes in favor of one that focuses on empathic reactions to the agents who bring about certain consequences.[3] Even so, we might still be able to use what Hume says about the *link* or *relationship* between feelings of approval and the moral judgments we actually make (or, so as not to presuppose cognitivism, the moral sentences we actually utter or write) to illuminate, or define, the latter. However, if we go this route, we should recognize that it loads us with an embarrassment of riches. Hume scholars and others have found a variety of different (inchoate) theories of the meaning of moral judgments/sentences (and of their relation to feelings of approval) within the *Treatise*, and some of these were original with Hume. But the theories are also all inconsistent with one

---

moral judgments involve approval and disapproval, they will be inherently motivating, and our sentimentalist metaethical approach will therefore count as a kind (*one kind*) of "moral judgment internalism."

In addition to accepting the "empathy-altruism" hypothesis, Martin Hoffman in *Empathy and Moral Development: Implications for Caring and Justice* (Cambridge: Cambridge University Press, 2000) claims that empathy can be psychologically tied to moral rules or principles, turning the latter into motivationally active "hot cognitions." But this assumes that we can understand and make general moral claims independently of any emotional involvement, so Hoffman isn't, in fact, a sentimentalist about moral judgment. However, I see no reason that he couldn't accept a sentimentalist approach to moral judgment of the sort advocated here. (More on this in later chapters.) For now, I am also ignoring questions (raised by Elizabeth Radcliffe) about the difference different agential capacities for empathy might make to reactions of approval or actual behavior.

3. One might also criticize Hume for regarding pleasure felt at the good someone does to others as a form of *approval*, but that criticism wouldn't be so telling against Hume's overall enterprise if he could show how that pleasure can ground and/or clarify the making of positive moral judgments. If he could accomplish *that*, then it wouldn't be so important whether we called the pleasure in question approval or ur-approval or even something else. Certainly, any pleasure tends to be regarded as positive and therefore resembles the "feel" of approval in most cases, but whatever we might say about these issues, the criticisms of Hume made in the text, if valid, make his overall metaethical approach seem at least somewhat unsatisfactory. I am indebted here to discussions with Charles Pigden.

another, and if one wants to be more consistent than Hume seems to have been, then one has to decide among these theories or advocate some different senti-mentalist account of (the relation between approval and) moral judgment. (As earlier, I will drop the qualification about moral sentences or utterances, because the reader who prefers that sort of formulation will know how to adjust what I say about "judgments" accordingly.)

Hume has been (not so unreasonably) viewed as a subjectivist ("x is right" means "I like x" and describes one's approval of x), as an emotivist ("x is right" means something like "hurrah for x!" and *expresses* one's approval of x), as an ideal observer theorist about moral judgment ("x is right" means something like "an impartially benevolent well-informed calm spectator would feel cor-rected feelings of approval toward x"), or as a projectivist/expressivist error theorist about moral judgments (they project our feelings of approval *onto* the world but always speak falsely about what they purport to characterize). And it is also possible for a sentimentalist to maintain a Kripkean reference-fixing view of moral judgments that sees "benevolence is morally good" and "cruelty is wrong" on analogy with a posteriori claims about sensible qualities like "red is what reflects such and such light frequencies." On such a view, which I myself have developed and defended in past work (but which Kripke himself has never endorsed), warm empathic feelings of approval noncircularly fix the reference of "morally right" (and "morally wrong") the way the experience of red(ness) fixes the reference of "red" for us.[4]

If one wants to offer a specific definition of "morally right," one certainly has to choose among these or possibly other theories of the meaning of moral sentences/predicates,[5] and some of the theories just mentioned seem implausible on their face and have seemed so to most recent metaethicists: I am thinking here

---

4. David Wiggins comes fairly close to such an approach in "Truth, Invention, and the Meaning of Life" in his *Needs, Values, Truth: Essays in the Philosophy of Value* (Oxford: Blackwell, 1987). And in *The British Moralists and the Internal "Ought": 1640–1740* (Cambridge: Cambridge University Press, 1995) esp. pp. 214f., Stephen Darwall claims that it is possible to see Francis Hutcheson as holding a Kripkean, reference-fixing view of moral concepts—*rather than* an ideal observer theory: Hutcheson says some things that indicate that he conceives moral goodness as *whatever* quality *in fact* causes approbation, that he thinks the nature of that property can be discerned only by *empirical* investigation, and that he also allows for the possibility of a world in which no one approves of what is good. For my own attempt to give a Kripkean reference-fixing account of moral terms, see, e. g., my "Moral Sentimentalism and Moral Psychology" in D. Copp., ed., *The Oxford Handbook of Ethical Theory* (Oxford: Oxford University Press, 2006), esp. pp. 236f. For reasons mentioned in the main text, I no longer think a purely Kripkean approach will work.

5. Almost all the semantic theories about moral terms have their parallel in semantic theories about sensory qualities like red(ness). There are subjectivist, ideal-observer, projectivist, and, of course, reference-fixing views of the meaning of color terms—but no one, to my knowledge, has ever come out with an emotive theory of the meaning of such terms. That fact is perhaps explained by the further fact that moral terms can be positive or negative, but color terms are neither. For a penetrating discussion of the emotivist and other tendencies in Hume's (confused, confusing, but deep) metaethical thinking, see Jonathan Harrison, *Hume's Moral Epistemology* (Oxford: Clarendon Press, 1976), chapter 7.

of (simple) subjectivism and (simple) emotivism. On the other hand, Simon Blackburn's projectivist error theory of moral judgment denies that moral utterances ever state moral truths or are objectively valid and does so with great panache and dexterity,[6] and it isn't easy to see what is wrong with that view, except, perhaps, for the fact that it *denies a deep-seated pretheoretical view of the nature of moral discourse*.[7] I think most of us would prefer a theory that did justice to that intuitive, commonsense understanding of things but that could also do justice to the motivational (positive/negative) force of moral claims. And I am trying to work out such a view in this book. So until and unless it more clearly appears that such a way of proceeding is on the wrong track, I think we should leave projectivism to one side and continue with the present project.

Now the ideal observer theory does allow for moral truth (and for moral falsity as well) and to that extent fares better in commonsense terms than projectivism does. However, ideal observer theories (and response-dependent theories) of moral terms typically treat ordinary moral judgments like "cruelty is wrong" as a posteriori, and this seems highly problematic. Since Kripkean reference-fixing sentimentalist approaches to moral judgments also have this problem, they, too, are somewhat dubious, and that leaves us at this point, therefore, without any definite account of the meaning of moral terms or claims.[8]

But that doesn't mean we can't work out such an account in a new way that is at least partly based on what we have said so far about approval and disapproval and their basis in empathy. However, before we do this (in chapter 4), I would like to show how what we have said so far *can usefully illuminate the general character of moral judgments or utterances*. Then, once some of the most important features of moral judgments have been explained in sentimentalist terms, we can try to be

---

6. See Blackburn's *Spreading the Word* (Oxford: Clarendon Press, 1984). To simplify matters, I have been downplaying the quasi-realist side of Blackburn's projectivism. That "side" of Blackburn's view is sometimes said to be in tension with (or even to be in some measure inconsistent with) its error-theoretic antirealism, but I won't here enter into these potential problems for Blackburn's approach.

7. For the idea that moral claims typically or conventionally lay claim to being objective, see, e.g., J. L. Mackie, *Ethics: Inventing Right and Wrong* (Harmondsworth: Penguin, 1977), p. 94. In *The Emotional Construction of Morals* (Oxford: Oxford University Press, 2007), Jesse Prinz argues that moral utterances *don't* so clearly lay claim to objectivity, but some of the cases/studies he mentions as calling the claim to objectivity into question don't seem to me to be well chosen for that purpose.

8. I am thinking here of an approach to moral predicates that treats them *exactly on analogy* with what Kripke says about "red" and other natural kind terms. Such a Kripkean approach to moral terms, which I shall discuss further in the next chapter, would allow moral judgments to be metaphysically necessary but a posteriori. And this doesn't really constitute an advantage over ideal-observer or response-dependent views, since these can be rigidified in such a way as to also allow for metaphysically necessary moral judgments. (I assume we like the idea that "cruelty is wrong" holds in all possible worlds.) But all such views have the disadvantage of making what seems a priori (like "cruelty is wrong") come out a posteriori, and so I shall be looking for an account of moral terminology that doesn't have this weakness. However, in the next chapter, I shall also be arguing that ideal observer and response-dependent views don't allow for as much *objectivity* as we intuitively believe in and as my own *semi-Kripkean* reference-fixing approach can provide for.

more specific about the meaning of moral judgments/sentences/utterances. Rather than rely on a (purely) Kripkean theory of moral language, we can explicate moral terms both by comparison *and by contrast* with the way Kripke treats the reference-fixing and meaning of color terms and terms for other natural kinds.[9] But we shall do this in the next chapter, and our task in the present chapter will be to show how (even) what we have said so far about approval and disapproval can help us cast a good deal of light on the nature or character of moral judgments/language.

Moreover, even in the absence, so far, of a more detailed elaboration or explication of the meaning of moral terms, the position I as a sentimentalist am in here is no worse, and may in some respects be better, than the position Kantians and intuitionists are in with respect to moral judgment. Kantians and intuitionists don't offer definitions or precise explications of moral predicates or sentences. (In fact, Moore explicitly argues that such definition is impossible.) But that doesn't make them deny that moral claims can be true or objective (or rationally compelling), and neither does it prevent them from holding that such claims can also be inherently motivating (and provide reasons for action).

Now J. L. Mackie has claimed that such "objective prescriptivity" is queer and defies genuine understanding.[10] But I think his view gives short shrift to the approach defended by Thomas Nagel in *The Possibility of Altruism* and developed further by John McDowell in various articles (published after Mackie's book).[11] When one considers, for example, what Nagel says about prudence, it does seem as if an ethical judgment can be both objective and inherently motivating (what Mackie calls "prescriptive"), for Nagel points out that the belief that one will in the future have reason to (want to) do something can quite naturally, or plausibly, be seen as giving one a reason, and motivating one, to do things now that will make it easier or possible to do what one knows one will want and have reason to do in the future. (For example, if one knows one will need to be able to speak Italian in the future, that automatically gives one a reason to study Italian now.) Yet the idea that we will in the future have such a reason doesn't seem to be necessarily subjective (nonobjective) or merely emotional, so Nagel's account of prudence seems to allow for "objective prescriptivity" in that realm and therefore undercuts the (general) claim that such prescriptivity is necessarily queer or unacceptable.

---

9. In *Naming and Necessity* (Cambridge: Harvard University Press, 1980), Kripke doesn't offer a definition or analysis of color terms or natural kind terms more generally, but the reference-fixing explication or explanation he gives of these terms is fully satisfying and makes one not want to ask for anything more (like a definition). I hope, in the next chapter, to offer an explication/explanation of moral terms that is as satisfying as what Kripke offers for natural kind terms. I won't be giving an ordinary analytic definition, but I hope and believe that what I do say won't leave the reader asking/hoping for such a definition.

10. See Mackie, *Ethics*.

11. Nagel, *The Possibility of Altruism* (Oxford: Oxford University Press, 1970). McDowell's arguably most important contribution, "Virtue and Reason," is reprinted in R. Crisp and M. Slote, eds., *Virtue Ethics* (Oxford: Oxford University Press, 1997).

Of course, and famously, Nagel goes on to argue for the "objective prescriptivity" (not his terminology, but it will do) of moral claims, and this part of his argument is generally seen as less successful than what he says about prudence. John McDowell then enters the picture (as I reconstruct the history) and offers what some regard as a better defense of the idea of objective prescriptivity *within the moral realm*. But because I don't want to rely on the specifics of McDowell's view of morality, I don't propose to say much more here about his ideas. I think it is enough, for our purposes, that Nagel has given us a/one very plausible case where objectivity and prescriptivity come together.

That case, which involves prudence rather than morality, shows us at the very least that there is nothing inherently dubious or counterintuitive in the idea of objective prescriptivity, and that leaves the way open, therefore, to the sentimentalist account of moral language and moral judgment that I am developing here. That account, as I have said, allows moral judgments to be both objective and motivating, and since I believe it is more plausible or promising as an account of morality than anything rationalists like Nagel and (at least in his earlier days) McDowell offer us, I shall simply present it in its own right, rather than dwelling on the details of other, nonsentimentalist views. But in any event, and from my particular perspective, these rationalists *point the way for sentimentalism*, and that is why I have invoked their example in explaining why the objective prescriptivity my own account will provide for is not inherently questionable and actually has, after all, the advantage of giving us just about everything we (initially) want or assume regarding the moral. Morality seems at first to be an objective matter, and it also seems to be inherently motivating, and it would, in fact, be philosophically desirable if we could combine these two features of our ordinary understanding of morality.[12]

Now I can't offer you a (traditional analytic) definition of moral predicates any more than Nagel or McDowell can. But on the basis of the views I defended in *The Ethics of Care and Empathy* (ECE) and shall be briefly summarizing in a moment, I think we can argue that empathy is involved in the making (and therefore in the understanding) of moral claims. And such a conclusion allows

---

12. Don't be too quick to add that morality is (also) inherently reason-giving. This claim is somewhat ambiguous, and once one disentangles it, it is not clear that moral judgments will turn out to give reasons for action in the way rationalists (like Nagel and Scanlon) seek to defend. (I am indebted here to unpublished work by Brad Cokelet.) More specifically, my *Ethics of Care and Empathy* (chapter 7) offers some reasons for thinking that there is nothing *irrational* in failing to comply with the dictates of a valid morality. Total immorality entails heartlessness, not irrationality or a failure to appreciate the reasons everyone has to behave in certain ways. The account to be offered in what follows allows for the possibility of supporting moral claims in an epistemically valid or reasonable way, but that doesn't translate into reasons for, say, a psychopath to do what is morally required, reasons that, given the epistemic support available for moral judgments, even the (intelligent) psychopath should be able to appreciate. As we shall see in just a moment, the sentimentalist regards nonempathic psychopaths as incapable of *understanding* moral claims or making their own moral *judgments*. So it isn't at all clear how such claims or judgments, however well others may be able to support them, can give the *psychopath* reason (or motivation) to act.

one to defend the objective prescriptivity of moral judgments from something other than a (Nagel-like) rationalist point of view.

In ECE, I defended a normative view of individual (and political) morality that based itself in ideas about empathic caring. I was there defending an ethics of care, and I argued that such an ethics, if it wants to account for or conform to the moral judgments we intuitively, or commonsensically, want to make, must make rather heavy use of the notion or phenomenon of empathy. If we talk just about caring, then it is not, simply on that basis, clear why it is worse to neglect one's children's health than that of strangers or why it is worse not to save a child drowning right in front of one than not to save a child by giving \$5 to Oxfam. (This assumes that Peter Singer is mistaken about such cases, but as I have already mentioned, ECE as a whole represents a reply to and critique of Singer.) However, and as I also mentioned earlier, if we introduce empathy into the mix, we end up with something that corresponds pretty well with intuitive moral judgment: for we (normal humans) generally feel more empathy, and more empathic concern (or caring), for those whose plight we witness than for those whose plight we merely know *about*, and for those who are related to (or intimately involved with) us than for strangers and people we know only by description.

In ECE, I also applied the idea of empathic caring/concern for others to questions of social justice, but let's leave such issues out of the picture for the moment (I shall take them up again in chapters 8 and 9) and concentrate here on individual morality. And what I would like the reader to accept, at least for purposes of the present discussion, is the idea that distinctions of empathy correspond pretty well with the moral distinctions we intuitively wish to make, a conclusion of ECE.

At the end of ECE, I speculated about this correspondence or correlation and argued that it gives us some reason to think that empathy enters into the making and understanding of moral judgments/utterances, for if this last hypothesis is correct, that would explain why there is a general correspondence between distinctions or differences in our empathic (caring) reactions and the moral distinctions we want, intuitively, to make. Thus (I argue in ECE that) empathy leads us to be more responsive to perceived pain or danger than to pain or danger we merely know about. But if our empathy and, in particular, our differential empathic tendencies also enter into our understanding of moral judgments/utterances, that would help to explain why we intuitively understand/judge an unwillingness, say, to relieve pain that we perceive to be (at least other things being equal) morally worse than an unwillingness to relieve pain that is merely known about. And similarly, as ECE argues, for a host of other cases. Putting the matter another way, if the very same empathy that leads us to respond differently to different kinds of situations enters into our understanding of (claims about) what is morally better and worse in those situations, it is no wonder that there is a correlation between our differential empathic tendencies and the moral distinctions we want to make.

So the idea that empathy enters into our understanding and making of genuine moral claims (what I call the empathy-understanding hypothesis) is

supported by its ability to explain the correlation or correspondence just mentioned—at least if we assume that the arguments for that correspondence given
in ECE, and rehearsed in chapter 1, are somewhat persuasive. In what follows,
I shall, in effect, be offering a deeper or further explanation of why such a
correspondence exists, so let me use the assumption that it does exist to continue
the present discussion.

A perceptive reader will already have noticed that what I am now saying about
moral judgment and what I said earlier about moral approval and disapproval are
similar in a very important respect: both discussions bring in empathy in a central
way. And from the sentimentalist perspective that is (and had better be) no
accident, for what I now want to claim is that the (in something, ironically, very
much like the Kantian sense) schema, or schematism, that connects approval and
moral judgment within a plausible ethical sentimentalism is the phenomenon or
idea of empathy, understood both as giving rise to differing agential reactions to
(other) people's situations and as a factor in our reactions to the ways agents react
to or treat (other) people. The empathy-understanding hypothesis seems plausible, at least given what I concluded in ECE, but what we have said here about
approval (and disapproval), together with the basic sentimentalist idea that (our
understanding of) approval grounds (our understanding of) moral judgment,
allows us to further clarify the implications and nature of that hypothesis. We
have argued that empathy enters into approval and disapproval, and since
sentimentalism holds that our attitudes of approval and disapproval enter into
the making of moral judgments, we can conclude that empathy enters into our
understanding of moral claims (which is what the empathy-understanding
hypothesis asserts) *because attitudes/feelings of approval/disapproval enter into the
making of moral judgments.* We thus end up with a strictly sentimentalist picture of
the relation between approval and moral judgment and of the character of moral
judgment "in itself," and far from making sentimentalism seem unsupported,
odd, or paradoxical, the picture we have painted seems plausible *as far as it goes.*

I say "as far as it goes" because what we have said so far can also help us
further illuminate the character of moral claims or judgments. It can, for
example, help explain how and why moral claims are inherently motivating,
and as I mentioned earlier, that is something that, other things being equal,
seems plausible and that we want to say. Although there have been arguments
against this view, none of them seems absolutely devastating, and the prepon-
derance of philosophical opinion, at least, is that allowing for the motivating
force of moral claims or utterances is a desideratum for or within metaethical
theory. And the particular explanation that we are now in a position to offer for
why moral judgments inherently motivate those who make them is that the
empathy inherently involved in making genuine moral judgments is precisely
the empathy that inclines us to do what we think of as right and avoid what we
think of as wrong.

For example, and as I also mentioned earlier, our being chilled by agential
indifference toward others requires developed empathy, and such empathy also

inclines us to not be indifferent ourselves (as agents) toward others. So when, on the basis of our disapproval of indifference, we (are able to) make an explicit moral condemnation of indifference, we are condemning something we are (to some extent) motivated to avoid in our own actions. Therefore, it is no wonder that we are inclined to *act in accordance with* negative moral judgments, and the same point can be made about positive judgments. Thus our sentimentalist view that approval and disapproval are based in empathy and themselves enter into the making of moral judgments helps explain why such judgments have motivating force for us, and this lends further support to the position being defended here. Moreover, nothing we have said about the nature of empathy and/or the way it operates in moral contexts argues *against* the possibility, the antecedently plausible view, that moral judgments are objective or cognitive, and so the metaethical sentimentalism being defended here seems so far to be *consistent* with the idea that moral judgments are objectively prescriptive. But we still need to nail down the idea that empathically motivating moral judgments are capable of objectivity (or cognitivity), and this I shall attempt to do in our next chapter, when I lay out a specific account of the meaning of moral terms. At that point, we will be able to more fully see that the present approach can allow and account for the objective prescriptivity of moral judgments and at least to that extent resembles what rationalist theories do or seek to do.[13] But for the moment, let us focus on what our discussion so far allows us to claim and explain.

For example, the account we have given can also help us explain—what, again, intuitively and other things being equal, it is desirable for us to be able to explain—how and why psychopaths cannot make or fully understand genuine moral judgments (but are confined, e.g., to "inverted commas" uses of moral predicates). If moral approval and disapproval essentially enter into the making of moral judgments, then if these attitudes involve empathy, psychopaths, who are usually said to lack empathy, will be unable to make or understand moral

---

13. In "A Sensible Subjectivism?" (reprinted in S. Darwall, A. Gibbard, and P. Railton, eds., *Moral Discourse and Practice: Some Philosophical Approaches* [New York: Oxford University Press, 1997]), esp. pp. 234f., David Wiggins espouses something like sentimentalism and says that moral judgments are both motivating and "cognitive." And in "Toward *Fin de Siècle* Ethics: Some Trends" (same volume, pp. 20–23), Darwall, Gibbard, and Railton (following John McDowell) accept the possibility that Wiggins's type of "sensibility theory" could allow moral judgments to have both objective/cognitive status and inherent motivating force. So my own sentimentalist commitment to objective prescriptivity is not at all idiosyncratic. (Sentimentalism can also treat moral injunctions as *categorical imperatives* in the basic sense of having validity independently of the desires, attitudes, intentions of those to whom they are addressed. See ECE, chapter 7.) Let me, in addition, note that objective prescriptivity may also exist outside ethics. It has been said, for example, that to perceive something's beauty is automatically to be attracted to contemplating (or aesthetically engaging with) it and to be reluctant to give up that experience too quickly. Yet this needn't make us say that judgments of beauty are not objective or cognitive. (The point is reminiscent of what Plato says about our being attracted to or moved by the contemplation of the Forms.) So clearly, objective prescriptivity has a wider and deeper appeal than Mackie's accusation of "queerness" grants.

judgments.[14] If I may invoke the often-invoked parallel with judgments about color, a psychopath can't make or fully understand moral judgments for something like the same reason that congenitally blind people are supposed to be unable to make full-blown claims about color or fully understand what others who speak of color are saying to them: they both lack the right sorts of experiences.[15] (It was this analogy that earlier persuaded me to develop a reference-fixing account of the meaning of moral terms that exactly paralleled what Kripke had said about color terms and terms designating other natural kinds.)

Finally, the sentimentalist theory/view that empathy enters into the making and understanding of moral judgment via states of moral approval and disapproval that are themselves empathic attitudes is supported by what we know about the general character and contours of normative moral judgment. Just to cite the most obvious instance, our commonsense moral judgments are self-other asymmetric in a way that has often been noted and never been explained. Thus we think it is wrong to negligently hurt another person, yet it isn't thought morally wrong—as opposed to imprudently inattentive—if one merely negligently hurts *oneself*. But why, one might ask, should such a distinction be made? There are forms of moral theory like utilitarianism that aren't self-other asymmetric in the way common sense is, and since each typical moral agent has the same kind of dignity, freedom, and welfare interests as the individuals morality tells him or her to be concerned about, why should our moral duties be more abundant and/or stricter toward others than toward ourselves, the way common sense says they are? (Jerry Fodor once said to me that it is *analytic* that morality involves concern just for others.)

But if empathy enters into the making of moral judgments, we have an explanation and potentially even a justification for the asymmetry of commonsense moral thinking. Empathy itself is self-other asymmetric: empathy for others is a much more understandable idea than empathy for oneself—in fact, the latter makes the most sense when one thinks of having empathy for one's

---

14. Psychopathic sadists may be able to "get inside" people's heads and on that basis find apt and exquisite ways to torture or manipulate them, but the empathy by "contagion" that lets us "feel" another person's pain involves a motivating emotional reaction, and the psychopath doesn't have this kind of reaction to other people's mental states. (On the inability of psychopaths to feel empathy, see, e.g., Hoffman, *Empathy and Moral Development*, pp. 35f.) Also, some may doubt whether nonempathic psychopaths are really incapable of moral judgment, but if the present sentimentalist metaethical approach seems plausible *as a whole*, that may give us (further) reason to suppose psychopaths can't make genuine moral judgments beyond any initial philosophical or intuitive reasons we may or may not have for that proposition.

15. I have been assuming that an adult who can't make moral claims can't understand the moral claims of others. If moral judgments require empathy, then a person lacking empathy not only will lack the ability to make moral claims but also won't fully understand the empathy involved in *other people's* making of genuine moral judgments. But this is parallel to what we think about the inability to see things as red: such inability makes it impossible for one to make full-blown claims about redness or to understand fully what others have in mind when *they* talk about redness.

much earlier unhappy childhood or adolescent self, and here there is something analogous to the distance or nonidentity that Hoffman (in *Empathy and Moral Development*) and others who study empathy have said is essential to empathy. So if moral judgment is grounded in empathy via psychological states of moral approval and disapproval as we have described them, we have an explanation of why our moral judgments tend to be self-other asymmetric, and the justificatory force of common opinion thereby helps to justify the sentimentalist metaethics we have been offering here.[16]

It is clear, then, that our sentimentalism allows us to explain a good many things we want to explain and doesn't seem to have any really implausible implications, and this, I hope, will make metaethical moral sentimentalism seem more promising than I think it recently has seemed to most philosophers. ECE worked mainly with, or at the level of, normative ethics, but the fact that it used empathy (or empathic concern) as criterial for normative moral distinctions means that the same factor that works (if it does) within the sentimentalist normative context also features within a sentimentalist metaethical approach of the kind offered here. So the present book takes us beyond the predominantly normative discussion of ECE and allows us to understand both the normative and the metaethical in sentimentalist terms. Sentimentalism in the larger sense that includes both metaethical and normative components, sentimentalism of the kind Hume was clearly committed to, can be redeployed or reworked in ways Hume didn't fully anticipate and is now, I believe, in a position to offer itself as a plausible, promising, and *fully systematic* alternative to rationalism and intuitionism about the moral. In the chapter that now follows, I will offer an explication of moral language that can help us see how moral judgments can be objective, while at the same time involving a motivational impetus, and my hope is that that will serve to further solidify our normative-cum-metaethical account and defense of sentimentalism.

---

16. On the self-other asymmetries of commonsense morality, see my *Commonsense Morality and Consequentialism* (London: Routledge and Kegan Paul, 1985), chapter 1. However, when I wrote that book, I didn't see the relevance of empathy to commonsense moral distinctions and to the ordinary making of moral judgments and so was unable to offer *any explanation* of why morality and moral claims are self-other asymmetric. What I am saying here allows me, in effect, to make progress on a project that began almost thirty years ago.

Note that empathy seems self-other asymmetric with respect to both first-order concern for people's welfare and second-order approval and disapproval. We can have empathy for the suffering someone else is at present undergoing, but (as we learn from Hoffman) it is hard to make sense of the idea of empathy for one's own present sufferings. And similarly, we can be chilled by what we see another person doing but not, I think, by what we ourselves are deliberately doing at a given time. (This won't necessarily rule out present-tense moral self-criticism if that doesn't involve occurrent chill.) Moreover, since what one does to oneself doesn't show or involve a lack of empathy (or coldheartedness), the chill one feels in regard to one's *past* (cold-hearted) actions has to focus on what one has done or sought to do with respect to others, not on what one has done with respect to oneself. (I am indebted here to discussion with Mark Warren.)

4

A NEW KIND OF REFERENCE-FIXING

In *Naming and Necessity*, Saul Kripke never offered a reference-fixing account of moral terms along the lines of what he said about natural kind terms, and he was no doubt wise not to do so. Such a view treats moral judgments like "benevolence is morally good" and "cruelty is morally wrong" as merely empirical, a posteriori, and that doesn't seem very plausible on the face of it: not nearly as plausible as Kripke's view that statements about the wavelengths reflected by red objects are empirical—though metaphysically necessary. However, I think it is possible to explicate moral terms/judgments by comparing and contrasting how we understand them with how, on Kripke's beautiful theory, we understand terms like "red" and "water." So let me say something briefly about how Kripke thinks we can and do understand/explicate terms like "red," then show what a view of moral terms that understood them exactly on analogy with color terms would entail, and finally and most importantly, use *something like* the Kripkean reference-fixing approach to show how the meaning of moral terms compares and contrasts with the meaning of color terms.

For Kripke (roughly and briefly), the experience of red serves to fix the reference of the objective term "red." (This, of course, assumes that talk of the experience of red doesn't depend on our understanding of red as an objective property.) And that is part of, a function of, the meaning of a word like "red." We may not be able to define "red," but we can at least say that it is an a priori truth that (objective) red(ness) is whatever causes or has tended to cause, and is perceived by means of, our visual experience of red (ness).[1] Moreover, it seems reasonable to suppose that one can't fully understand the color word "red" unless one has been in a position to (help) fix its reference for oneself via one's own experience of red. That is why a congenitally blind person presumably doesn't fully understand color terms. And these last two claims/truths are themselves also a priori. (Here I am going somewhat beyond what Kripke explicitly claims, but at various points in *Naming and Necessity* he does indicate that blind people may very well not have our concept of color.)

Given the preceding, it is nonetheless a posteriori/empirical that objective red is the color that reflects light of such-and-such wavelength(s) because it is a posteriori that what reflects such wavelength(s) is causally responsible for (and perceived via) our particular experience of red. What is and remains a priori, however, is that whatever turns out to be causally responsible for our experience of redness will turn out to be objectively red (in all metaphysically possible worlds). And though these ideas were early on subjected to lots of questioning and criticism, they are accepted or treated as plausible today by a great number of philosophers. I am inclined to accept them too, but the account of moral terminology I mean to offer won't absolutely depend on my doing so. What I want to maintain about moral terminology contrasts in important ways with what Kripke says about color terms and also bears important *similarities* to what he says about them. But my semi-Kripkean reference-fixing approach can, for all that, I believe, stand on its own. It might be correct or on the right track even if Kripke were wrong about natural kind terms.

However, before I introduce what I hope and take to be the correct account of moral language, let me first present a purely Kripkean explication of moral terms, one that treats "right" or "morally good" exactly on analogy with Kripke's view of color words. I have already indicated that such an account has implausible implications. But if we pay attention to the details of such an account, we might learn how to vary it in such a way as to avoid those implications. I have been trying to do that for more than five years now, and I believe I have finally found a way to make it work. So let's begin with the kind of pure Kripkean view of moral terms I *used* to think was promising.

We have previously spoken a great deal about warm feelings of approval and cold or chilly feelings of disapproval. These quasi-tactile feelings are analogous with the experience of red(ness) inasmuch as they have a certain

---

1. For Kripke, what a priori fixes the reference of "(objectively) red" is (roughly) a phrase like "whatever has tended to cause our visual experience of red(ness)." But we also need the experience of red itself in order to understand "(objectively) red" and in order for its reference to be fully fixed for us, so it is natural to extend Kripke's terminology and allow that the experience of red itself fixes or helps to fix the reference of the color term. This extension needn't cause any misunderstandings or unclarities, and making it is actually useful for expository and argumentational purposes. It allows us to say things more simply and succinctly than we otherwise could, so I shall be speaking of reference-fixing in this extended way in much of what follows.

subjective phenomenology and seem like purely inner states. So if Kripke explicates (objective) "red" by saying that its reference is fixed a priori by our subjective experience of redness and by saying, more specifically, that it is an a priori truth that redness is whatever tends/has tended to cause our subjective experience of redness, then we can proceed analogously with "right" or "(morally) good."[2] We can say, for instance, that the reference of "right" is fixed a priori by the subjective feeling of warmth we feel in regard to certain actions, and we can hold, more specifically, that it is an a priori truth that rightness is whatever tends/has tended to cause such warm feeling(s). Our explication can continue, moreover, with the claim that it is an a priori truth that one can't understand "right" (what rightness is) unless one has experienced the feeling of warmth with respect to certain actions, and that, presumably, would explain why psychopaths cannot make full or genuine moral judgments. (All this holds mutatis mutandis for the term "wrong" and other moral words.)

Continuing the analogy with what Kripke says about "red" (and assuming a sentimentalist care-ethical account of the normative content of right and wrong), we can say that it is a posteriori that acting caringly or benevolently is right because it is a posteriori that other people's acting caringly or benevolently (is what) tends to cause us to have warm feelings. (We can also say that it is metaphysically necessary that acting caringly is right because the theory says that it is a priori true that whatever causes our warm feelings in the actual world will count as right in every possible world.) But as I mentioned earlier, it seems implausible to suppose that it is only an a posteriori truth that caring/benevolent action is morally right (and cruel, malicious action wrong). So what I want to suggest now is a way of varying the just-given account just enough so that it retains some of its useful explanatory analogy with Kripke's views without entailing the conclusions about what is a posteriori that seem appropriate for color concepts but inappropriate for moral concepts.

I think the problem with the reference-fixing account of "right" that we have just given is that it uses too thin a basis for that fixing. It assumes that we should fix the reference of "right" or "good" in relation to a purely subjective experience of warmth that is indeed exactly analogous with the subjective experience of red

---

2. Actually, when Kripke talks of fixing the reference of a term like "red," he speaks not only of what causes red sensations but of what, in the object, is *perceived* via such sensations (and by means of one's eyes). However, the simpler account I am giving makes things easier to follow and doesn't substantially affect the argument; at one point (*Naming and Necessity* [Hoboken, N.J.: Wiley-Blackwell, 1981], 131), Kripke himself talks of identifying objective *heat* via the sensation it gives (i.e., causes) without referring to perception and its organs—perhaps he, too, was just doing this for simplifying purposes. On the same page (and the previous one), Kripke also makes it clear that he is talking not just about language but about how concepts have their reference fixed, so the claims I am making in the main text about what is a priori of certain terms can perhaps be made more accurate by talking of what is a priori of certain concepts.

that Kripke uses for "red." It is the purely subjective character in both cases that delivers up the supposedly a posteriori character of certain judgments, the judgments that red objects reflect light of a certain wavelength and that rightness is a matter of acting benevolently or caringly. (Obviously, we need to say more about rightness than this, but this simple expression of the kind of thing the sentimentalist wants to say is convenient for stating the argument I want to give.) If we wish to avoid the conclusion that it is a posteriori that acting caringly is right while retaining the idea of reference-fixing, then, I submit, we need to thicken our account of what does, or helps to do, the fixing. It can't, it shouldn't, be a mere, sheer feeling of warmth (or of chill in regard to negative moral evaluations); it needs to be something thicker or more robust, something less purely subjective and phenomenological, and I think what we have said about how empathy works in delivering warm and chilly feelings/sentiments may suggest a way of doing this.

Let me begin with the thought that it may be a priori that if a person fully has the concept of rightness and/or moral goodness, they are capable of empathy with others and capable via empathic mechanisms of being warmed (and chilled) by what others do. Now any rationalist who doesn't think empathy to be of moral-psychological importance might deny this claim, but I don't think that that fact *undercuts* what I have just said. Something can be (correctly regarded as) a priori even though some philosophers deny that it is. The truth will depend on how philosophical issues get argued out and resolved. So although the claim I have just made about what is a priori is philosophically controversial and would be denied by theorists opposed to (my kind of) sentimentalism in moral philosophy, it may be true, and it is all the more likely to seem so to anyone who finds the general argument of the present book convincing or even just plausible. The idea, therefore, is that if everything I have been saying here makes sense and seems promising, then the claim, made just above, that it is a priori that a person with the concept of moral rightness or goodness will be capable of being warmed by others' actions via mechanisms of empathy will not seem odd or implausible.

But this can be, and perhaps needs to be, clarified further. What is a priori is relative to the possession of the concepts involved in a given proposition, so what I am saying, basically, is that anyone who fully possesses moral concepts will have to be capable of empathy, will have to have had the experiences of being warmed and chilled by the warmth and cold-heartedness displayed by others in their actions and attitudes, will (therefore) implicitly understand what empathy is, and will also have to be capable (if they are intellectual enough and what I say is cogent enough) of seeing how the *philosophical arguments* in what follows support a reference-fixing view of moral terms/concepts of the sort I am defending. Even if the term *empathy* wasn't invented till the twentieth century, that just means that if people from an earlier period had our notion of rightness, the term *empathy* could be explained to them and that would enable them to recognize the analytic truth that when we are warmed by others' empathic warmth, that involves a kind of empathy.[3] The phenomenon of being warmed (or chilled) by the warm-heartedness (or cold-heartedness) of others is very familiar (though Hume may have been the first *philosopher* to talk about it), and I don't think it is implausible for a sentimentalist to hold that it is the grounding basis of our having moral concepts and making moral judgments. So a recognition or awareness of (what can be described as) empathy is also part and parcel of, or a priori to, our understanding of morality.[4]

If we say this, then, and as a way of indicating how the reference of a moral term like "morally good" or "right" is fixed, we can also say that it is a priori that moral goodness (or rightness) is whatever feelings of warmth directed at agents and delivered by mechanisms of empathy are caused by. Alternatively, it is a priori that goodness (or rightness) is whatever causes us to be warmed by the warmth displayed by agents, and since it is trivial and obvious that it is agential warmth itself that causes this warming, it follows that agential warmth, as displayed in actions, is just what the goodness (or rightness) of actions consists in. So unlike Kripke's account of redness and other natural kind terms, we have an a priori but in some sense causal and reference-fixing theory of what moral rightness or goodness is, and this permits us to avoid the criticism that can be directed at any purely Kripkean account of moral terminology—the criticism, namely, that it treats claims like "benevolence is morally good" and "cruelty is wrong" as a posteriori truths.[5]

3. When Hume spoke (*Treatise of Human Nature*, ed. Selby-Bigge [New York: Oxford University Press, 1978], 605) of our being warmed by the warmth others display in their actions, he was just being more articulate than most people are about (what is to them) a familiar phenomenon, and I want to say that that empathic phenomenon is fundamental to our understanding of morality. It can be known a priori that being warmed by the warmth displayed by others is a kind of approval and that rightness is what makes for such approval. The rationalist, of course, will disagree, but I want to maintain that that if (without rationalist commitments) we think carefully and perceptively about certain of our reactions to others, we can recognize (a priori) that the psychological phenomena I have been describing are central to morality. To be sure, it is a question of *a priori theorizing* whether these empathic phenomena ground our use of moral language, but the present book is offering theoretical/philosophical reasons for thinking that this is the case. These reasons are no more (immediately) available to perceptive ordinary folk than Kripke's theory of natural kind terms is, but that doesn't mean that Kripke's theory or my own can't give us a plausible philosophical account of the meaning of certain terms.

4. Kripke says it is a priori that objective redness is whatever causes and *is perceived via* sensations of red, and the role of perception here is at least partly analogous with what my view of moral terms says about the role of empathy in fixing moral concepts. In both cases, the reference-fixing takes one beyond the mere idea of causally explaining certain experiences and builds on or involves a more specific psychological notion.

5. On the theory just stated, a person can genuinely claim that some (kind of) act is wrong without *at that time* feeling (cold) disapproval toward that (kind of) act. This seems perfectly acceptable, and we certainly want to make a parallel claim about judgments of objective redness. Note, too, that although the reference-fixing view of moral terms just offered differs from Kripke's account of natural kind terms, both see the application of certain terms as dependent on and focusing on certain experiences and what causes them. That analogy makes it seem natural to characterize the view I am defending as a reference-fixing (and causal) account of moral terms.

But don't we have to say more about agential warmth? It may be a priori and obvious that indifference, malice, and cruelty toward others aren't warm and equally obvious that kindness and parental love *are* warm. But what about a mother who prefers to help someone else's child rather than her own because (she says) she can do somewhat more good for the other child. This doesn't seem to us like warmth; in fact, such a mother strikes us as cold-hearted (as making "cold utilitarian calculations") and perverse, among other things. Yet such a mother may be committed to the maximization of impartially reckoned good, and isn't such concern for general human happiness a kind of warmth, something deeply different from malice and indifference concerning the welfare of others?

Well, it certainly is different from the latter. But such a mother's attitude nonetheless strikes us as cold or cold-hearted (toward her child), as rather chilling. Similarly, for the sort of case, mentioned in an earlier chapter, where miners are trapped underground: if someone (e.g., Charles Fried in *An Anatomy of Values*) says that we should use whatever money is available to install safety devices in the mine rather than save the contemporaneously trapped miners *because that will save a somewhat greater number of lives in the long run*, their attitude will strike us as (to that extent) cold-hearted (or worse).[6] So I think it is an a priori (and necessary) truth that a basically warm-hearted agent will not prefer the general good to that of particular individuals or groups of individuals in the ways (or cases) just spoken of. In fact, I think our judgments here follow the contours of ordinary empathy. We tend to empathize more with miners who are right now in danger than with a somewhat larger group whose plight lies (however certainly) in the future, and a (normal) mother will feel more empathy for her own child than for the child of other people (strangers) and thus be inclined to take care of her own child's needs, even when she can do more good for some other child. So our empathic tendencies as agents seem to inform our intuitive sense of what is more or less cold- or warm-hearted. In other words, the same empathy that leads us to certain preferences or choices *as agents* also governs our empathic reactions of chill and warmth *as spectators or contemplators* of what (other) agents do. And this is not so surprising when one considers that for an attitude to be experienced as warm, it has to resemble ordinary physical warmth at least to the extent of affecting what is (metaphorically) near more strongly than what is (metaphorically) distant. We can conclude, I think, therefore, that it is a priori (and necessary) that agential warmth consists in empathy-driven or empathy-based concern for others—and also a priori (and necessary) that agential coldness or cold-

---

6. Charles Fried, *An Anatomy of Values: Problems of Personal and Social Choice* (Cambridge: Harvard University Press, 1970), 207–227, esp. 226. I might just add that we also tend to find Fried's attitude in the miners' case somewhat *chilling*.

heartedness consists in various specific ways of lacking such empathic concern.[7]

We argued above that it is a priori that actions are morally good if and only if they express or reflect agential warmth, and the argument depended on an a priori fixing of the meaning of "morally good" (or the concept of moral goodness) in relation to the experience of being warmed by the warmth of (evinced by) an agent or agents. But if what we have just been saying is correct, then it is also a priori for us that always preferring impartial good is not a form of warmth and is even (to a substantial extent) chilling or cold-hearted. In fact, it is more generally a priori for us that going (in various ways) against the flow of empathy is a sign of (some degree of?) coldness or cold-heartedness. And since failing to help oneself typically doesn't go against the flow of empathy, we tend not to be chilled by and not to morally criticize such failure. So we can conclude that it is a priori that actions are morally good or right if and only if they express or reflect empathic concern *for others* on the part of the agent. And all these things will seem like necessary truths as well.[8]

Let's take stock. The account just given is a reference-fixing account of "right" or "morally good" and, by extension, of other moral terms. But what fixes or helps to fix the reference is not some thin, subjective notion of experience but, rather, certain experiences *as directed toward others* and *as reflecting what others feel*. These latter notions are both causal and both contained within the idea of empathy, and we can, therefore, say that on the present account a certain phenomenon of empathy understood as a causal mechanism serves (or helps) to fix moral reference in an a priori way. This seems very much in keeping with what we have previously said here about approval, empathy, warmth/chill, and moral judgment, and as I have indicated, it is more plausible than a reference-fixing view that works via (or fails to work because it implies) an exact analogy with reference-fixing in the case of color and natural kind terms.

---

7. The full contours of empathy, of our empathic reactions, don't emerge till the teenage years, when, e.g., empathy with disadvantaged *groups* emerges as a psychological disposition or possibility. I am prepared to say that full possession of moral notions doesn't occur till this late period. But I would certainly want to grant that such notions may be partially or imperfectly realized in younger individuals: after all, young children often use terms like "right" and "wrong." Nonetheless, I am inclined to think that these uses may just represent/express "training wheels" versions of adult moral concepts.

8. What we are saying fits moral goodness better than rightness, if we assume that an act (like tapping one's fingers) can be morally (all) right if it merely doesn't express an *absence* of empathic concern for others. We can say, therefore, that an action is morally wrong only if it *does* exhibit a lack of full-blown empathic concern for others on the part of an agent. And notice that a person lacking in such empathy can do many right things: if they go to bed, their behavior doesn't have to express, exhibit, or reflect their lack of empathy. The present account would also probably have to be complicated in order to deal with actions that have both good and bad aspects and in order to treat the vexed topic of moral dilemmas.

Here is another way to see what I have just been saying. The pure Kripkean view of rightness treated feelings of warmth and chill as a priori to having the concept of rightness (or goodness). But the view I have been defending here holds that *there is more that is a priori to having the concept of rightness than having certain feelings.* What (among other things) is more largely or capaciously a priori to our understanding of moral judgments and to our fully having the concept of moral rightness or goodness is *our capacity for empathically feeling or reflecting what others (and, in particular, agents) feel.*[9] Our account, in any event, explicates moral terms by using the notion of reference-fixing and to that extent is similar to Kripke's approach to natural kind terms. But it also differs because it uses a much thicker reference-fixer than Kripke found appropriate to the terms he was interested in, and the result has been a theory that avoids the problems that arise when one strictly carries over all of Kripke's ideas about redness and the like to moral notions like rightness. It is a theory that allows us to say that claims like "empathically caring actions are right" are both a priori *and* metaphysically necessary.[10]

---

9. Interestingly, if we simply say that it is a priori that those with the full concept of rightness will have the capacity for warm and chilly feelings, that seems less plausible (perhaps because it is so vague or indefinite) than if we make the larger claim that it is a priori that anyone with the full concept of rightness will have the realized capacity, via mechanisms of empathy, to feel warmed or chilled by what others do. Such a person will then be able to *say* that certain people's actions are chilling or cold-hearted and that other actions are heart-warming and show warmth (toward other people) or a warm heart. People do say such things, and I want to claim that this is part and parcel of their/our having moral concepts. And these facts, these phenomena, then allow us to give a reference-fixing account of moral terms that makes the connection between moral rightness/goodness and empathic concern for others both necessary and a priori.

10. For Kripke, experiences of red fix the referent of "red" a priori, but the a priori truth that objective redness is what is responsible for those experiences is nonetheless a contingent one: some other phenomenon *could* generally cause red sensations. By contrast, Kripke thinks it a posteriori but *necessary* that red objects reflect such-and-such wavelengths of light. However, my view sees it as both a priori *and* necessary that rightness is whatever it is about actions that causes any empathically derived warm feelings we have in reaction to what moral agents (may) do; sees it as both a priori and necessary that such feelings, if they occur, are caused by empathically warm caring actions; and so sees it as both a priori and necessary that any and all right actions will reflect warm (empathic) concern for others (or not reflect the opposite). What Kripke allows as metaphysical possibilities—namely, that something other than red objects and something other than objects reflecting particular wavelengths should cause red sensations—has no moral counterpart because it just isn't possible that we should be empathically warmed by something other than (what we take to be) agential warmth or empathically caring right actions. Likewise, what Kripke says is a posteriori—namely, that red objects reflect light of such-and-such wavelengths—has no parallel in the moral case because we can't say it might have turned out that actions expressing empathic warm concern for others were morally wrong. We had to find out about the physical bases of color via empirical experiment, and there is nothing parallel to this in the moral case.

Note, finally, that it *isn't* a priori that whenever we feel warmth toward someone, that feeling is due to empathy with the warmth they display and is thus a form of approval. As I indicated earlier, personal feelings can interfere with the empathic mechanisms of approval, and there are times when we can't be sure whether the warmth we feel toward someone is derived from empathy with their warmth or is simply based in our affection for the person. But I assume there *is* a fact of the matter as to whether a given feeling of warmth has the right causal origin to count as approval, and we can

Such a view allows one to avoid the problems that Terence Horgan and Mark Timmons have pointed out about certain reference-fixing accounts of moral terminology that have been put forward by moral realists.[11] If the reference of a term like *right* is fixed via causal notions in a way that allows it to pick out different properties for groups of speakers in different possible worlds, then we could have someone in the actual world using the term *right* to refer to the property of having overall good consequences, but someone else in another possible world using the same term to talk about some general deontological property. And (disanalogously with what Kripke says about natural kind terms) it would then be far from obvious that the person in our world, the actual world, could reasonably claim that the person in the other possible world wasn't really talking about what they (the person in the actual world) meant by morality or rightness. In that case, certain reference-fixing forms of moral realism may lead toward some sort of relativism, rather than giving us what they purport to give us, namely, an account of what (we can plausibly say) morality really and essentially is. But Horgan and Timmons are able to raise these issues because the causal reference-fixing theories they discuss allow terms like *right* to pick out different properties in different possible worlds, and on the semi-Kripkean theory defended here, our moral reference-fixing practices *don't* permit or require different properties to be picked out in the differing speaker-circumstances of different possible worlds. In particular, what causes our warm empathic reactions to what others (or we ourselves) do doesn't, on our theory, vary from world to world, so moral rightness and goodness remain constant across possible worlds, and relativism of the kind Horgan and Timmons raise as a possible threat to causal/reference-fixing theories doesn't threaten our own brand of reference-fixing. All this depends on the fact that we have placed causality within the reference-fixer rather than leaving it entirely

---

often have reason to believe that our feelings reflect the warm agency of the other person, that we are in fact being warmed by their warmth. I am indebted here to discussion with James Harold.

11. See, e.g., their "Troubles on Moral Twin Earth: Moral Queerness Revived" (*Synthese* 92, 1992, pp. 221–260) and their "Copping Out on Moral Twin Earth" (*Synthese* 100, 2000, pp. 139–152). I am dealing with what I take to be the most troublesome aspect of their rather complex arguments. But let me also just briefly point out a couple of other things that can be said about moral-twin-earth possibilities.

If intelligent beings on a Twin Earth were to understand and use the term *warm-hearted* in purely utilitarian terms and/or without reference to empathy as we know and understand it, then I think we could say that their "warm-heartedness" could only ground a sense of "right" different from our own. We could and, I think, would regard their "warmth" as (in certain ways) cold-hearted and as giving rise to wrong actions, and I don't think that there would be anything parochial or narrow-minded in our saying so or that such cases force the present view toward some form of repugnant relativism. In other words, I think we can and would stand by our own moral judgments in the face of such radically different views on the part of (possible) others, and I think we could plausibly say that such beings weren't really talking about morality in our sense of the term. Similarly, if Twin Earthlings somehow defined the word *empathy* impartialistically or very narrowly, they wouldn't be using it in our sense, and any "morality" they defined in its terms would not, I think, contain words meaning the same thing as our "right" and "wrong."

outside of it.[12] And just as Kripke's theory tells us what we need to know about the meaning of natural kind terms, the present account or explication of moral language and concepts is specific enough so that I don't think anyone who finds it basically attractive will feel the need for more.[13]

But it is worth noting a couple of important implications of our account. If empathy-derived agent-directed warm feelings are crucial to the reference-fixing of "right" or "good," then, given our judgment-free sentimentalist conception of moral approval, we can also say that moral approval plays a major role in fixing the reference of that term. What is right (or morally good) is what causes or tends to cause nonjudgmental approval. In the last chapter, I said that empathy and approval enter into the meaning (into our understanding)

12. Here my extended use of the notion of reference-fixing might be misunderstood. I have just said that the theory of moral terminology I am offering differs from one that treats such terminology exactly on analogy with what Kripke says about natural kind terms, in placing causality within the reference-fixer rather than outside it. But even the purely Kripkean account of "morally right" uses causal language within the reference-fixing phrase "whatever has tended to cause feelings of warmth." Nonetheless, that phrase distinguishes between certain feelings and what causes them, and the causality is outside the feelings (of warmth). So if one then, by extension, talks of the feelings' helping to fix reference, one is talking about something that contains no causality. On the view I am defending, however, and still speaking in an extended way, reference is fixed by something "thicker" that contains causality within it, namely, by feelings of warmth as derived from empathy vis-à-vis agents. Using Kripke's original terminology, we could say that the view I am defending incorporates (at least) two references to causality within the phrase that fixes the reference of "right," the phrase "whatever causes our warm empathic reactions to what people do." For empathy itself is a causal notion. By contrast, and as I indicated a moment ago, the phrase that fixes the reference of "right" on a purely Kripkean theory contains only one reference to causality.

13. On the present view, it is possible that intelligent beings in other (possible) worlds might be *more*, or *less*, empathic than we are. I am not talking of beings who are (for example) more responsive to heard-about pain than to pain they actually perceive. That would be weird and would mean that such beings weren't responding via what we would regard as empathy. I mean, rather, beings whose empathic mechanisms are like ours but slightly more or less sensitive. It is not clear how to avoid a parochial view of such differences: e.g., one that says that moral judgments have to be relative to such differences or (another form of parochialism) that says our own human empathy sets the moral standard for beings with different levels of empathy. But it is important to realize that these issues create difficulties for *any* plausible theory of our obligations to help. If a given normative theory argues that a certain level of concern for distant people is obligatory, it must eventually face the issue of whether other beings who were "by nature" more or less inclined than we are to help distant others would have the same obligations of beneficence that we do. I don't think we (yet) really know how to deal with such issues, but that doesn't particularly count against sentimentalism.

Note also that the sentimentalism defended here will want to say that rationalists have to be capable of feeling empathy if and when they make moral judgments (or show concern for their children or friends)—*even if they are misled by their own rationalism into believing that this is not the case*. But ordinary people, too, can be misled about what it is appropriate to criticize or praise in moral terms. Kantianism, Aristotelianism, and sentimentalism all have to acknowledge the existence of many putative moral opinions that fail to fit in (easily) with what those views say about moral concepts. Many people think that homosexuality, masturbation, or overindulgence in food is morally wrong or disgusting, apart from any ill effects on human lives. And it is difficult but not, I think, impossible to explain away all these (putative) opinions in the light of various philosophical views about moral concepts. But of course, Kantianism, Aristotelianism, and sentimentalism will all have *different ways* of working this out.

of "morally right" and used that claim to account for a variety of familiar facts about rightness—for example, that it is self-other asymmetric and that beliefs about rightness motivate (though not always effectively). As a result of what has been said in the present chapter, however, we are now in a position to explain how and why empathy and approval enter into the meaning of "right." They do so because it is part of the very meaning of "right" that its reference is fixed in relation to empathy and (what our theory says constitutes) moral approval, that it is understood as referring to a property that causes or tends to cause approval, that is, warm feelings toward agents resulting (in the ways described previously) from the operation of empathy.

Hume is sometimes accused of committing the naturalistic fallacy (or making some other fundamental mistake) when he moves as freely as he often seems to do from talk about what we approve to talk about rightness or virtue. (See *Treatise*, pp. 471, 574f., 590, for just a few examples.)[14] However, if the present view of "right" and other moral terms is correct, the very meaning of those terms allows for this to happen; if some other sentimentalist theory of moral terminology—say, the ideal observer theory—were correct, that, too, would permit one to move from claims about approval to claims about rightness. But of course I am saying all this against the background assumption that approval doesn't presuppose a moral judgment of rightness and so can be used, in one way or another, to explain the meaning of "right."

On the present view, moreover, moral rightness, wrongness, and goodness are real properties of agents and their acts, attitudes, and motives. Moral claims don't describe our (tendencies toward) attitudes of approval or our (tendencies toward) empathic reactions of warmth or chill; rather, these attitudes and empathic reactions (are used to) fix the (objective) reference of moral terms and utterances. And the contrast here with ideal observer and response-dependent views of moral terminology is instructive. Such views entail that moral utterances are at least as much about the (actual or hypothetical) reactions of observers as they are about the actions or agents being observed (or judged), and to that extent, these views treat moral claims as less objective than we ordinarily think or want to think they are. But the present reference-fixing form of sentimentalism regards moral claims as *not* being about our observer-reactions to acts and agents and sees them, rather, as being primarily *about the acts or agents* we react to, and for that reason, it clearly allows for the objectivity of moral judgments in a way that ideal observer and response-dependent views do not. So on the present approach, our experiences of warmth and chill (and, quite possibly, of color, given Kripke's views) serve, in David Wiggins's felicitous phrase, to "light up" properties that are objectively there in acts or agents (or physical objects), rather

---

14. On Hume's tendency to move from talk of approval to evaluative talk of what is right or virtuous, see Jonathan Harrison, *Hume's Moral Epistemology* (Oxford: Clarendon Press, 1976), 122ff.

than functioning as the basis for (possibly rigidified) dispositional self-descriptions or as the basis for moral (or other) projections.[15]

In conclusion, then, it turns out that the notion of empathy is absolutely basic and crucial to sentimentalist metaethics, and as I have argued in ECE, it also seems to be crucial to making the claims and the distinctions that a commonsense normative sentimentalism would wish and need to make. ECE argued, in particular, that we can use facts about the differing empathic responsiveness of agents to *justify* (or as *criterial for*) normative moral claims and distinctions, but that argument, that discussion, can be deepened or solidified in the light of the fuller metaethics offered here. If empathy-derived approval and disapproval fix the reference (and help constitute the meaning) of moral terms, that gives us *more* reason than ECE ever offered to think that we can justify normative moral claims by reference to how we as agents empathically respond to different situations (though I won't go into further specifics here). This allows metaethical and normative sentimentalism to tie up fairly neatly together. Since Hume was the first philosopher to make use of empathy (sympathy) for such systematic moral-theoretic purposes, my own overall approach is distinctly Humean—both in its tone and in its substance. My hope, at any rate, is that it can serve to revive something like Humean sentimentalism in promising contemporary terms.

But have we gone too far? Hume famously worried about the possibility of deducing or deriving an "ought" from an "is" (*Treatise*, 469f.), and yet I have argued here that our reference-fixing explication of moral terms allows one to move automatically from statements about what we approve and disapprove to statements about what is right or wrong, and that *is* deducing an "ought" from an "is." In addition, I have pointed out that ideal observer theories also allow such derivations. How can all or any of this be Humean? And how, indeed, can it really be *true*? In our next chapter, we shall have to consider these issues.[16]

15. See Wiggins's "A Sensible Subjectivism?" 238. Wiggins thinks the metaphor of "lighting up" is apt for (what I take to be) a certain subtle form of ideal observer (or response-dependent) approach. But I think it makes more sense, is more illuminating (excuse the punning!) when applied to the more objectivistic semi-Kripkean approach taken in these pages. For views about the implications of ideal observer theories that are very similar to what I have been saying about them here, see, e.g., J. L. Mackie, *Hume's Moral Theory* (London: Routledge, 1980), 58f.; Michael Smith, "Objectivity and Moral Realism," in J. Haldane and C. Wright, eds., *Reality, Representation and Projection* (Oxford: Oxford University Press, 1993), esp. 241; and (on color) John Locke, *An Essay Concerning Human Understanding*, II, viii, 25.

16. Harrison, in *Hume's Moral Epistemology*, points out the ways in which several metaethical views that can be attributed to Hume allow the (analytic) transition from "is" to "ought" (whereas other views that can be attributed to him do not). And in the light of the worries Hume raises in his discussion of "is" and "ought," Harrison (like me) is mystified about what is going on in Hume. The "threat" (my word) of Hume's turning out to allow the derivation of "ought's" from "is's" is also mentioned by J. L. Mackie in *Hume's Moral Theory*, 69.

5

HOW TO DERIVE "OUGHT" FROM "IS"

The title of this chapter is taken, of course, from a famous article by John Searle.[1] And if the reader doesn't feel skepticism about what the title (and what I have previously said) indicates that I am going to attempt to do, then there is something wrong. They *should* feel skepticism or disbelief about the idea of deriving an "ought" from an "is"; indeed, until the various arguments of the present chapter occurred to me, I was very skeptical, too. But when I go through the argument step by step, it all seems to make sense. To me, it seems fairly convincing, so I hope you will give me a chance to convince you.[2]

Searle's article was roundly criticized by a number of critics around the time it appeared. But the critics disagreed among themselves as to (precisely) where in Searle's argument things go astray, that is, as to which inference Searle makes is faulty. That disagreement is, in my opinion, a mark or measure of how clever the argument is, but I don't want to critically engage it myself because, whether it works or not, I have another, more purely semantical and clearly sentimentalist

---

1. "How to Derive 'Ought' from 'Is'," *Philosophical Review* 73 (1964): 43–58.

2. In *Hume's Moral Theory* (London: Routledge and Kegan Paul, 1980, esp. 69), J. L. Mackie takes the fact that ideal-observer and subjectivist interpretations of Hume's metaethical views entail that "ought" can be derived from "is" as evidence against interpreting Hume in this way (and as a reason to prefer an emotivist or projectivist interpretation). And that is because of the strong worries or doubts Hume expresses about the idea of such a derivation. But what may not do as an interpretation of Hume might nonetheless fit the semantic/moral facts, and that is what I shall be attempting to show here. Let me also, however, mention Jesse Prinz's discussion of whether one can derive an "ought" from an "is" in his recent *The Emotional Construction of Morals* (Oxford: Oxford University Press, 2007), 1–10. I find much to disagree with in Prinz's assumptions and arguments, but what he says constitutes an interesting contrast with the approach taken here.

way of deriving "ought" from "is" that is more relevant to the purposes of the present book.

Given what has been said in the last three chapters, I think we are in a position to deduce moral claims from factual ones about human tendencies of approval and disapproval (which, as I previously indicated, is just the kind of inference Hume is constantly making in the *Treatise*). The argument I shall give will be conceptual rather than linguistic. I am not going to say that because language is used in a certain way, such and such moral claims are true. That would be a mistake. Paul Ziff pointed out many years ago, in a book called *Semantic Analysis*, that we can't properly say that a certain painting is beautiful *because* all critics think so; what (or the most that) we should say is that the fact all critics think the painting beautiful is evidence for its actually being beautiful.[3] Similarly, putative facts about how we use the term *empathy* or *right*—facts mentioned in our last chapter—may (I hope) give us some reason to believe that acting cruelly is wrong, but they can't be the *reason why* it is morally wrong. The facts about linguistic usage are contingent, and the wrongness of cruelty is presumably an a priori and necessary truth. It is because of potential slips or confusions like this that I won't chiefly be talking about language but rather about concepts, attributes, and propositions. And yet I do want to say that citing facts about how we use moral language can give us reason to hold that certain normative moral propositions are true. The fact that language is used in a certain way gives us reason to accept, and perhaps may even allow us to prove, certain moral claims, and if moral terms have their reference fixed in the way I specified in the last three chapters, then I think we have reason in particular to believe that compassion is right or good and cruelty wrong or morally bad. (None of this amounts to a proof, though or as yet, because what I have said about the way language works is just a working hypothesis, not something that has itself been proved or that is immediately obvious.) But having made these points, let us move on to our main, nonlinguistic, conceptual argument(s), and let us begin by seeing what would follow if an ideal observer theory of moral concepts were correct.

Let us assume, in other words and taking things very roughly, that the concept of rightness is the concept of what would be approved by a(ny) fully informed, calm, impartial, human observer. This conceptual analysis, if correct, would seem to allow us to deduce an "ought" from an "is" if we allow that conclusions about right and wrong count, in a sense that is fair to Hume's original intentions in the famous "is-ought" passage, as "ought's." I think that we should count them as such—or at least that an ability to deduce a moral "right" or "wrong" from an "is" would be a sufficiently surprising and important philosophical result to be worth pursuing in these pages. So, given the conceptual analysis, an "is" statement or proposition about human dispositions to approve (or even a singular claim or proposition about what

3. Paul Ziff, *Semantic Analysis* (Ithaca, N.Y.: Cornell University Press, 1960), chapter 6.

a given fully informed, etc., observer approves) enables us to deduce a statement about what is morally right. And similarly about disapproval and wrongness. To be sure, and as someone might point out, the argument goes through only if one (also) assumes that (it is conceptually analytic that) if fully informed, calm, impartial, human observers would approve of an action, it is morally right. But since this is or is supposed to be analytic, assuming it as a premise (if one feels one can or should do that) doesn't undercut the validity or soundness of the deduction or derivation of "ought" from "is."

However, there is reason to be suspicious of this argument. If the ideal observer theory or approach is supposed to be helpfully analyzing a concept, then the notion of approval it mentions had better not be (analytically) equivalent to the idea of what the ideal observer *thinks is right*. It had better be conceived in a way that allows the definition not to be circular and unhelpful: for instance, in the way in which Hume in the *Treatise* conceived it. But even then, we may wonder how we can really deduce an "ought" from an "is" (from now on, I shall simplify by dropping the quotation marks), given the emotive, normative, or motivational force that the conclusion seems to possess and the premise(s) to lack. A statement or proposition about what fully informed, calm, impartial people would approve lacks emotive/motivational force, whereas the conclusion that a certain (kind of) act is morally right seems to have such force, and so it may seem impossible in any valid manner to have really gone from the premise to the conclusion. But I think this would be a mistake and would now like to explain why I think so.

The ideal observer theory holds that moral claims or utterances can be true or false, and perhaps the most important question before us is whether we can accommodate emotive meaning to this assumption about moral claims. Obviously, if moral or other evaluative utterances are merely expressive of emotions (or are imperatival), they can't be true or false in the sense that common sense appears to assume—and if that were the case, not only our ordinary view of morality and value but also something very desirable in itself would have to be renounced or repudiated. The ability to make true value claims, if it exists, is part of our heritage or birthright; it allows us to think in ways that we often think and often want to think, and the armamentarium of our understanding of and responding to the world would be much diminished if it turned out we couldn't make true (and false) moral or other evaluative judgments.

In chapters 3 and 4, I argued that the motive force that attaches to empathy and to moral claims based in empathy can be conceived as fully consistent with the making of objective, "cognitive" moral judgments. But at this point, and for reasons that will emerge in what follows, I want to talk of emotive/evaluative meaning in a sense broad enough to encompass both moral and other value judgments. If we accept some standard version of the ideal observer theory, we accept the "factuality" and cognitive import of moral judgments, and we obviously can't then accept a theory of the emotive meaning that attaches to value utterances that undercuts such factuality and cognitive import or the ideal observer theory itself.[4] In particular, then, I want to maintain a view of emotive meaning that is consistent with Philippa Foot's idea that value judgments don't automatically "commit the will" in the way that Hare's view (not to mention Stevenson's and Ayer's) pretty clearly implies.[5] So what we are looking for is a way of conceding the existence of emotive meaning and conceding that such meaning attaches to moral (or other) value claims in a way that it doesn't attach to the *analysans* (or *analysantia*) in ideal observer theories of morality—without undercutting the cognitive import or factuality that ideal observer theories hold to characterize moral claims or utterances, and without undercutting the ideal observer theory itself.

Many years ago, I defended a view of emotive/evaluative meaning that would allow us to do all these things and also (therefore) allow an ideal observer theory to deduce an ought from an is in the way mentioned earlier.[6] I (still) believe that the account of emotive meaning I offered is a plausible one, so let's see how well it can work in the present context.

On that account, we should conceive emotive meaning as a kind of Gricean implication or implicature. According to Grice in his famous article, "The Causal Theory of Perception," statements we make can have implications that are not part of what makes them true or false.[7] If, for example, I say that my wife is either in the kitchen or in the bedroom, I imply that I don't know which of the two she is in, but if I in fact do know, then my original statement can still be true. According to Grice, the original statement's implication of ignorance is *cancelable*, because, after all, one can, immediately after making the statement, add that one isn't saying which room she is in. In other words, one can make the total statement: my wife is either in the kitchen or in the bedroom, and I'm not saying which. The last part does the canceling, and according to Grice, it shows that when one just says "my wife is either in the kitchen or the bedroom," the implication that one doesn't know which isn't a truth condition of what one is asserting.

Grice went on to also talk about *detachable* implications. For example, "he was poor, but he was virtuous" implies that poverty makes it more likely that someone will be a criminal (or immoral), but if it turns out that this sociological generalization is incorrect, that wouldn't presumably affect the truth value of what one said when one said of someone "he was poor, but he was virtuous." If, in fact, the person referred to was both poor and virtuous, I believe most of us

4. In chapter 4, I argued that ideal observer views don't allow for as much moral objectivity as we crave and implicitly believe in, but they do allow moral statements to be cognitive, factual, and true and to be to some extent about the entities that are morally evaluated.

5. See Philippa Foot, "Goodness and Choice," reprinted in her *Virtues and Vices* (Berkeley: University of California Press, 1978).

6. See my "Value Judgments and the Theory of Important Criteria," *Journal of Philosophy* 65 (1968): 94–112.

7. H. P. Grice, "The Causal Theory of Perception," *Proceedings of the Aristotelian Society* 35 (1961): S121–S153. Grice developed his ideas about implication much further in subsequent work.

would call the original statement true—irrespective of anything that turned out to be the case on the sociological issue or question that the statement implies an answer to. However, the implication in this case is not only irrelevant to truth but also actually detachable. That is, one can say the same thing (in truth-relevant terms) that one says when one says "he was poor, but he was virtuous" without implying a sociological contrast between poverty and virtue: namely, by saying "he was poor, *and* he was virtuous."[8]

Applying these ideas to ideal observer theories, we can say that the (positive) moral claims that such theories allow us to deduce imply that we like certain things in a way that statements about what an ideal observer would approve do not, but that this implication isn't part of the truth conditions of moral claims. Thus the assertion that a certain act is right implies that the person making the assertion likes or has a favorable attitude toward that (kind of) action, but the holding of that implication—the truth of the assumption that the asserter *does* like that (kind of) action—may not be a condition of the truth of the original moral claim. Further, if the ideal observer theory is correct, we can say that the claims about what an ideal observer would like or approve that moral statements are analyzed in terms of lack the implication that the person making the claim likes a given (kind of) act. There seems to be no reason that people shouldn't dislike calmness or impartiality as a trait in themselves or others, and so when people say that a fully informed, impartial, calm, human observer would approve or like something, they needn't at all be saying or even implying that they themselves like it.[9] In Gricean terms, this would mean that the implication of liking (on the part of a speaker, etc.) that moral claims have is detachable, because a statement can be made with the same truth conditions but lacking the implication of (speaker) liking. In other words, an ideal observer theory might correctly specify the analytic truth conditions of moral claims in terms of claims about what ideal observers would approve or like, even if the former claims imply that the person making the claim likes some (kind of) act, but the latter do not.

Now if, given an ideal observer theory, the implication of liking that attaches to moral claims is detachable, does such a theory also treat it as cancelable? Can someone properly say, "This is right, but I don't mean to imply that I like this sort of action"? Given ideal observer theory, I don't see why one couldn't say

8. Let me hasten to add that "he was poor, but he was virtuous" doesn't *always* imply that poverty makes for a lack of virtue. If you say: "both she and he were poor and morally vicious," I can respond by saying: "I disagree; he was poor, but he was virtuous; on the other hand, I am willing to grant what you said about *her*." In cases like these, the contrast implied by the use of "but" refers, not to some difference between things spoken about, but to the difference between what some other person has said and what the speaker believes to be true. And there are probably other sorts of uses of "but" as well.

9. If they had to be implying such a thing (because, e.g., everyone really does have to like calmness and impartiality), then there would be no difference between what moral claims and claims about hypothetical observers imply, and we wouldn't face a problem in going from is to ought in such a case, at least if we assume, as I shall argue in just a moment, that the implications are what emotive/evaluative meaning amounts to.

such a thing, and the reason is actually very simple. (Certain) ideal observer theories may well be consistent with the externalist thesis that sincere, full moral judgments aren't necessarily motivating, because (for the reasons just mentioned and for others as well) it is not at all clear that the belief that a given act would be approved by a calm, fully informed, impartial observer would necessarily motivate someone toward doing the act in question. In that case, there would seem to be no reason that people claiming that some act is right shouldn't cancel the conventional implication of liking by adding, for example, that they don't themselves like or feel favorably toward such acts.

We now need to make one further, important step. In my earlier article, I argued that emotive/evaluative meaning can be understood as (nothing more than) a Gricean implication of moral and other evaluative claims. "This act is wrong" has emotive meaning in virtue of the fact that it conventionally implies that we dislike, disapprove of, or have an unfavorable attitude toward the act in question.[10] And similarly for positive moral/evaluative claims. So if, as per the ideal observer theory, we can analyze such claims in terms of claims about the reactions of ideal observers, and if, given my theory of emotive meaning, an implication of favorable or unfavorable attitude is what emotive meaning amounts to, then claims of rightness have an emotive meaning that claims about hypothetical ideal observers seem to lack, but the two sorts of claims can be analytically equivalent, nonetheless. Which is all an ideal observer theory actually needs to claim.[11]

So if some form of ideal observer theory offers a correct analysis of moral concepts, the fact of emotive meaning needn't get in the way of deducing an ought from an is. The ought (of moral rightness) may imply liking or a favorable attitude in a way that the is (of approval by a hypothetical ideal observer) arguably does not, but the latter may still offer a correct (truth-conditional) analysis of the former, and we will still be able to go validly from an assumption about hypothetical approval to a conclusion about rightness, *at least as far as the issue of truth and necessary truth preservation is concerned.* And presumably that is all that *does* have to concern us when we are thinking about valid deduction or

---

10. The theory of emotive meaning I offered didn't have sentimentalism built into it, so one could, without pain of immediate circularity, speak of evaluative claims implying approval and disapproval, and not just liking or disliking.

11. My article argued that certain evaluative claims have emotive implications that can be canceled. I can sincerely and correctly say that someone is a good Catholic and immediately add that I don't approve of Catholicism or of being a good Catholic. Similarly with "he was very good at conning people." So in some cases, emotive/evaluative meaning may be both detachable and cancelable, even if we have reason to wonder whether it ever makes sense to cancel the evaluative implication/meaning of a (sincere, non-inverted-commas) moral claim. I shall later return to this issue in the main text.

Notice, too, that on simple subjective theories of the analysis of moral claims, the distinction between the evaluative implications and the actual content of a moral judgment collapses. "I like this act" doesn't just *imply* that one likes it. "Hurrah for that act!" may, on the other hand, imply, but not say, that one likes a certain act, but it is *clear and obvious* that this implication *isn't* cancelable.

derivation. But of course, this whole argument depends on assuming the theory of emotive meaning I have just been working with.

Note, however, two things. First, as I previously indicated, the ideal observer theory can escape circularity only if the notion of approval or liking that it uses doesn't presuppose moral judgment, and that moves the theory in the direction of moral sentimentalism. But second, chapter 3 mentioned another reason for doubting any ideal observer analysis, namely, that it allows basic moral claims like "cruelty is wrong" to be a posteriori. So even if the correctness of an ideal observer analysis would allow us to go from is to ought, our doubts about such analyses should make us hesitate and more than hesitate to base a claim about how one can deduce an ought from an is on any ideal observer theory. This moves us or can move us in the direction of a sentimentalism that allows basic moral claims to be a priori, a sentimentalism of the kind defended in the previous chapter.

Thus our use of the ideal observer theory may help us see how one *might conceivably* be able to go from is to ought, but it pretty clearly doesn't much help us actually do that, and if I want to defend the idea that we actually can go from is to ought, then I had better base the argument on something more promising and less questionable than the ideal observer approach. In the present instance, that means, I think, using the sentimentalist views defended in the past three chapters as a basis for the argument. This will entail making use of a semi-Kripkean theory of moral reference-fixing, rather than a typical, explicit analytic definition, to make our case, but that is precisely what I hope to do in what follows. In other words, I hope and believe that what was said in previous chapters is fairly plausible or promising, and I shall now argue that if those ideas are correct, then we can indeed deduce an ought from an is. Now, of course, one person's modus ponens is another's modus tollens, so if my earlier ideas can be shown to entail that oughts follow from ises, some may conclude that there is something deeply wrong with the earlier ideas. But I don't think people should or necessarily will react in this way if each step in the overall argument from the earlier ideas to the conclusion that an ought can be derived from an is is made in a clear and plausible way. So let me try to make the argument go.

The is-premise of our argument is the claim or assumption that we approve (e.g.) of fully kind actions. The analytic, inference-permitting further assumption in the argument is our reference-fixing theory of the meaning of moral terms, of the content of moral concepts, a theory that doesn't involve us in making any normative moral claims but that entails, basically, that what causes approval in us is morally right or good. The conclusion, then, is that fully kind actions are right or good. This is a clearly normative moral claim, and I will assume here, as earlier, that if we can derive it from factual and semantical assumptions, we have in a meaningful and important sense deduced an ought from an is. And the same, of course, would hold if we used a factual premise about disapproval and came to a conclusion about what is morally bad or wrong.

Now the (assumed) semantical theory/truth that this argument relies on was itself defended in terms of other assumptions in our last chapter. The idea that what causes approval in us is right or good depends on the assumption that it is a priori that approval is empathically based warm feeling directed at agents. And we also have to assume that the notion of rightness cannot be understood unless one is capable of approval and (therefore) of empathy and, further, that it is a priori that empathic caring in the form of kindness, love, benevolence, compassion, humanitarianism, and the like involves warm feeling toward others. These are assumptions I defended earlier, and I won't try to defend them again here, but if one is willing to accept them, then I think one should be able to see how they support the metaethical assumption that our derivation of ought from is explicitly relies on. In effect, that assumption is nothing more, or less, than the claim that the reference of moral concepts (or terms) is fixed in the semi-Kripkean way I described in chapter 4 and that this mode of reference-fixing is analytic of moral concepts (or, if you will, of the meaning of moral claims).[12]

But this fact then leads to a difficulty. If the second premise of the argument from is to ought is just a statement about how the reference of a concept is fixed, then presumably it lacks emotive or motivating force. And the factual assumption that we approve of fully kind actions also seems to lack motivating or emotive force. But since the conclusion of the argument, according to what I have said in previous chapters, *does* have motivating force, it is difficult to believe that it could properly have been derived from the two claims or statements I used to derive it. One could, of course, claim that the motivating force doesn't have to "come in whole." Philippa Foot wanted to allow for this sort of possibility in her early paper "Moral Arguments,"[13] but I hesitate to rely on such a relatively untested notion. Let me see if we can say something more immediately plausible to defend our is-ought derivation from the just-mentioned objection.

The objection can, I think, be answered if we realize that it takes empathy to make or fully understand the claim that one can't make a genuine moral claim or genuinely approve or disapprove of something without having empathy for others—just as it takes experience of red to fully understand the claim that a congenitally blind person can't fully understand what red is. If one can see this, one will also be able to see that one cannot make the factual claim/assumption of our is-ought derivation without also having empathy. If approval requires an empathy-based experience of warmth, then (on analogy with what we want to say about redness) one can't make or fully understand statements about approval unless one knows what approval is, and that requires one to have the relevant experience of warmth. It follows, then, in particular that one can't meaningfully claim that people approve of fully kind actions unless one can approve things oneself and thus possesses empathy for others.

---

12. In *Naming and Necessity* (Oxford: Blackwell, 1980, esp. 130f.), Saul Kripke makes it clear that reference-fixing can occur with respect to concepts and even phenomena, and not just with respect to terms or words.

13. See Philippa Foot, "Moral Arguments," reprinted in her *Virtues and Vices*.

This is not a very unusual thing to be saying. We think one needs to have experienced anger to fully understand the claim that anger is an important human feeling, and we think that someone who lacks moral concepts cannot fully understand what it is to say that kindness is morally good. And the claim that someone who doesn't really know what approval is cannot fully understand what it is to say that people approve kind actions is not all that different. So the idea that understanding approval requires us to have experienced warm feelings derived from empathy is no more far-fetched than the idea, defended in previous chapters, that approval *is* a certain kind of empathically derived feeling of warmth.

But once one grants these points, our derivation of ought from is may no longer seem as suspicious as the objection raised earlier might lead one to think. One can't in fact understand its factual premise unless one has empathy and is motivated, therefore, to do the kind of thing that the conclusion of the argument says is right. So the premise might not itself be motivating, but it presupposes that any person who assumes it is motivated to do what the conclusion says is right. Therefore, the argument, the derivation, doesn't lead to a conclusion that involves a certain kind of motivation on the part of someone who accepts it, from premises that *don't* involve such motivation on the part of someone who accepts *them*.[14] There isn't, at least, that kind of reason for being suspicious of the is-ought argument we have given.

More generally, once one sees that certain factual premises that entail claims about empathy cannot themselves be understood without one's having the sort of empathically derived motivation that attaches to making genuinely normative moral claims (or having moral beliefs), the supposed gap between is and ought will seem like less of a gap. And here, as elsewhere in the argument of this book, it is empathy that does the trick. Empathy is a factual phenomenon, part of the world that "is's" describe. In fact, it is a psychological phenomenon, and one aspect of empathy, the warm or cold feeling that empathy involves or makes possible, cannot be understood except by someone who is empathic and has empathically reacted to certain human actions or situations. So one cannot understand empathy and claims about it unless one has had a certain kind of experience, just as one cannot fully understand claims about red—even claims about what people without certain experiences cannot fully understand—unless one has had those experiences. But empathy also underlies and powers certain sorts of motivation, so someone who understands what approval and empathy are must, on the present view, also have certain sorts of motivations, motivations that, on that same view, characterize that person as, at least to some extent, morally good (not morally terrible). Thus assumptions about people's states of approval and other aspects of their psychology are tantamount to conclusions

---

14. Don't say that it is suspicious that the derivation/argument goes from an a posteriori premise to an a priori conclusion. After all (the a priori) "that mathematical proposition is true" follows from (the a posteriori) "Hilbert proved it."

about their (at least partial) moral goodness. One can't be in the factual or is-like state of approval unless one instantiates an ought-like moral property, and this very claim should encourage us to think that we may be able to make a logical transition from an is to an ought.

However, at this point, I would like to return to our previous discussion of emotive meaning. In my early article, I said that statements like "he is a good Catholic" and "he was very good at conning people" have such meaning in the form of a cancelable implication to the effect that one likes or has a favorable attitude toward the person called a good Catholic or toward (the actions of) the con artist. After all, one can (with complete linguistic propriety) sincerely call someone a good Catholic but immediately go on to say that one doesn't like Catholicism or approve of someone's being a good Catholic, thereby canceling the implication of liking, or of a favorable attitude, that normally attaches to calling someone a good Catholic. And similar things can be done with "he was very good at conning people." When we discussed ideal observer theory, I was inclined to say that it too (if true) allows for the canceling of the implication of a favorable attitude that attaches to positive moral judgments. But some Gricean conventional (non-truth-affecting) implications *aren't* cancelable, and I believe that the form of metaethical sentimentalism I am defending also doesn't allow one to cancel the implication of a favorable attitude that conventionally attaches to positive moral judgments. Let me explain.

We saw earlier that the implication of contrast that conventionally attaches to "he was poor, but he was virtuous" is detachable via a sentence like "he was poor, and he was virtuous." But it is not at all clear that the implication of contrast or incongruity between poverty and virtue is *cancelable*. People who say "he was poor, but he was virtuous," implying such a contrast or incongruity, cannot cogently or sensibly go on to say that they don't intend or believe in that implication. If one *doesn't* believe in the contrast or incongruity, then, obviously, one can and should just say "he was poor, *and* he was virtuous," and for that reason, it would be perplexing and even mystifying if someone said: "he was poor, but he was virtuous, but I don't intend to imply, or at least I don't believe, that there is any contrast or incongruity between poverty and virtue." It doesn't make good sense to say "he was poor, but he was virtuous" and then cancel what it implies, and so I am inclined to conclude (on general linguistic/pragmatic grounds) that the implication in question is not a cancelable one.

Though the case is a somewhat different one, the (conventional) implication of a favorable or approving attitude that attaches to moral judgments is also not cancelable. I believe that all value judgments or claims possess some sort of emotive meaning, positive or negative, but moral claims depend on empathy in a way that other evaluative claims do not, and this makes a motivational difference to them. If empathy isn't involved in sincerely saying that someone was good at conning people (or burglarizing their homes), then there is no reason that the implication that one has a favorable attitude toward the person or what the person did can't be immediately canceled. But empathy cannot be canceled; it is a habitual, long-term, and in some measure involuntary state.[15] So claims about what is morally good or bad have an underlying motivational component that isn't subject to or open to immediate conversational cancelation or abrogation.[16] Someone who sincerely claims that an act is morally good or right has to be empathically disposed in its favor, and it doesn't make any sense for such a person to go on to claim that they don't have a favorable attitude toward that (kind of) act.

Thus morality is distinctively emotional and motivating, because of the empathy it distinctively involves, and (assuming the theory of emotive meaning I have been using) moral claims have an emotional/motivational force that other value claims lack. But the other value claims still have some emotive/expressive meaning, and as I have argued, that emotive/expressive meaning consists in a conventional Gricean implication of favorable or unfavorable attitude. In fact, as I indicated earlier, this sort of implication attaches to *all* value claims, including moral claims/judgments. But the latter also have a more deep-seated emotional/motivational aspect or component that doesn't allow their Gricean implications ever to be canceled. So one might say that there are, overall, two distinct degrees or levels of emotive meaning: the *expressive* (Gricean) kind that attaches to all value claims and the *motivating* (sentimentalist) kind that attaches specifically to moral claims.

In chapter 6, we shall see that all value claims have a tendency to make others (who initially don't accept them) think and act in accordance with them. As we shall see, this tendency works via empathic transmission or osmosis, and it seems to have a particular effectiveness in the case of moral claims, with their deeper or greater degree of emotive meaning/force. But to return to the concerns of the present chapter, it is worth pointing out that moral sentimentalism has absolutely no reason to object to the idea that nonmoral value judgments involve a lesser degree or kind of emotive meaning than that involved in moral value judgments, for moral sentimentalism need only be a view about *morality*. Hume tended to treat all evaluations in the same terms as moral ones, but a sentimentalism resting on empathy directed at and felt by moral agents can and probably should restrict itself by and large to the moral realm and say that other sorts of value

---

15. I am speaking somewhat loosely here (and elsewhere in the present chapter). I think empathy should be primarily regarded as a psychological mechanism and, as such, doesn't entail or include (the actual having of) warm or cold feelings. The looser kinds of things I have been saying about empathy won't do any harm if we remember that they *are* somewhat loose and that empathy is, most basically, a mechanism.

16. Even the implication of having a favorable attitude that attaches to claims about beauty seems to be cancelable. If one woman calls another woman beautiful, thereby implying a favorable attitude toward her, she can still in the next second add that "of course, I have no use for beautiful women; they are usually spoiled, vain, etc.," thus canceling the original implication. (I apologize if this illustrative example seems distasteful.)

judgment have to be understood and justified in different terms. And that is just what I want to say here.[17]

Of course, much (though hardly all) of what I have been saying here depends on the Gricean theory of emotive/evaluative meaning, and I haven't directly, or frontally, defended that theory. Rather, I have made use of it to clarify a number of issues. But in the course of doing so, I don't think its implications or applications have seemed implausible in any way, and I think the theory is in fact rather commonsensical. The defense of moral sentimentalism and of reference-fixing offered here doesn't in itself depend on assuming a Gricean account of emotive meaning. But what I said earlier does permit us to see how differently ideal observer theory and reference-fixing sentimentalism accommodate the idea of deriving ought from is. And seeing *that*, I think, makes the case for the reference-fixing possibility of deducing ought from is seem less odd or idiosyncratic than it otherwise might.

I had no antecedent desire to show how such a deduction could or might occur, and that was in part because it seemed to me, as to so many others, that if someone purported to derive an ought from an is, there would be a catch, something suspicious or tricky, about the deduction. But even if people have reacted in just that way to Searle's purported deduction, I don't think our (fuller) description here of how, on different accounts of moral language, one might be able to derive an ought from an is should make people think there is something suspicious going on. Or at least, I hope not. And in any event, since I don't accept ideal observer theory and prefer reference-fixing sentimentalism along the previous lines, our argument, to the extent it doesn't seem suspicious, shows how and why the phenomenon of empathy, as central to the moral life and moral concepts, allows a transition from is to ought. I believe that this new way of deriving ought from is is less dubious and more plausible than some of the others that have been proposed.

---

17. If emotive meaning is cancelable for most value judgments, one might well wonder why we have to say that "he is a good Catholic" is a positive evaluation, and one might well need to explain why it conventionally implies liking rather than disliking. This may have something to do, linguistically, with the fact that, in the moral case and a number of others (think of the uncancelable implication of a favorable attitude that attaches to "Good for you!"), the positive implication of saying that something is right or good can't be canceled and with the fact that the judgment of moral rightness or goodness itself (via the connection with empathy) entails motivation to do, rather than avoid, the kind of act called right or good. But a full and explicit explanation would have to be more complicated and would, in any event, take us away from our main purpose of better understanding morality, something that doesn't seem to require us to have a theory of the nature of evaluation generally.

I might just add, finally (a point made in my 1968 article), that the conventional implication of a favorable attitude that attaches, e.g., to "he is a good Catholic" is cancelable not only by a speaker's further remarks but also by what a speaker has said in the past or is known to think. If people know that I am anti-Catholic (and most particularly, if they know that I know that they know about this antipathy), then they *won't* initially assume I have a positive or favorable attitude toward those I call good Catholics—far from it. In such cases, it is perhaps most idiomatic to speak of what *undercuts* a conventional implication rather than of what cancels it.

But it is time now to move, or start moving, our discussion away from semantic issues and in the direction of normative ethics. The form of sentimentalism I have been defending accounts for the meaning of moral language in terms that allow moral claims or utterances to be at one and the same time both objective(ly valid) and inherently motivating. For reasons I have already mentioned, this is highly desirable from a metaethical (and perhaps even a normative) perspective, and I hope what we have said will put to rest, or at least calm, some doubts about sentimentalist metaethics. But there are, or traditionally have been, other worries about sentimentalism that we haven't yet addressed here. For example, we need to say more about how a thoroughgoing sentimentalism can understand or explain the possibility of living morally, that is, in a morally good or acceptable way. Rationalists often assert that the emotions are an inadequate guide to what is morally right and that even when they aim us toward what is right, they are incapable, by themselves, of ensuring that we eventually do act rightly. We need to answer those criticisms, and to do so, we will also have to clarify (in sentimentalist terms) the role that moral injunctions and moral principles can or do play in the life of someone who is acting or will act morally. And beyond those issues, there are strictly normative questions that also have to be addressed. Chapter 1 discussed some reasons for thinking that a form of moral sentimentalism that relies on the normative significance of empathy can explain why we should be more partial to some (groups of) individuals than to others. And somewhat more surprisingly perhaps, I also outlined some reasons for thinking that the emphasis on empathy and empathic concern for others can give normative support to deontology. (The reasons I gave were a briefer form of what I argued at considerable length in chapters 2 and 3 of *The Ethics of Care and Empathy*.) But to fill out the normative picture, we also need to consider what a sentimentalist care ethics can say about such (presumably) essential moral/political topics as respect, autonomy, and justice, and in later chapters, I want to focus on these sorts of normative issues.

But given our emphasis, in previous chapters, on the nature and meaning of moral judgments, I think our first task now is to clarify the role of moral claims, moral injunctions, and moral principles within the moral life, and it is to that task that I turn in the next chapter.

6

THE USE OF MORAL JUDGMENTS

Kant famously emphasizes the importance of conscientiousness, of conscious adherence to moral principle, as a basis for human actions. He holds that one can act rightly in following or exhibiting natural motives like benevolence or self-concern, but that such actions fail to exemplify moral worth or goodness. Kant also seems to hold that one can *never validly criticize* someone who acts conscientiously or, equivalently, from a sense of duty, and this view directly contradicts the reaction most of us have to the kind of example Bernard Williams (also famously) has given of the husband with "one thought too many," the husband who, upon seeing his wife and a stranger both drowning in nearby water, considers whether he is morally permitted or obligated to give preference to his wife before he decides to go in and save her. Most of us think there is something wrong with (the attitude and motivation of) this husband, and the force of Williams's example seems, therefore, to indicate a grave, great weakness in Kantianism.

Most moral sentimentalists, both historically and recently, would, I think, agree that there is something unappealing about or wrong with the husband in Williams's example—though they would perhaps tend to agree for different reasons. For example, Hume speaks of the natural motives and virtues of family affection, and he indicates that someone who lacks such motives and acts only from a sense of duty has reason to "hate himself," whereas Francis Hutcheson might actually question the rightness of saving the wife rather than the stranger, if it turned out that the stranger's life was more important to the good of society. Hutcheson advocates a version of the principle of utility and thinks that morally right action has to promote the greatest overall human or sentient good or well-being. But Hutcheson also thinks that there is something wrong with and morally criticizable about conscientiousness in general: he holds—antithetically to Kant—that conscientiousness is selfish (roughly, because it involves an egotistical desire to look good in one's own eyes and ipso facto less concern than one should have for those who need one's help). So I believe he would criticize the husband of Williams's example, but he would also hold that universal benevolence is or would be a better motive than either conscientiousness or spousal affection in such cases and all others.[1]

More recent sentimentalists would also see much to criticize in the husband with one thought too many. In *Caring*, for example, Nel Noddings says that conscientious adherence to principles or rules gets in the way of affectionate or warm concern for other people,[2] and in my own book *Morals from Motives*, I seconded this opinion in further detail and with further arguments.[3] Noddings thinks that we sometimes need to use or rely on moral principles, rules, standards, injunctions, or (self-)exhortations, but that the very fact we do is less than ideal from a moral standpoint. And in the just-mentioned book, I argued that principles, rules, injunctions, and the like are in fact less needed than many ethical rationalists—and perhaps even Noddings—seem to suppose. Rationalists assume that when emotions/feelings/motives like caring or love flag or cease to exist, the use of or adherence to moral principles and injunctions constitutes an important fail-safe device for ensuring that one acts rightly.[4] But I want to argue (as I did in *Morals from Motives*—henceforth, MFM) that we don't need principles or injunctions to act rightly in most cases where our natural moral motives weaken. Later on, I shall claim, in addition, that moral injunctions, principles, and rules aren't as generally available in a first-person way to moral agents as Kantians and/or rationalists assume, but we shall also see that moral injunctions and the like *have an important second-person use that I never recognized in MFM*. However, before we take up these further issues, let's first consider whether we really need moral injunctions and rules as much—or as often—as is usually thought.

Imagine a son who is helping to take care of a very sick aged mother who is in the hospital. In addition to trying to keep her in good spirits and helping her when nurses or orderlies aren't (and even when they are) available, the son may also have to consult with doctors, find out about second opinions, keep her affairs at home in order, investigate issues about her will, and on and on. All of these things can take time and energy and be very wearing, and at a certain point of what the psychology literature calls compassion fatigue, it would be understandable if the son were tempted to skimp on these activities in a way that would allow him to have more free time to see friends, have a really good meal, or have one evening, finally, to himself. One might think that such a son will need to rely on available-to-him

<hr />

1. For Hume's view, see *A Treatise of Human Nature*, ed. Selby-Bigge, esp. 479. For Hutcheson's, see *An Inquiry into the Original of Our Ideas of Beauty and Virtue*, 4th ed., 1738.

2. Nel Noddings, *Caring* (Berkeley: University of California Press, 1984), 5, 13, 25f.

3. Slote, *Morals from Motives* (New York: Oxford University Press, 2001), chapters 1–2.

4. For two examples of such ethical rationalism, see Marcia Baron, *Kantian Ethics Almost without Apology* (Ithaca, N.Y.: Cornell University Press, 1995), 127; and Stephen Darwall, *The British Moralists and the Internal "Ought": 1640–1740* (Cambridge: Cambridge University Press, 1995), 280f.

moral principles or injunctions in order to resist acting, at that point, in a morally unacceptable way. But I don't believe this to be so, and I want to explain why.

If one is tempted, sorely tempted, to give one's mother short shrift, then one counts as less morally praiseworthy than if one weren't tempted. But even someone with that sort of impulse or facing that sort of temptation may have inner resources for resisting it that don't involve a reference to or use of moral rules or injunctions. For example, one afternoon, as the son is about to drive his car to the distant office of a doctor whom he may need to engage to give a second opinion about some aspect of his mother's condition, he may say to himself, "To heck with this! I think I will just go and see a good movie." But he may still not succumb to that temptation if he deeply cares about or loves his mother. If he does love and care about her, then those feelings or motives are very likely to *reassert themselves* after he has expressed to himself the desire to throw everything over for a movie (after he has blown off moral steam in this fashion). If he thinks about going to a movie and actually forms the intention to do so, that may give the son a kind of psychological respite from the physical and emotional burdens of caring, but it can also serve to make him more vividly aware of the likely consequences of his going to the movie and missing the appointment for a second opinion. The doctor is very busy and successful and won't soon be available for another appointment, and the son never entirely *forgets* these facts. But more important perhaps, once one actually intends to do something and takes, say, a few first steps toward doing it, its nature and consequences typically become more vivid and real than they were before the intention was formed, and the son who decides to go to the movies rather than keep the appointment with the doctor is likely to become more vividly aware of the consequences of not seeking a second opinion and of the fact, in particular, that that will mean taking chances, taking unnecessary risks, with his mother's whole future. And when a genuinely caring or loving son realizes, in a more vivid way, these implications of his going to the movies, that very realization is very likely to reengage or reawaken his warm or affectionate feelings and motivations vis-à-vis his mother and lead him to keep the appointment with the doctor rather than go to the movies.[5]

When an antecedently strong feeling/motive momentarily weakens and one is tempted to act in ways that threaten its goals, one naturally or usually becomes aware of the threat, and that very fact is likely to alert and send an alarm to one. Fatigue, temptation, and impulse may make us for a while forget our kindness or our love for another, may tip us, in effect, toward a moral capsizing, but if we are genuinely and appropriately caring, the tipping boat will also have a built-in tendency to right itself, regain its balance, a tendency activated by realizing the dire consequences of acting

---

5. In *Friendship, Altruism, and Morality* (London: Routledge and Kegan Paul, 1980, 37ff.), Lawrence Blum considers a somewhat similar case of someone's deep-seated concern or feeling's (eventually) overcoming the temptation to do (what most of us think of as) wrong without there being any use of moral claims or principles.

on the felt (countermoral) temptation. Thus as he is driving toward the movies and as the consequences of his present course of action become more vivid to him, the son may say to himself, "What am I doing? This might really hurt my mother's chances." And that realization, as it becomes vivid or even panicky and thereby helps to revive his usual empathic concern for his mother, might lead him to turn his car around and head for his appointment with the doctor. And the thought specifically of right and wrong needn't have come into the matter.[6]

Now some sons will go to the movies, despite the risk to their mother. But this will show that their love, their affection, is less than one might hope for or expect from a son. Such a son is very likely to feel guilty after the fact, and I certainly don't want to say that every mother has or even deserves the full love and affection of her son. But assuming that it is or would be in a given instance wrong to go to the movies rather than see the doctor, I believe that typically strong natural (in Hume's sense) affection is (eventually) sufficient for preventing such immoral action. Does that mean that thinking of that very wrongness wouldn't help the son make the morally right decision in the end? Not at all. Because our sentimentalist account of explicit moral thinking holds that such thinking is essentially emotional and motivating, the recognition that going to the movies would be wrong could certainly, on its own or by way of reinforcing reviving natural feeling, help the son decide not to go to the movies. But I don't see that such thinking or recognition is necessary to this result, and I have just been explaining why.

More important, if the son is one whose natural feeling isn't strong enough to revive in a direction that will make him (do the right thing and) help his mother, it is not at all clear to me that explicit moral thinking is likely to occur to him and make the moral difference. Kant tended to assume that (the same) moral principles are known and practically available to everyone, but in our case of the son, compassion fatigue (or general tiredness) and resurging self-concern or selfish impulse can (temporarily) put relevant moral principles out of his mind in much the same way, I think, that it can put *his mother* and *her welfare* out of his mind. (This is a point that Lawrence Blum made many years ago.)[7] It is a mistake, I believe, to think that the moral principles and injunctions one is familiar with and accepts have a reasonable chance of occurring to one in every circumstance and in every condition one may be in. And of course, given the present account, such principles will *never* be available to people (like psychopaths) who lack certain relevant dispositions of feeling and motive. In the kind of case where a generally decent individual is sorely tempted to do what is wrong because (for instance) they are compassion-fatigued, (self-addressed) moral injunctions and moral principles may be just as (temporarily) unavailable as natural motives like love or caring concern for another.

6. To the extent that the son steps back from and effectively questions what he is doing and intending to do, he shows a self-reflexive autonomy or self-governance that may be (one) distinctive (feature) of the human moral life. But Kantians assume this sort of thing happens or is accomplished by means of explicitly moral thinking, and I am saying this needn't be so.

7. Blum, *Friendship, Altruism, and Morality*, 22–29.

However, I can also see a way in which they just *might*, at least sometimes, turn out to be *more* available and morally helpful than the natural motives. Consider again the son with the sick mother. He has been paying emotional attention to his mother, and like reflexes and other responses that can become inhibited or temporarily disabled through frequent repetition, *this particular response, this particular form of caring attention* might become temporarily disabled even while *other* responses and motives were not. Now, as Hoffman points out in *Empathy and Moral Development* (chapter 6), the moral injunction to care for those one loves and who need one's help (even when that is very tiring or exhausting) can, through inductive discipline and the habituation of "scripts," accumulate a motivational force that is to a substantial extent independent of any relevant particular instance. That injunction speaks to one's caring relationships generally, not specifically or merely to what one feels and wants to do regarding one's mother, and to use a possibly useful metaphor, this injunction and one's commitment to it may constitute a kind of reservoir of moral(ly good) motivation that can or might be drawn on *when one's feelings and intentions in a particular given direction are exhausted or inhibited through their own repetition and the through the tiring or bad consequences (for the agent) of having acted on them.* This takes us a bit beyond anything Hoffman explicitly says, but it makes sense, I think, in the light of what he *does* say about the ways empathy supports the use of moral principles or rules. And if we accept these ideas and what I said in earlier chapters about the emotional underpinnings and content of moral claims/beliefs, then we may have reason to think that moral injunctions *are* more likely to be available and useful to the son in our example, during his initial period of compassion fatigue, than (ex vi terminorum) his compassion and feeling for his mother are. That indicates a potentially important role for moral injunctions and rules in the moral life, though, as I also argued, that role may be *more* limited and *less* important than Kantians and many others have conceived. But my argument here has been somewhat speculative about empirical matters, and it would be useful to see how well the idea that learned moral rules constitute a reservoir of motivation can be corroborated in psychological studies or experiments.[8]

---

8. We learn motivationally charged scripts through induction (e.g., the association of hurting people with guilt), and (as Hoffman says) these scripts can attach themselves to and motivate adherence to moral rules or principles. But on my view (and unlike Hoffman), the full understanding of moral claims/principles/injunctions requires the second-order empathy (approval and disapproval) described in chapter 2. This serves, however, to reinforce the points being made in the main text. If the son of our example understands and is (often) motivated by moral principles/claims, those principles will be more general than his concern for his mother and will probably contain motivational force not only through inductively learned scripts but also through the empathic chill and warmth involved in subscribing to moral principles. This suggests more strongly than anything explicit in the text that the principles (or some principle) that the son subscribes to might represent a substantial source of potential motivational energy—a motivational reservoir—for him to draw on, if his (first-order) feelings toward his mother were weakening or temporarily silent.

But consider, too, that *almost nothing we have been or will be saying about moral education or the uses of moral injunctions depends on the specific reference-fixing theory of moral meaning defended in* chapter 4

In any event, I would like to turn now to a quite different use and usefulness of moral principles and injunctions, one that I think is less speculative and/or more obvious than what I have just been saying about their first-person uses. I think moral claims or injunctions expressed *to others*—what I shall call *second-person uses* of such claims or injunctions—are a very real and rich source of moral motivation. They represent a way in which someone with good motives and a sense of morals who is tempted to do wrong may be called back from such wrongdoing and led to do what is right or even good, instead.

Now when I said a moment ago that moral injunctions or rules may constitute a kind of reservoir of empathy—what one might think of as potential energy for the kinesis of empathy—I was assuming that someone like the son in our example might well on his own think of a moral injunction/rule against doing what he is thinking of doing, even while not feeling any direct empathic concern or compassion for his mother. And we can see how this might or would lead him to reconsider and even recoil from his intention to go to the movies when he should be seeking a second medical opinion about his mother's treatment and prospects. But usually a reservoir can be tapped only if one tries to tap it, and it is not clear to me exactly how someone like the son would tap into his reservoir of principles, how he would come to think of a moral injunction or principle that indicated the wrongness of what he was intending to do. I'm not saying it wouldn't happen; I'm just saying that I am not sure how it would happen—and saying further that it might well *not* happen in the circumstances we described. A moral injunction or principle can constitute a reservoir of empathy or empathic concern that has (to switch metaphors) been built up out of past empathic reactions to and in other circumstances, but it can affect the son's behavior or actions only if he actually draws on that reservoir, and that means, for example, paying attention to the moral injunction in circumstances where his concern for his mother has temporarily flagged or failed. Of course, the son would still have other resources for pulling himself back into doing the right thing by his mother—emotional/motivational resources that we have described at some length. And that seems to me to be a good thing precisely because I don't think one can rely on the assumption that any moral principle or injunction *will* occur to him in the situation we posited.

But there is another way in which moral principles or injunctions might affect, for the morally better, the behavior of the son in our example. Other people might find out what he was intending to do and tell him that and/or why what he is intending

---

rather than on sentimentalism as such. If approval, e.g., is seen as a kind of empathy with empathy, then however we relate such approval to the meaning of moral claims/utterances—whether we think of it as what is expressed, described, projected, or used to light up moral properties, when we make moral claims—there will be emotional/motivational force to the claims, and our account of moral education and the usefulness of moral claims relies on *that aspect* of the claims for most or all of its conclusions. So our account of moral education and thinking is sentimentalist in the broadest sense—and not just in relation to my particular theory of sentimentalist moral semantics.

to do (namely, go to the movies rather than seek a second opinion) is wrong.[9] And such a second-person use of a moral injunction, rule, or principle might be quite efficacious in bringing the son back from the brink of what I think we would consider a moral shipwreck. Other people's opinions and attitudes influence our own—a fact that Hume greatly emphasized. And for reasons that I shall describe in just a moment (and that Hume was to some extent aware of), other people's *moral* opinions and attitudes have a very strong tendency to affect our own.[10]

Charles Stevenson's ideas about the emotive meaning and "magnetism" of value judgments/utterances is particularly relevant here.[11] Stevenson held an emotivist theory of evaluative utterances, according to which (very roughly) value claims express positive and negative emotions on the part of those who (sincerely) utter them. In their second-person usage, they in effect tell others to have an emotion or reaction similar to that of the speaker, and given human nature, they tend to have that effect. But Stevenson doesn't say much about how this works, how it happens. At one point, he notes the possibility that the feelings expressed in a moral judgment or utterance may spread via contagion to another person, but he doesn't mention Hume or the notion of empathy/sympathy in this connection. His chief purpose is merely (but what a merely!) to point out that evaluative and moral judgments (including, presumably, both negative judgments like "killing is wrong" and positive ones like "it was good of you to help that poor woman") are often successfully used to influence others to have similar opinions or attitudes, and he uses this fact, and others, to defend his form of emotivism.[12] But Stevenson didn't think one could combine cognitivism and emotive meaning/magnetism together in a single (sentimentalist) theory—and that is precisely what we attempted to do in earlier chapters. And for reasons I mentioned earlier, I think sentimentalism does better to reject emotivism in favor of a view that makes some sort of room for moral cognition and/or objectivity.

Moreover, our previous discussion of empathy helps to provide Stevenson's theory with a (more explicit) mechanism for the emotive effects he describes: the mechanism, of course, being empathy. In fact, and without having terms like

9. Perhaps the son tells others what he is intending to do because he already knows that and why it is wrong and wants to be forcefully reminded of that fact and thereby helped to do what he is, at least momentarily, finding it difficult to do. (Anticipatory guilt would also probably enter in here.) This would complicate matters in an interesting way. But surely there are other ways in which people might find out what he intends to do—someone might call his cell phone and ask him where he is or what he is doing—and I think we should confine our attention to this latter sort of psychologically simpler case.

10. As I mentioned earlier, (some of) Hume's views about the way others' (moral) opinions influence our own can be found in the *Treatise*, ed. Selby-Bigge, 320–324, 346, 499, 589, 592, 605.

11. See Stevenson's "The Emotive Theory of Moral Judgments," *Mind* 46 (1937): 14–31. Stevenson also introduces the idea that evaluative claims are "dynamic," but I won't distinguish between dynamism and emotive meaning or magnetism here.

12. Hoffman's inductive discipline focuses on preventing harmful actions, and Hoffman doesn't mention any ways that good behavior/actions can be empathically reinforced. But if we bring in Hume's ideas about the general empathic transmission of (moral) opinions and enrich the discussion with some of Stevenson's ideas, we can see a way for positive reinforcement in the form of praise to play a role in moral education. I am indebted on this point to discussion with Dennis Arjo.

emotive meaning and *magnetism*, Hume already saw that moral judgments are emotively influential and that that influence occurs via empathy, and we can now bring what we said earlier about empathy to bear on what we have just been saying about the use and efficacy of second-person moral judgments. Of course, other sorts of value judgments also have emotive meaning/magnetism, and empathy can help account for that, too, but even if further discussion of that point might be very interesting, it would take us away from our present main purpose: understanding how second-person uses of moral rules or injunctions can influence (hopefully for the better, but sometimes, of course, for the worse) what people who are tempted to do something (believed to be) wrong will end up doing.

If and when someone (sincerely) tells the son who has been taking care of his mother that it would be wrong of him to go to the movies (because his mother needs . . . , etc.), the son may, through empathic osmosis, pick up on what they are feeling about his intended action and to some extent start to feel the same way himself. His recognition of the force or truth of what they say (assuming that is what happens) will contain or mirror the negative emotion or chill they are feeling about what he is intending to do and may well then cause him to recoil from doing it. In empathizing with the chill another person feels at the thought of what he (the son) is intending to do—a chill that itself, as we have seen, involves and is based on the other person's tendency to not do that sort of thing—the son may have that same tendency reinforced in himself and thereby be led to not do what he had been intending to do. Empathy, then, seems to be the mechanism of second-person emotive meaning, and the frequent usefulness or efficacy of second-person moral injunctions in pulling an otherwise moral individual back from doing what would be wrong is further testimony to the moral importance of both empathy and the second-person use of moral principles or injunctions.

But more can be said. If someone, say it is a friend, tells the son that it would be wrong of him to go to the movies and thereby worsen his mother's life chances, the fact that a moral injunction (roughly) against harming those we love is active in the friend can, by empathic contagion or osmosis, *activate* the same (or a very similar) principle in the son. In that case, not only will the son then feel some of the repugnance at the doing of what he plans to do that his friend feels but what the friend says will also *elicit or bring out* all the emotional/motivational associations or content that the moral principle of not harming a loved one contains for the son. And this is to (get him to) draw on the accumulated reservoir of emotion and motivation that the principle constitutes for him. Even if, while he is sick and tired of helping his mother, he isn't likely on his own to draw on that reservoir, the intervention and influence of another may allow or cause him to do so and thus be further efficacious in getting him (more quickly) to abandon his plans to see a movie.

So there are two ways in which a second-person use of a moral injunction can influence action, that is, lead a person to act in accordance with the injunction. The injunction can express the feelings and motives of the one who issues it and thereby empathically induce similar feelings and motives in the hearer.[13] And it can elicit and draw on the (reservoir of) feelings and motivations that the hearer already associates with that injunction (or others like it). These influences are likely to occur together and to interact and possibly reinforce each other in ways that would need to be further investigated and elaborated. But what we have said in any event shows that and how the second-person use of moral principles or injunctions may sometimes influence people to act in ways they wouldn't have acted if such directives hadn't been addressed to them. And all of this would occur in a way consistent with, and indeed supporting the truth of, moral sentimentalism.

However, I am afraid that this already complex picture has to be complicated a bit further. In previous chapters, I argued that moral approval and judgment involve a second-order empathy about empathy. I also pointed out that when we feel the chill of (someone's) disapproval (of us), we are in effect feeling a third-order empathy: empathy with the second-order chill that others feel with respect to the first-order lack of warmth of our own intentions or motives. Now the chill of disapproval can be conveyed by a look or a glance, but in the case we have just been describing, the son is explicitly told that something he intends to do would be morally wrong. Since this moral judgment contains empathically conveyable chill, any chill it makes the son feel about what he is proposing to do is third-order, too: it is a chilly empathic response on the part of the son to the second-order chill that someone else feels (and expresses in a second-person moral judgment) about a first-order cold-hearted intention that the son himself has. Of course, I am making what I take to be the plausible assumption that if the son is told that what he is intending to do is or would be wrong, his empathic juices may flow in response, even if he doesn't at that point immediately feel any

---

13. It turns out, then, that moral assertions not only rest on second-order empathy with first-order empathy but also depend on empathic osmosis for some of their ability to influence others. Note, too, that the empathic effects of someone's stated moral opinions aren't limited to opinions stated in the grammatical second person. General and impersonally stated moral injunctions and grammatically third-person (and even first-person) claims about what it was/would be wrong for someone (else) to do can also empathically seep into hearers or even readers (and according to the usage adopted here, they would then be functioning in a second-person way). But let me just add one small point that might be of interest to epistemologists. It has been said that children are inferentially justified in believing what their parents tell them (e.g., about God) because they are able to rely on their parents in so many areas of their lives—both practically and epistemically. Others hold that the acceptance of (this kind of) testimony isn't inferential, but immediate. But I wonder whether anyone in the recent literature has suggested that the immediate, noninferential character of such childhood acceptances results from empathic processes à la Malebranche and Hume. Keith Lehrer tells me that Thomas Reid thought of children as gullible regarding statements made by others, but if empathy is at work here, then various childhood beliefs may (for that reason) be beyond rationality and irrationality/gullibility, and it seems to me that this possibility deserves to be explored further. Of course, I have spoken somewhat generally about the beliefs children take in from others and have assumed that they can acquire nonevaluative beliefs, and not just evaluative ones, via empathy. But in chapter 10, I shall be arguing that it is possible to empathize not only with empathically charged moral claims but with nonevaluative claims/beliefs as well—and it turns out that one doesn't have to be an empiricist/sentimentalist like Hume in order to defend such a view.

empathic concern for his mother.[14] As before, the fact that it is a different source (someone other than his mother) and a somewhat different and more generalized kind of response that is involved may allow or cause an empathic reaction, even if the particular response of empathic concern for his mother has been temporarily inhibited or exhausted. But in any event, if the son feels a chill analogous to and caused by the chill someone else experiences in regard to his (the son's) intended behavior, he will presumably experience (in a reawakened form) the strong reluctance to do the kind of thing he has been intending to do that that other person, the one expressing a negative moral judgment, presumably feels. And that will motivationally inhibit that intention to at least some extent and make it more likely that the son won't in fact do what he had originally intended but instead will keep the appointment to get a second opinion.

Note, too, that injunctions expressed by those we know or love may be (even) more efficacious in changing or influencing our behavior than anything a stranger tells us. And the reason, once again, has to do with empathy. It is easier to empathize with the plight of those who are near and dear to us than with the plight of

---

14. I am also assuming that the son fully understands moral judgments. But the scripts that Hoffman says result from induction presumably start accumulating motivational/emotional power before someone is fully capable of understanding such judgments. Empathy with empathy or its lack and whatever else is cognitively necessary for full moral judgments may come later than the more primitive empathic responsiveness to people's difficulties that is enhanced by inductive discipline and that, as a result of such discipline, leads to motivationally charged scripts. More particularly, moral injunctions may be addressed to children before they are capable of fully understanding them but at a point when, as a result of induction, they have learned to be more empathic in a first-order way with others. Since a genuine moral injunction requires the sincere speaker to be reluctant to violate the injunction, the child hearer may pick up on that reluctance before fully understanding the injunction as a moral judgment, and the child's induction-influenced tendency not to do the kind of thing in question may be strengthened as a result. But the hearing of such an injunction may *also* increase the capacity of the child to empathically respond with a sense of chill to the unempathic or wrong actions of others and so to disapprove of and morally criticize such actions. The person who utters a moral injunction typically displays such chill, and why shouldn't the child empathically pick up on *that*? The theory defended in earlier chapters says that a tendency to be empathically chilled and warmed by actions is essential to making moral claims, and it also holds that the idea that we can be chilled or warmed by (contemplating or witnessing) various actions that exhibit cold-heartedness or warmth is part and parcel of our ordinary understanding of morality. But these ideas and tendencies may in great part derive from some combination of receiving inductive discipline (a largely first-order process) and witnessing or hearing the moral claims others make (which involves or can involve both second-order and third-order empathy). Both these parts of moral learning help increase moral motivation, but more needs to be said about how these factors integrate, and it would also be nice if psychologists could do studies to test some of what I have been saying. (Also compare note 17 in chapter 2.)

Finally, let me briefly mention how what I have been saying differs from Hoffman's views. Although both he and I regard empathy as necessary to moral motivation, Hoffman assumes that moral principles can be *understood* independently of whether one has any empathic motivation to live up to them. So Hoffman is a moral externalist and appears to reject sentimentalist views of moral meaning. By contrast, my approach claims that concern for others and our understanding and application of moral principles or injunctions both derive from empathy's development (together with other factors).

strangers or people known only by description, but this difference presumably carries over to the influence of moral opinions and attitudes. We can empathically pick up other people's moods, attitudes, and opinions, but it is a familiar fact that this happens more readily with people one knows or loves, and this illustrates the more general fact that empathy tends to work more strongly or efficaciously between people who know or love each other than between people who don't.[15]

We have here been describing how second-person injunctions can reinforce or even jump-start moral behavior, and that makes them a significant part of the moral life. I earlier described various means by which we can educate children and, in particular, students to an empathic awareness of and concern for the frequently dire situations of (groups of) people they have never met. I spoke of the ways in which such inductive education can occur, and I believe such education, in the forms described earlier, can be largely efficacious. But I think the use of moral principles can make a positive difference to that efficacy. People with fully developed empathic concern for others will concern themselves not just with those around them but with (groups of) people whom they are not personally acquainted with and who may live at some distance from where they live. Although this doesn't mean that we should or can help everyone who needs help (given limited resources, one has to pick one's causes), it does mean that (general) concern for people who are sick, suffering, starving, or endangered will play a substantial role in lives of morally decent individuals, and since it is harder to keep people who are far away (or whom one never sees) in mind than to do so with those one sees all the time, it seems to me that self-directed or other-directed moral injunctions can and perhaps should play an important part in helping us fulfill our moral obligations toward such people.

The empathy-based sentimentalist conception of morality I am defending says in effect that it is morally wrong to act—that one has an obligation not to act—in ways that express or exhibit a lack of fully developed empathy. That doesn't mean that one shouldn't have a special concern for one's own welfare and for the welfare of those who are near and dear to one (a point argued at great length in chapter 2 of ECE). But failures to act on behalf of distant others who need one's help can sometimes manifest a lack of full or well-developed empathy, and the use of first- or second-person moral injunctions can take up the slack created by the (temporary)

---

15. When parents use inductive discipline with their children, they typically show their concern for some other person that their child has hurt, and concern for the good of others both inside and outside the family is what typically motivates parents to instill empathic concern for others into their children. They may also think that their child will benefit from being concerned with others—will be more likely to be accepted and to thrive in social groups if they are not selfish. But unlike Rosalind Hursthouse in *On Virtue Ethics* (Oxford: Oxford University Press, 1999), I don't think that is the *principal* reason that children are taught to be morally virtuous and don't, therefore, accept Hursthouse's consequent defense of eudaimonism as something parents show themselves to believe in.

nonvividness of disadvantaged people's situations and help one fulfill (what our sentimentalism regards as) one's obligations to those people.[16] Later on, I also want to take up some moral issues about humanitarian foreign aid with an eye to questions of global or international justice. But for the moment, I think it is important that I try now to put some of what I have just been saying into perspective.

The use of moral injunctions in the form of or based on rules or principles can be quite helpful. And we have said something about how and why that is so. But one shouldn't forget that sentimentalists put a moral premium on direct concern for other people, for (what we could call) the natural virtues of caring. If empathy causes people to flinch from causing harm or killing (more than from allowing harm or death), then those with developed empathy don't in most cases need a moral principle that tells them that it is wrong to kill (or worse to kill than to let die) in order to refrain from, even recoil from, killing. Similarly, and as we have seen all along, our desire to help those we can see need our help—for instance, a child drowning right in front of us—can lead us to act without involving us in using or referring to some moral rule, principle, or injunction. Williams's example of the husband with one thought too many also illustrates the way in which moral principles don't have to play a role in getting a normal loving person to do what is morally right or required.

And we could go on and on with other examples. The fact is that through large swaths of the moral life, rules and injunctions don't have to be involved—and when they are, that can be a sign of moral inferiority, moral danger, or moral failure. So having described (some of) the ways in which moral injunctions, explicit moral thought, can be useful, I still want to say that explicit moral thinking is *less* important or central to the moral life than many philosophers,

---

16. In comments on a symposium talk, "Global Caring, Global Justice," that I gave at the Eastern APA in 2007, Sarah Clark Miller criticized my approach for not saying in advance how to resolve all conflicts between helping loved ones and meeting the dire needs of people one doesn't know. But I think that is actually a good thing. Ceteris paribus, one has a greater obligation to people one loves, and our theory accounts for that. But there will be times when helping distant others at the (lesser) expense of one's loved ones will not reflect a lack of fully developed empathic capacities, and similarly vice versa. In such cases, either choice will be acceptable on our view, and it needn't, therefore, dictate a particular choice. We shouldn't expect a moral theory to always dictate a single obligation because there are (many) circumstances where a variety of choices are morally permissible. (The same point holds for choices about *which group* of distant or not-so-distant people in need one should help.)

In other circumstances, however, there is a right answer: either one should help one's family or one should help those one doesn't personally know. But at this point, we can at least say that we have as yet been given no reason to think that when someone spells out some new case in which a person has to choose whom to help and it is obvious whom *she should* help, one isn't going to be able to undergird that intuition by reference to the empathic factors we have been talking about. I do think the burden of proof is on those who want to show that the present approach *doesn't* give us a reliable motivational criterion of right action in such cases. And I might just also mention my belief that considerations of developed empathy do a better job with these issues than my earlier appeal (in *Morals from Motives*) to the idea of *balancing* self-concern with concern for intimates and humanitarian concern more generally. Empathy gives us a better map of the intuitive moral domain, and when balancing is relevant, empathy can explain how and why.

especially Kantians and other ethical rationalists, have supposed. We have seen that a great deal of moral education can work, and work successfully, without reference to moral principles or judgments: both inductive discipline and the empathic identification with (or modeling on) parental caringness that tends to accompany it can be described and explained without bringing in explicit moral thinking. And even if moral principles and injunctions can strengthen or reinforce empathic concern for other people, they seem less basic and less central to (the) sentimentalist (view of) moral education than the inductive process and the modeling (empathic imbibing) that naturally or normally accompanies induction. So for the sentimentalist (who doesn't emphasize artificial virtues à la Hume), moral education and moral development are more a matter of becoming sensitized by, and taking in attitudes/dispositions from, those around one than of becoming more sophisticated in the use of moral principles. Kantians and rationalists see moral development to a large extent as a matter of developing one's ability to understand and apply universal (abstract) principles.[17] But the sentimentalist (and others) will wonder how the rationalist can account for the motive to conform to or follow such principles—and will in any event think that the sentimentalist approach to moral education and development makes moral motivation a good deal easier to understand than anything offered by the rationalist or Kantian.[18]

In the next chapter, however, we need to consider an important criticism that Kantians and rationalists in general have made of sentimentalist approaches.

17. For an influential Kantian/rationalist account of moral education, see Lawrence Kohlberg, *Essays on Moral Development*: Vol. 1, *The Philosophy of Moral Development*; Vol. 2, *The Psychology of Moral Development* (New York: Harper and Row, 1981, 1984). For a briefer version of similar ideas, see Kohlberg's "Moral Stages and Moralization: The Cognitive-Developmental Approach," in T. Lickona, ed., *Moral Development and Moral Behavior: Theory, Research, and Social Issues* (New York: Holt, Rinehart and Winston, 1976), 31–53.

Contemporary Kantians (e.g., Barbara Herman in *The Practice of Moral Judgment* [Cambridge: Harvard University Press, 1993] and in *Moral Literacy* [Cambridge: Harvard, 2007]) often don't think of moral development as centered around the inculcation or appreciation of very general/abstract moral principles to the extent that Kohlberg (following Piaget) does. They are often more concerned with the specification of our moral thought in particular (historical) circumstances. But such Kantians still think that some version of the Categorical Imperative is fundamental to (operates as the background of) our moral thinking, and their ideas about how to approach particular decisions place less stress on emotional sensitivity than care ethicists would. (Still, contemporary Kantians pay *more* attention to such sensitivity than earlier Kantians did. In the light of various criticisms brought by virtue ethicists and others, they have to some extent moved closer to the views of their critics.) I am indebted here to discussion with Jonathan Adler.

18. For doubts about the motivational adequacy of Kohlberg's account of moral education, see, for example, Randall Curren's entry on "Moral Education" in L. Becker and C. Becker, eds., *The Encyclopedia of Ethics*, 2nd ed. (New York: Routledge, 2001), 1129. I should mention, however, that Kohlberg himself in various places grants that purely cognitive development cannot ensure (substantial) motivation and even talks about empathy as (somehow—he isn't very specific) involved in moving beyond the cognizance of moral norms to reliable moral motivation. But as far as I know, he never nails any of this down, and that seems to me to represent a major difficulty with the way he approaches moral education and moral development more generally.

It can be and has been wondered whether the sentiments are really reliable enough to constitute the basis for the moral life—for living in a morally acceptable or good way. And though our discussion of the son taking care of his mother does something to allay such worries, more, much more, now needs to be said.

7

BETWEEN MOTIVE AND MORALITY

The idea that natural motivation in the Humean sense is insufficient or inadequate to ensure moral action is familiar from the literature of Kantian ethics (including Kant himself), but part of the appeal of that literature depends on the intuitive or commonsense plausibility of that assumption. The sentimentalist would need to do a great deal of work in order to show it to be mistaken, but I in fact believe this is something that can be done—and done in a way that can permanently weaken and indeed undercut the intuitions that lead one to think sentimentalism has to be inadequate for understanding the distinction between right and wrong and for specifying human moral resources for reliably doing right rather than wrong. Since much (though hardly most) of the force and plausibility of Kantianism and of ethical rationalism more generally depends on this assumption of inadequacy or insufficiency, what I shall be saying in what follows can and should affect how rationalism is viewed, and if what I say is at all on the right track, then there will be a lot less reason to see Kantian or rationalist ethics as the only game in town. That last idea seems to have flourished in the wake of historical sentimentalism's well-known inadequacies, but it has also depended on the absence of any more recent attempt to show how and why natural sentiment actually can function as an adequate basis for moral thinking and the moral life.

The charge Kantianism and ethical rationalism more generally make against moral sentimentalism can be summarized in the thoughts that sentimentalism makes the connection between good motivation and right action somewhat accidental and/or that natural motives are an unreliable guide to what is right and an unreliable basis for right action(s).[1] These charges or criticisms involve two ideas in essence: first, that even benign sentiments like empathic concern for others don't always lead us toward right actions and away from wrong ones and, second, that even when such sentiments or motives lead us in the right direction, they often lack the force or momentum needed to ensure that one actually does the thing that (on the basis of one's motives) one originally intended to do. The first idea can be summarized in the thought that natural motives are morally problematic with respect to their *direction*, and the second in the thought that natural motives are problematic with respect to their *momentum* (or, if one prefers, *force*).

Now much of what we have said so far in this book can be seen as providing at least a partial answer to these rather Kantian thoughts or criticisms. What was said earlier about the empathic basis of deontological distinctions is a way of showing Kantians and other rationalists that empathic concern for others can direct us toward the actions deontology requires of us. This may come as a surprise—when I first came to think that it was possible, it came as something as a surprise to me, too. But one should also add—I can't forbear adding—at this point that Kantian efforts to justify deontology over the past few decades seem to have run into more difficulties and perplexities than one might have originally expected, given the historical or traditional understanding of Kantian ethics as a form of deontology par excellence. So it might turn out that sentimentalism offers us the best or only way to defend deontology in philosophically adequate terms, and that eventuality would certainly be ironic, to say the least. In any event, my main purpose is to defend sentimentalism, rather than directly criticize other approaches to ethics, and what the example of sentimentalist deontology shows is that in the area of deontology at least, our natural motivation isn't problematic with respect to its direction in the way one might have initially supposed it would be.

Our earlier discussion of the (other) modalities of empathic concern for others also indicates that empathic concern for others is properly targeted onto what intuitively seem to be right actions, rather than wrong, and of course, the account I offered of moral approval and disapproval and of how the meaning of moral terms is *generally determined* also constitutes a defense of the nonproblematicness of empathic concern with respect to its *general direction*. In other words, our metaethical discussion supports the idea of empathic concern or caring as a general (normative) criterion of right action, and what we have done here (and is done at greater length in *The Ethics of Care and Empathy*) is show, with

1. For relevant discussion and references, see Justin Oakley, "A Critique of Kantian Argument against Emotions as Moral Motives," *History of Philosophy Quarterly* 7 (1990): 441–459. Also, for two (more recent) examples of the sort of rationalist objection to sentimentalism I have just been describing, see Marcia Baron's *Kantian Ethics Almost without Apology* (Ithaca, N.Y.: Cornell University Press, 1995), 127; and Stephen Darwall's *The British Moralists and the Internal "Ought": 1640–1740* (Cambridge: Cambridge University Press, 1995), 280f.

respect to a wide variety of cases, that what reflects or expresses adequate empathy (or at least doesn't reflect a lack of full empathy) will generally be thought of as morally right and justified.

But we still need to consider issues or problems about the moral momentum of natural motives; we need to address the well-known criticism that good motives (like good intentions) can flag or fail before they have led one to act rightly.[2] This supposition has led many rationalists and, especially, Kantians to hold that we need to consciously follow or adhere to (correct) moral principles or judgments in order to ensure that we act rightly, and our discussion of the son with the sick mother in the last chapter focused directly on this issue. What I believe we showed there is that normal, good, caring motivation toward a mother is more than likely to eventually lead one to doing the right thing by her: even if a genuinely devoted son can get tired of helping and temporarily lose any (conscious) feeling of concern or empathy for his mother, his empathic concern is very likely to revive before he does something that threatens her future well-being in a serious way and thus before any serious wrongdoing occurs.[3] In this case, and as we have seen, a moral injunction not to do what would threaten her future well-being may or may not surface in the son or be directed toward him by third parties, but such explicit moral thinking doesn't appear to be necessary as a supplement to natural motivation. The latter seems to be able to ensure right action on its own.

In this one case, therefore, the use of moral principles doesn't, despite initial appearances or suspicions, appear to be necessary to right action—unaided natural motivation seems sufficient. But there are other cases, some relatively

---

2. Sometimes our concern for others weakens without even temporarily leading us toward acting wrongly. If one of my friends does something underhanded and damaging to me behind my back and I find out, my affection for that friend will probably diminish and lead me to not do things for the friend that I otherwise would have wanted to do. This doesn't represent a "momentum" problem for sentimentalism, because we don't think the lesser concern for one's friend is morally questionable, and sentimentalist care ethics can explain why (we think) it isn't wrong to do less for that particular friend. In *Empathy and Moral Development* (Cambridge: Cambridge University Press, 2000), Martin Hoffman describes the anger that arises toward those who hurt us or hurt those we care about as naturally (e.g., in terms that the moral development literature can describe and to some extent even quantify) limiting the empathy and concern we feel toward those who do the hurting, and it doesn't seem that the lesser concern shows a lack of fully developed empathy, any more than the fact that one may stop helping a stranger if one is attacked with life-threatening force by some third party indicates that one isn't fully empathic. These limitations are built into our empathy, and one sees this same sort of limitation, though on a larger scale, in the public's desire for criminals to be appropriately punished. This, too, isn't unjust or wrong on our care-ethical account because, again, such a desire doesn't in itself indicate a lack of fully developed empathy. Note, finally, that if empathy works in the manner just indicated, it is both forward- and backward-looking: it seeks to improve people's future situations, but also takes account of what a potential intended recipient of its concern *has done in the past.*

3. I use the term *likely* because it is possible, after all, that the son should have a heart attack or stroke and die before his empathic concern has a chance to revive. And there could also be a terrorist attack that made it impossible for him to do anything further to help his mother. But these occurrences would, of course, not open him to the charge of having acted wrongly.

similar to that of the son with the sick mother, where it isn't as obvious or clear that natural motives are enough to ensure right action. The son with the sick mother suffers from what in the literature of moral development is called "compassion fatigue," and the most well-known kind of compassion fatigue is that associated with health care professionals.[4] Such cases involve special moral issues of their own.

So consider the health care professional who, after caring for many patients over a short period (during a medical crisis or emergency) or after a longer, sustained, but somewhat less intense period of involvement with patients, finds herself unable to feel much for or take much interest in those who still need her help. The professional may then do less for such people than she had been doing and than she is generally expected to do, and the question then naturally arises whether the fatigue or burnout justifies or excuses the lesser concern and lesser helpfulness. But this question is subtler or more complex than may first appear. If we assume that this is the first time the professional has ever experienced compassion fatigue, we will respond differently to the example than if we assume this sort of thing has happened to her before. So let's investigate both possibilities and see where they lead us.

If compassion fatigue has never before happened to her and if (to simplify matters) we assume that she had no reason (based on what she had heard about other health care professionals' experiences) to think that such a thing was likely to happen to her, she has a certain moral excuse for the resultant temporary slackening of her interest in and helpfulness toward other patients *this first time*. Such a case is, I believe, the moral analogue of the (somewhat controversial, but far from implausible) legal doctrine of "one free bite," according to which a dog owner isn't legally liable for the damages caused by a dog's unanticipated *first* biting of someone.

What the health care professional won't have any excuse for, however, is not being sufficiently helpful in the future (and analogously for the dog owner and the dog's later bites). If she is at all normal, her concern for patients will revive, and she will then realize that to help those she wants, professionally, to help, she is going to have to find ways to budget and manage her concern so that similar fatigue and burnout won't occur in the future. But there are such ways, and many health care professionals have figured them out and told us (and other professionals) about them. Thus, to take just one example, a normally compassionate health care professional who becomes aware of his own tendency toward

---

4. On compassion fatigue, see Martin Hoffman, *Empathy and Moral Development*, 200ff. Hoffman also describes the sort of "empathic overarousal" that can lead someone perceiving another person's horrible condition or situation to attend to their own empathic distress rather than try to help the person whose plight led, via empathy, to the distress. I believe that in such cases empathy doesn't invariably lead to morally wrong action, and what I shall be saying about the moral character and implications of compassion fatigue applies analogously to cases of empathic overarousal. But I won't go into the details.

compassion fatigue might actually try to feel less about any given patient, and such a keeping of distance would then serve the aims of compassion indirectly.[5]

If a health care professional who has experienced compassion fatigue and the falling away from normal professional helpfulness that that usually entails *doesn't take steps to avoid such a thing happening again in the future*, then at that point, she is acting wrongly and criticizably, from the standpoint of any plausible sentimentalism, because her refusal at that point to make an effort to prevent such a thing's happening again shows her to be lacking or deficient in empathic concern for her patients as a group or class. And if, knowing what she knows and having failed to make relevant efforts, she once more gets overinvolved with her patients and eventually experiences a compassion fatigue that leaves her unable or unwilling to help her patients in normal ways, then this subsequent failure of helpfulness will presumably count as morally wrong, even if the earlier failure did not.[6]

This kind of example seems to involve moral problems both of direction and of momentum. If great empathic compassion by its very nature tends to lead to its own burnout and if a health care professional's first-time compassion burnout/fatigue makes him act in an unhelpful way toward patients, then in a sense compassion seems to move us in the morally wrong direction—and a greater reliance on principles may well seem to be the antidote. However, the problem here can also appear to be one of momentum, since if compassion gives out in the form of compassion fatigue, one can say that the original compassion wasn't strong enough, persistent enough, to ensure later helpful action. But despite these appearances, if the first instance of lesser helpfulness doesn't have to be seen as morally wrong or criticizable, then (strictly speaking) we don't have a problem either of direction or of momentum regarding that lesser helpfulness. And in any

---

5. In "Lessons in Empathy: Literature, Art, and Medicine" (in H. Spiro, M. Curnen, E. Peschel, and D. St. James, eds., *Empathy and the Practice of Medicine* [New Haven: Yale University Press, 1993], 135–146), Helle Mathiasen and Joseph Alpert say that a good physician is empathic but also knows how to limit his [*sic*] empathy. However, I probably should also mention the common complaint that empathy and involvement with patients are medically less helpful than a more detached and "professional" attitude. If correct, this might be a reason for health care professionals to avoid empathy with patients as much as possible. But there is a growing literature favoring the view that empathy needn't interfere with professionalism and actually facilitates the (present or ideal) goals of medical treatment. For one very interesting and persuasive book that makes this point, see Jodi Halpern's *From Detached Concern to Empathy* (New York: Oxford University Press, 2001). Moreover, as Raul de Velasco has recently pointed out (in as yet unpublished work), medical treatment may be facilitated or enhanced not only by the physician's having empathy toward the patient but also by the patient's empathically feeling that empathy and responding with (greater) trust toward the physician.

6. Actually, one might say that the later failures of helpfulness (under renewed conditions of compassion fatigue) aren't themselves morally wrong but rather stem from a morally wrong earlier failure to take steps to prevent compassion fatigue from recurring. This would be like saying that the actions of a totally drunk individual aren't themselves wrong (because they aren't under his control) but rather stem from the previous wrong action of getting totally drunk. This way of putting things would not, however, affect our main argument.

event, the sentimentalist take on this example seems far from implausible. It involves saying that one can't be held responsible or seriously criticized for the (normal) results of unanticipated first-time compassion fatigue, that is, that what one does as a result of such fatigue shouldn't be viewed as morally wrong.[7] The compassion fatigue doesn't demonstrate a lack of full empathic concern—it may even indicate the contrary, and so the actions it immediately leads to don't, on our sentimentalist criterion, count as wrong or immoral. What does, or would, count as immoral on our criterion is a failure, on the part of the health care professional, to budget himself in the future, to change his ways. That would really indicate a lack of or weak empathic concern for patients and so count as immoral in sentimentalist terms, and none of this seems to be counter-intuitive or implausible. Our approach does seem to be able to handle this (initially or seemingly) problematic kind of case, and what we have said about it carries over in substantial measure to other kinds of cases that may seem to pose problems for moral sentimentalism.

I am thinking here of negligence and of cases, in particular, where through negligence one ends up acting (or failing to act) in a way that most of us would criticize or condemn. Thus consider the person who backs his car out of his driveway and accidentally kills a small child who is walking behind the car. That person surely doesn't intend any harm to the child—there is a total absence of what the law calls mens rea, and yet we think the person has acted wrongly.[8]

---

7. I have been assuming that the health care professional of our example had no way of knowing that she might be subject to compassion fatigue—and this means assuming that no one ever mentioned this possibility to her in professional school and that none of her new colleagues (at the hospital) ever broached the subject with her. This seems a slightly far-fetched assumption, but if it is incorrect, if the subject *had* been previously broached, then the *first instance* of compassion fatigue *will* be morally criticizable in sentimentalist terms. If the health care professional doesn't pay sufficient attention to the warnings and doesn't make an effort to guard against compassion fatigue (by budgeting time or emotional connection), then she shows a lack of sufficient concern for her prospective and actual patients. But as I said, if she in fact has no way of knowing about the risk(s) of compassion fatigue, then she can't be criticized in this way, and what she does during her first experience of compassion fatigue vis-à-vis patients won't be morally objectionable or criticizable because it won't show a lack of appropriate initial concern for those patients.

8. If the man backs out heedlessly, but doesn't hurt anyone, then we will think of what he has done as less *seriously* wrong than if he *has* killed or injured a child. This is one aspect of the problem of moral luck, and if common sense is right to make this sort of moral distinction, then external factors do enter into our moral thinking, even if they don't, say, affect what we call wrong tout court. But commonsense thinking may not be right here—I just don't know, and I don't think *anyone* really knows, how to handle the problem of moral luck. But notice two things. If common sense is *right*, then what it is right *about*, the greater seriousness of actually killing a child, is something we are empathically very sensitive and reactive to and something, therefore, that we might hope to understand and eventually explain in sentimentalist terms. But then, second, if common sense is mistaken, and acting negligently (or heedlessly) in backing out of one's drive determines equal(ly serious) wrongness no matter what *actually* eventuates, then what *is* wrong can clearly be unpacked in the sentimentalist motivational terms employed in the main text. Either way, given the emphasis placed on motivation as determining right and wrong, our sentimentalist approach *does* appear to be a form of virtue ethics. But to be focusing on whether or why that approach counts as virtue ethics would distract us from our main task of developing sentimentalism in a contemporary way.

And surely, it could be argued, such a person might have entirely good motives, might be fully empathic and caring, and that would mean that, in this sort of instance, such motives don't serve to ensure right action. (Moreover, the moral problem with such motives doesn't exactly seem to be one either of direction or of momentum in this kind of case.) We might then side with the Kantians or other rationalists in claiming that greater attention to a moral principle would have prevented (wrongfully) running over the child. If one had borne in mind (the principle) that one should look about to see if small children are around before backing out of a driveway, then the human and moral disaster would have been avoided, and such considerations appear overall to strongly favor a Kantian reliance on injunctions and principles over a sentimentalist reliance on empathic concern as a motive. But I think this is a mistake. The just-given description and analysis *misdescribes* what is at stake in cases of negligence.

The driver who negligently kills a child while backing out of his driveway doesn't desire or intend the harm he causes. He is ignorant (until it is too late) of the child's presence behind his car, and that ignorance is clearly culpable, morally criticizable. And his lack of attention to the *possibility* that a child might be there is also morally criticizable. But contrary to what was suggested before, I think all these valid moral criticisms are based on motivational assumptions, and if we look in the right direction, I think we will see that the negligent driver can be (correctly) accused of having lacked sufficient empathic concern for others. For example, the driver presumably knows that cars are dangerous and knows that, because children are usually more heedless or less circumspect than adults, someone who drives has to be especially concerned about the safety of children. He has been told things like this and presumably has some direct experience of relevant facts—has, just to take two possible examples, seen children run heedlessly out into traffic or ignore dangers that are coming right at them.

So what does it mean if, knowing these things, he backs up in his driveway without checking to see if there is anyone small behind him or moving swiftly in that direction?[9] What I think it means is that when he was told or observed that children act heedlessly, he didn't really take that knowledge to heart. By contrast, someone who really cares about the welfare of (the) children (in his neighborhood) will impress upon himself the dangers of driving a car in an area where children live and will not drive as negligently, carelessly, or incautiously as the driver who kills the child has driven. If someone cares enough, cares in the way that a fully empathic concerned person *would* care, then the possibility of children will be on her mind (or in the back of her mind) when she backs her car out of her driveway. Or alternatively, she will have instituted a habit-checklist of things to do when she drives that includes automatically or always checking around the back of her car when she backs out of her driveway. Such a practice or habit might

---

9. Of course, it is possible for a child to dart out into traffic or dart behind a car in a way that no careful (nonnegligent) driver could have anticipated. But I assume that there is or need be no wrongdoing in such cases.

allow her to not be thinking about children at the precise moment she backs out of the driveway. But then her habituating herself to using such a checklist will itself be a sign of the concern she has for children and free her from any charge of (culpable) negligence or ignorance.

The point can perhaps be reinforced by considering another kind of example. People driving a car in summertime with groceries in the back might suddenly realize that they have a quick errand to do and then drive to where the errand is to be done. They might park their car and then, after doing the errand, get caught up in a way they hadn't anticipated in some activity that leads them to forget the groceries. As a result, when several hours later they return to their car, they could easily find that much of the food had spoiled. All or most of us have had such things happen. But contrast such a case with one in which a person who is driving during summertime with his child in the backseat has to do a quick errand. Imagine that he leaves the child in the backseat while he does the errand and then gets distracted by some further activity or interest, forgets the child, and returns several hours later to find that the child has died of suffocation due to heat and/or lack of air. Such cases are very rare (thank heaven!), much, much rarer than cases where one neglectfully allows groceries to spoil. And there is a reason for this difference in frequency.

We care much, much more about the lives of our children than about any bundle or bundles of groceries, and although we know both that groceries can spoil and that children can suffocate or die from heat, the latter knowledge is much more vivid to any decent parent than the former. A parent who would allow a child to die of heat in a car while he was distracted by activities in the vicinity treats the child like a sack of groceries, simply doesn't love and care about the welfare of his child the way a parent should. If we are good or even halfway decent parents, we don't *let* ourselves entirely forget (for some hours) a child we have left in our car. And we don't leave a child in a car at all unless the errand we have to run is very, very quick and the neighborhood where we park is entirely safe, and so forth. Any parent who acts otherwise lacks the kind of motivation we think of as necessary to being a morally decent person, because every parent knows that there are dangers in leaving a child alone in a car on a hot summer's day.

Thus the person who negligently runs over a child and the parent who negligently or neglectfully allows his child to die of suffocation in a car lack adequate empathic concern for (certain) others and manifest that lack of concern in their neglectful/negligent actions. Negligence turns out to be less of a challenge to sentimentalism than might initially appear to be the case, because relevant motivational factors lurk just below the surface in cases of wrongful or culpable negligence. (Any differences there are between wrongness and culpability aren't relevant, I think, to the present example.) And in cases where ignorance leads to bad results, but we don't think anything wrong or negligent has been done, that will be because one cannot attribute morally defective motivation to the person whose ignorant actions or inactions lead to those results. (I am thinking of cases where one has no way of knowing, for example, that the milk one is giving one's child has been poisoned with arsenic by a disgruntled factory worker.)

But there is a further point to be made. Our ability to deal with cases of compassion fatigue and negligence in terms of natural motives shows how difficult it is to undermine sentimentalism on the grounds of the unreliable, or merely accidental and intermittent, connection that obtains between the natural motives it favors and actions we intuitively think of as right. But we have also seen that the efficacy of such motives can be enhanced or reinforced by the use of self-directed or other-directed moral injunctions, and since (the force and operation of) these injunctions can (also) be understood in strictly sentimentalist terms, that gives us a further and a deeper reason to think that sentimentalism can give a good explanation of how people can (come to) generally act in a morally right or acceptable manner. Kantians and not just Kantians have believed and claimed that sentiment is inadequate or insufficient to ensure moral action, and they have in effect pointed to problems both of direction and of momentum with understanding morality in terms of good motives like benevolence, compassion, love of humankind, and (various kinds of) caring. But when one examines the specific sorts of cases that are supposed to give sentimentalism problems and/or to show what those problems are, we see, as we have seen previously, that sentimentalism has ample modes of self-defense and even self-justification. In particular, I hope the picture I have painted in the present chapter and previous ones (including what has been said about the *meaning* of the terms *right* and *wrong*) will indicate why I think and how one might justifiably think that the connection between developed empathic caring and morally good or acceptable human behavior is neither accidental nor unreliable.

One final point: An important part of Kant's reason for holding, in the *Groundwork* and elsewhere, that actions based on natural, that is, nonconscientious, motives are never morally good or praiseworthy is that such motives are only accidentally and unreliably connected with right action. Kant has other reasons, of course, for denying that such action, and such motivation, is morally praiseworthy—for example, the fact that he considers our capacity for morality to (depend on formal rational considerations that) transcend the natural realm. But if the sentimentalist picture of morality I have been drawing is on the right track, then Kant's misgivings about natural motives and his conclusions about what counts as morally good may be misguided. Even if explicit moral thinking and conscientiousness play a significant role in ensuring moral behavior or action, we have seen that such thinking can be explained in terms of the same natural motives that operate separately or exclusively when we help someone out of sheer love or out of humane concern for their welfare. So our sentimentalism adds fuel to the fire of criticism that from the very beginning (e.g., in some mocking poetry by Friedrich Schiller) has been directed at Kant's claim that sympathy, love, and compassion cannot on their own give rise to morally good actions.

It is one of the putative weaknesses of Kantian ethics that it regards compassionate, loving, sympathetic action(s) in this way, but we have also seen that there is some reason, a reason we can all in fact appreciate, why Kant held such a view. If the connection between natural motivation and moral action is as unreliable as Kant thinks, or as most of us are initially inclined to believe, then there is at least reason to wonder whether compassionately motivated action is really morally good.[10] So our discussion of why natural, empathically sensitive motives are generally reliable as guides and means to moral action helps support the initial, commonsense moral view that conscientiousness isn't a necessary condition of morally praiseworthy action, and this conclusion clearly helps the sentimentalist's case against the opposed, Kantian view of what is praiseworthy and (since such a view is integral to Kantian ethics) against Kantian ethics as a whole.

But having said all of this, I think it is now time to move more decisively, and in a more expansive fashion than we did in chapter 1, into issues of normative ethics. Our whole discussion during the past two chapters has, roughly speaking, concerned ought implies can problems, and I want in the next chapter and the one to follow to concentrate on the normative side of the oughts and to say less about the cans and the issues of "implementation" that they raise.

---

10. There is something in us that recoils, e.g., at the idea that Hitler's compassion for particular *Aryan Germans* could have counted as morally praiseworthy—assuming such compassion on Hitler's part to have been possible and given all the other things Hitler thought and did. But this may just indicate that it isn't compassion in isolation or on a limited basis that we find praiseworthy, but compassion in the context of overall (natural) motivation that is sensitive to human need and/or the moral distinctions we find basic or compelling. It is a reason for accepting, in a certain limited form, the idea of the unity of the virtues, but not a reason for thinking actions based on natural motives/motivation can't be praiseworthy or for rejecting sentimentalism as an approach to morality. (For more on this issue, see my *Morals from Motives* [New York: Oxford University Press, 2001], 35f.)

8

PATERNALISM AND PATRIARCHY

In chapter 1, I sketched out the implications of a sentimentalist care ethics based on empathy, for normative/moral issues concerning individual action. I spoke of our special obligations to those near and dear to us, and I also explained how empathic care supports the notion that it is morally worse not to save a child drowning in shallow water right in front of one than not to save a child one has never met by offering a contribution to Oxfam. These ideas run counter to Peter Singer's impartialistic moral views on these matters, but the whole point about empathy is that it *is* partial, and our metaethical account of morality in terms of empathy therefore justifies and *grounds* a partialistic conception of the morality of individual action (and of political morality as well, but that will be made more explicit in our next chapter).

In chapter 1, we also saw how considerations of empathy correlate with the most important deontological distinctions we commonsensically make, and our subsequent metaethical discussion provided philosophical/moral foundations for deontology—something that Kant and recent Kantians have had a surprisingly difficult time doing. What I presented in chapter 1 was a somewhat truncated version of the parallel normative ethical discussion(s) of *The Ethics of Care and Empathy* (ECE), but the present book also offers a much deeper and more foundational justification of a care ethics based on empathy than anything to be found in ECE. (Its concluding chapter made a good start, but it was just a good start, on the ideas about metaethics we explored in chapters 2 through 5 of the present book.)

Now, however, I think it is time to broaden out our discussion of normative issues in two ways. First, I would like to relate moral sentimentalism to feminist ideas and ideals. The ethics of care is perhaps the most influential and interesting form of sentimentalism now extant, but the ethics of care has also taken up issues of morality and justice that specifically concern or affect women and other disadvantaged groups or classes of individuals. And though I want to focus attention mainly on feminist thought and aspirations, much of what I shall be saying carries over in substantial and interesting ways to discussions of race, ethnicity, gender orientation, and facts about oppression and previous injustice. (In what follows, I shall sometimes note those connections.) At any rate, my focus, in the present chapter, on feminist ideas will broaden the subject matter of our discussion by getting us to address moral issues that were quite far from our consideration in chapter 1.

Second, I want (to some extent in the present chapter but especially in the chapter that follows) to deal with the topic of social and international justice in an entirely general but completely sentimentalist fashion. This discussion will include considerations having to do specifically with women or other disadvantaged groups, but it will take up a large number of other social/political issues as well.

However, our first task, here in the present chapter, will be to explore feminist moral ideas in relation to some important moral concepts we have not yet considered. Kantians place great emphasis on deontology, and we have spoken about how sentimentalist care ethics can understand and justify deontology. But Kantians and many others also attribute great importance to notions like respect, autonomy, and respect for autonomy, and I believe a sentimentalist care-ethical account of these notions can help us better understand some of the deeper parts and aspects of feminist moral thought.

Now Kantians often say that we owe people respect on the basis of their autonomy (or their moral worth or dignity) as rational beings, and so they conceive respect for individuals as (most fundamentally) respect for their autonomy.[1] But the idea that we owe people respect goes beyond the Kantian tradition. It seems *intuitively* plausible to suppose that we ought to respect other people and (also) that we should respect their autonomy, and I think an ethics of care needs to make sense of these notions. But I shall be reversing the Kantian order of explanation. Respect *is* respect for autonomy (or for the capacity for autonomy), and if we can first understand respect, I think we can use that understanding to clarify what autonomy is.

1. Respect

The notion of caring about or concern for (the welfare of) others is widely regarded as different from that of respect. The former is seen as focusing on

---

1. I shall focus mainly on respect for autonomy and autonomy itself, leaving dignity and worth pretty much to themselves. But I assume that if the former notions can be accounted for, the latter are either inessential or can be explained in similar terms. (See reference to Seyla Benhabib in note 5.)

human (or animal) welfare or well-being; the latter seems to invoke or involve some other (distinctive) aspect of human beings. And we see this assumption, for example, in *Taking Rights Seriously*, where Ronald Dworkin argues that justice requires the state to treat all its citizens with equal concern *and* respect.[2] Traditional utilitarianism is a welfare-oriented approach to morality, and it has no room for any notion of respect beyond the minimal one of treating all individuals (including animals) the same in consequentialistic welfare calculations. But an ethics of care also focuses on welfare, and so it is natural to think that it has no way of accommodating our intuitive moral thinking about the respect we owe to individuals. And there is also another reason for thinking this.

Care ethics is, after all, a form of moral sentimentalism, and it is difficult to see how respect for others can be grounded in (mere) sentiments, emotions, or feelings. I can feel compassion or concern for another person, but these feelingful motives seem focused on the other person's welfare, and respect seems, or has been thought, to involve something more than or different from any such emotion. Indeed, the fact that respect seems such an intuitive notion with us has been used as an argument against utilitarianism and moral sentimentalism, given the somewhat natural assumption that these approaches can't make sense of what we almost all think about respecting others. But I believe a sentimentalist ethics of care can in fact ground respect, and respect for autonomy, in its own terms. Those terms don't, of course, include the Kantian idea that autonomy represents a noumenal feature of human beings. But contemporary Kantian liberals also shy from Kantian metaphysics, so the real issue is whether an ideal of respect that goes beyond (mere, sheer) concern for well-being and that can be plausibly regarded as involving respect *for autonomy* is derivable from sentimentalist sources.

In chapter 1, we saw that moral sentimentalism has some perhaps surprising resources for dealing with deontology. In what follows, I hope to show you something similar about respect. Both deontology and respect can, I believe, be conceived and justified by reference to the idea of empathy. And this then leads to a conception of autonomy that likewise falls within the terms and traditions of sentimentalism.

Now this latter point is perhaps not surprising from the standpoint of a sentimentalist ethics of care. Some feminists and/or care-ethicists have developed their own (relational) notion or notions of autonomy to replace what they take to be the more atomistic and putatively less adequate views of autonomy to be found within the (male or masculine) tradition of rationalist/Kantian liberalism—or within Kant's own thinking. However, I shall be going further than other care ethicists have gone. As far as I know, other care ethicists haven't sought to give a theoretical account of respect (for autonomy) in sentimentalist terms, and neither have they explicitly attempted, as I shall be

2. Ronald Dworkin, *Taking Rights Seriously* (London: Duckworth, 1978), 180–183, 272–278.

attempting, to *understand (relational) autonomy itself* entirely in care-ethical terms.[3] So I shall end up defending a (relational) conception of autonomy that sits well with the views other care ethicists have about autonomy but that is more thoroughly grounded in care ethics and in sentimentalism overall than those other views have been. However, our first step toward this conclusion requires us to see how respect might be understood in sentimentalist, care-ethical terms.

Concern for well-being and respect are often thought to clash when issues of paternalism arise: for instance, when someone acts against another person's wishes "for their own good." Now obviously we all think there are times when paternalism is justified—parents sometimes have to act like parents. But at other times, paternalistic interventions against the expressed wishes or desires of another individual seem morally invidious and unjustified, even though the person who acts in this way can be seen as acting out of caring concern for the well-being of the person whose wishes are thwarted. And we typically and intuitively describe what we object to here in terms of respect: we say that the person who intervened showed a lack of respect for the person whose wishes were thwarted, indeed a lack of respect *for their autonomy as individuals*. Here, very roughly, autonomy is regarded as the capacity for making and acting on one's own decisions, and the lack of respect at the very least involves not letting the person exercise that capacity. However, when a *parent* insists, against a child's loudly expressed wishes, on taking that child to the doctor's or dentist's, we *don't* think they are necessarily showing a lack of respect for the child. So what makes the difference?

I believe the most important part of the difference relates to empathy. There is a lack of empathy in cases where a putative concern for well-being is accompanied by a failure of respect, and if we enrich the notion of caring to make it include empathy, then the ethics of caring will be in a position to account for respect. To see this, we need a more detailed example of how putative concern for well-being can involve a lack of respect.

I pointed out in chapter 1 that empathy is typically regarded as *not* involving the merging of two souls or personalities. Someone who is overinvolved with another person may have difficulty in separating their own needs and desires

---

3. Jennifer Nedelsky's "Reconceiving Autonomy: Sources, Thoughts and Possibilities" (*Yale Journal for Law and Feminism* 1 (1989): 7–36) offers a groundbreaking defense of relational autonomy that seeks to model such autonomy on the mother-child relationship. But even though Nedelsky's piece shows the influence of care ethics, it doesn't explicitly espouse an ethics of care or (therefore) attempt to integrate relational autonomy into such an ethics; neither does it tie relational autonomy to empathy or respect. These are all things I shall be doing here. Grace Clement's *Care, Autonomy, and Justice: Feminism and the Ethics of Care* (Boulder, Colo.: Westview Press, 1996, chapter 2) anticipates the present book in stressing the importance of (empathic) parental caring to the development of relational autonomy but makes the further claim that autonomy *cannot* be entirely understood in care-ethical terms. Clement holds that the ethics of justice (conceived separately from caring) is also essential to understanding autonomy, and that is just what I am going to be denying here.

from those of the other, and this may mean that they fail to respond empathically to what the other needs or wants. One familiar example of such overinvolvement can be found in the attitudes some parents have to their children. Parents with a weak sense of self often seek to live through (the successes of) their children and have a difficult time separating their own needs from those of their children. Such parents ipso facto have difficulty empathizing with the individual points of view—the needs, wishes, and fears—of their children. (If the child says he wants to do something different from what the parent has planned for him, the parent will often say, and believe, something like "you don't really want to do that" or "I know what's best for you and that isn't it.") The problem with such parents is not the absence of an emotional connection with their children (they are not like the so-called distant father) but, rather, *too much connection*. Such overinvolvement or overconnection has recently been labeled "substitute success syndrome" (henceforward "sss").[4] And it has been recognized that sss involves an inability to recognize or understand the individuality or wishes of one's children (or others). To that extent, however, it also seems plausible to say that sss parents *fail to respect their children*, since respecting individuals is naturally thought of as requiring respect for their wants and fears and what is individual or distinctive about them.

I am inclined, then, to hold that respect for individuals can be unpacked in terms of empathy. Speaking roughly, one shows respect for someone if and only if one exhibits appropriate *empathic* concern for them in one's dealings with them. Furthermore, we saw in particular that sss parents lack empathy for their children's own burgeoning desires and aspirations, and since autonomy—again very roughly—is readily seen as involving a capacity for deciding things on one's own, we can also say that sss parents show a lack of respect for their child's nascent *autonomy*. (Or we could say that they show a lack of respect for their child's *capacity* for autonomy. For our purposes, it won't make much difference which way one puts it.) In that case, it would appear that a morality of empathic caring requires one to respect other people's autonomy and not just or simply to be concerned with their welfare.[5] A normative care ethics based on empathy will condemn an action as morally

4. On substitute success syndrome, see L. Blum, M. Homiak, J. Housman, and N. Scheman, "Altruism and Women's Oppression" in C. Gould and M. Wartofsky, eds., *Women and Philosophy* (New York: Putnam, 1976), esp. 238. And for helpful relevant discussion, also see Clement, *Care, Autonomy, and Justice*.

5. In "The Generalized and the Concrete Other: The Kohlberg-Gilligan Controversy and Feminist Theory" (in S. Benhabib and D. Cornell, eds., *Feminism as Critique: On the Politics of Gender* [Minneapolis: University of Minnesota Press, 1987], esp. 89–92), Seyla Benhabib argues that recognizing the dignity of the "generalized other" necessitates seeing things from the standpoint of the "concrete other." This comes very close to the view I am defending here, and there are also similarities between what I am saying and Nancy Sherman's "Concrete Kantian Respect," *Social Philosophy and Policy* 15 (1996): 119–148.

Also, I assumed at certain points in the main text (though not at others) that it is possible to be genuinely concerned about another's welfare *without* taking up their point of view or respecting their autonomy, but that was a concession made, basically, for expository purposes. I mention some strong

wrong if it reflects or expresses a lack of full-blown empathic concern for other people, and failures of respect can be seen as one form of such wrongness, as acts that show or reflect a lack of empathic concern *for someone's autonomy*. So what is wrong (and, as we shall see, unjust) with a lack of respect can be fully understood in the sentimentalist terms offered here (and in ECE).[6]

But what is one to say, then, about cases where paternalism is justified—cases, for example, where a parent has to override a child's wishes and entreaties in order to ensure her health? Our theory of respect suggests that such paternalism doesn't show a lack of respect for the child('s autonomy) because the parent in question can be fully empathic with the child's fear of the doctor and nonetheless decide to take the child to see the doctor. Such a parent can be visibly upset at what she has to do to her child, and this would show a sensitivity to her child('s point of view) that the sss parent seems to lack. According to the present theory, then, taking one's unwilling child to the doctor needn't show disrespect for the child or for the child's developing autonomy. (I shall consider issues of paternalism and respect vis-à-vis grown-up children and other adults later on in this chapter.)

However, we have so far been basing that theory on one kind of example: cases where parents act or do not act respectfully toward their children. It is time to broaden the discussion. A lack of respect can also be shown at the social and/or political level, and the theory I am developing applies very comfortably in this larger sphere. Consider, then, religious autonomy, or freedom of religion.

It is often said that sentiments like benevolence and love of fellow human beings can motivate people or societies to unjustly *deny* certain people various important forms of religious freedom or liberty and can lead, in effect, then, to a failure to respect individual and group (rights to) autonomy within the religious sphere. (The same point can be and perhaps has been made about caring.) During the Spanish Inquisition, for example, the religious practices and beliefs of heretics were said to threaten the stability of the state, and it was claimed that the use of torture to force confessions and recantations was necessary for the eternal salvation, and thus the ultimate well-being, both of those with false beliefs and of those whom they might corrupt. This is certainly paternalism, and of a kind that most of us find horrifying. But the paternalism here may seem to spring and is often allowed to have sprung from good sentiments, and many philosophers and others have argued on that basis that a just social order that respects autonomy and freedom has to go beyond sentiments/motives like

---

reasons for questioning (or qualifying) it in *Morals from Motives* (New York: Oxford University Press, 2001), esp. 131f.

6. In ECE (chapter 2), I argued that full-blown or fully developed empathy doesn't require one to be as empathic as anyone could possibly be or actually is—just as one can be fully capable of driving a car yet be less skilled, less capable, as a driver, than certain chauffeurs and others. Empathy-based care ethics can allow for supererogation.

benevolence and concern for others and acknowledge (on rational grounds) an independent order of rights to various freedoms and liberties.

One can find views like this in J. L. Mackie's *Hume's Moral Theory*[7] and also—spelled out at greater length—in Thomas Nagel's *Equality and Partiality*.[8] But in fact, I think there is reason to believe that religious intolerance and persecution *don't* arise out of (otherwise admirable) human feelings/motives in the way that Mackie, Nagel, and so many others have assumed. In cases like the Inquisition, the "dry eyes" (in John Locke's wonderful phrase) of those who persecute and torture others show that such people aren't really concerned about the welfare of those they mistreat but have other, egotistical or selfish reasons for doing what they do.[9] And this begins, I think, to give us some reason to suspect that we may not need to go beyond sentimentalist considerations and invoke independently justifiable rights to religious freedom and autonomy in order to explain what is morally repellent and seems unjust about the denial of religious freedom and autonomy.

However, the main reason for believing this can be stated in terms of empathy. There is something extremely arrogant and dismissive in the attitudes and actions of those who feel they are justified in coercively suppressing the religious beliefs and practices of others. Those who persecute others in this way clearly don't try to understand things from the standpoint of those they persecute, and I think what most strikingly characterizes (arrogant) attitudes and acts of intolerance toward others is a failure to empathize with the point of view of those others.[10] (In the most extreme, but hardly atypical, case, intolerance is accompanied by actual, though perhaps unacknowledged, *hatred* of the other, and hatred is a strong barrier to empathy.) In that case, religious intolerance involves a morally criticizable lack of respect for others that can be understood in terms of an ethics of empathic caring. One needn't go beyond sentimentalism and the sentiments in order to say what is disrespectful, wrong, and unjust about the denial of religious liberty or autonomy.[11] (I intend to be much more specific

7. J. L. Mackie, *Hume's Moral Theory* (London: Routledge and Kegan Paul, 1980), 28.

8. Thomas Nagel, *Equality and Partiality* (New York: Oxford University Press, 1991), 154–168.

9. See Locke's *Second Essay on Government* in *Two Essays on Government*, ed. Peter Laslett (Cambridge: Cambridge University Press, 1960). Notice the contrast here with the empathic parent who is *really upset* at having to take an unwilling child to the doctor's or dentist's.

10. Marilyn Friedman has pointed out to me that a torturer may need to understand her or his victim's feelings and reactions to be able to really hurt the victim, and by the same token (and as I mentioned in an earlier chapter), it is often said that psychopaths can understand what makes people tick with exquisite precision and that this is precisely what enables them to use or abuse unsuspecting victims. But a cold and sadistic/manipulative understanding is not the same thing as empathy, and it is generally agreed, and we have already said, that psychopaths lack empathy for *anyone*. Likewise, those who torture classes of victims whom they hate or contemn arguably don't (fully or substantially) empathize with those victims, but more needs to be said, and some of this will be considered in note 12.

11. Since empathy is, and is supposed to be, more strongly evoked toward people one personally knows, the empathic concern that constitutes respect for (the autonomy of) fellow citizens or compatriots will tend to be less than what is necessary to respect for (the autonomy of) one's own

about how issues of justice relate to empathy and sentiment in our next chapter, which is mainly on the subject of justice. But the claims about justice I am and have been making here will, I think, seem intuitive in the light of what I have otherwise been saying about the foundational moral importance of empathy.)

Now opposition to religious freedom may be compatible with certain kinds and degrees of concern for others, and certainly those who coerce and persecute the adherents of other religions or sects may manage to view themselves as primarily concerned with the welfare of those they coerce and persecute. But the dry eyes make one wonder about egotism, rationalization, and self-deception here, and the concern—even granting that it *is* concern—for those persecuted leads to something that is clearly not morally acceptable.[12] So-called concern for those one persecutes involves or is accompanied by an attitude that is arrogantly dismissive of, and lacking in empathy for, the viewpoint of the other. And that is why the idea that empathy is a necessary basis for respect allows us to criticize religious persecution and coercion in care-ethical terms.[13]

2. Autonomy

I would like now to say something more about the nature of autonomy and to do so, as I promised earlier, in the light of what we have just said about respect, which we have understood as equivalent to respect *for* autonomy. Feminists who criticize or condemn (what are considered) male notions of autonomy typically offer a relational theory of autonomy, and the theory I offer will be relational in

---

children. Still, our empathy for compatriots who adhere to a different religion can easily be strong enough to allow us to understand religious matters from their point of view and be tolerant of their beliefs and customs, and that seems all that respect requires in this instance. Our theory entails that what respect for someone requires depends both on that individual's particular needs and desires and on one's particular *relation or connection* to that individual, but although this may not be typical of views about respect, its implications seem quite plausible.

Let me at this point also quickly add that since (even) *tolerance* can sometimes coexist with hatred, one shouldn't put too much weight on that notion in describing the attitudes and actions characteristic of empathic respect for others. (I am indebted here to Susan Brison.)

12. Notice, however, that *wet* eyes don't necessarily indicate that one is really empathically concerned with those one is crying about. Certain members of the Nazi SS and SA sometimes wept after they had brutalized, tortured, or murdered certain (groups of) victims, but full-blown empathy works in a preventive way before, rather than after, violent harmful actions are perpetrated, and there is no reason to deny that the Nazis just described were lacking in empathy (or that they were giving vent to a kind of *narcissistic* grief). I am indebted here to discussion with Stephen Angle.

13. In *Morals from Motives*, chapter 5, I describe a science fiction case in which a refusal to grant certain religious liberties would be justified and in no way demonstrate a lack of empathy. But it is difficult to think of a single case in actual human history where religious persecutions or intolerance *didn't* reflect a failure of empathy. So if we wish to defend religious liberties in the circumstances of actual human life, our sentimentalist approach may give us all we need. (For further discussion of the idea that religious persecutions and intolerance reflect a lack of empathy toward "out-group members," see Albert Bandura, "Reflexive Empathy: On Predicting More Than One Has Ever Observed," *Behavioral and Brain Sciences* 25 [2002]: 24f.)

at least one of the senses (to be described in what follows) that feminists have relied on. But the theory of autonomy I shall offer will also be grounded (entirely) in sentimentalist care ethics, and this is not true of any other relational conception of autonomy that I know of. We have specified respect for autonomy in terms of empathic factors that are absent in sss parents but present in good or healthy parenting, and we can in the first instance say what autonomy is by claiming that it is what empathic parenting tends to produce and sss parenting tends to preclude.

Think of the sss parent who imposes things on a child and who rides roughshod over the wishes, fears, and desires of that child.[14] If the parent fails to respect those wishes or even to acknowledge them, it will be difficult for the child to accept or acknowledge them, too,[15] and it is likely that the child—if not totally and self-thwartingly rebellious—will learn to submit in large part to the authority, the wishes, the priorities of the parent. Such children will be less likely than others to grow up thinking and deciding things for themselves, and in that case, they will lack the kind (or one kind) of autonomy that features centrally in contemporary discussions. In contrast, parents whose empathy with the growing child allows them to care about and encourage the child's maturing aspirations and individuality are showing respect for the child, and such empathy and respect make it more likely that the child *will* grow into an adult who thinks and decides things autonomously. (I am assuming here that rebellion for its own sake doesn't demonstrate autonomy and represents a kind of *negative submission* to actual or displaced parental authority.)

However, I don't want to leave the impression that it is only sss parents who discourage autonomous thinking and aspirations. Many children start to question religious dogmas or rituals, for example, and some (but not all) religious parents strongly discourage such tendencies, making it likely that their children will either accept what their religion tells them "on faith" or else become rebels against (their) religion. Similarly, sexist attitudes in the early twentieth century led many parents to discourage their daughters from even considering a career in medicine. If a talented girl expressed the desire to become a doctor, she would often be told that she "would really prefer to be a nurse," and such a reply is highly reminiscent of the way sss parents tell their children that they don't *really* want to do certain things (that are inconsistent with what the parent has planned for them). So earlier social mores, attitudes, and institutions can be said to have

14. Much of what I am saying also applies to parental substitutes who may be raising a child.

15. Since the notion of empathy for oneself is somewhat strained (unless, perhaps, we are talking about one's much earlier or much later self), I don't propose to understand self-respect in terms of empathy. Rather, given the account offered here, the conditions of self-respect may turn out pretty much to be the conditions of autonomy itself. A failure of parental respect undermines both the child's (progressive realization of the capacity for) autonomy and the child's earlier and later self-respect. But perhaps it is most accurate to say that self-respect involves a sense of the importance of one's own aspirations and beliefs and that autonomy, in the sense of actually deciding things for oneself, causally depends on such self-respect.

shown a lack of empathy and respect for the aspirations of many girls, and as we shall see more clearly in chapter 9, this represents a form of (sexist or patriarchal) injustice.[16]

What I have just been saying also ties in with some major themes in Carol Gilligan's work. Both in *In a Different Voice* and elsewhere, Gilligan points out that patriarchal societies treat many of the thoughts and aspirations of girls as if they were mistakes or involved misunderstandings on the girls' parts.[17] This can lead girls to doubt or deny their own "voices" and to a state of dissociation from their own thinking and desires that can result in (or constitute) their becoming to a substantial extent selfless, self-denying, or self-abnegating—these are all terms she uses—in their relations with others. If this is correct, then, making use of our earlier analysis, we can say that selflessness and the like typically result(ed) from the disrespectful way in which some or many girls were or are treated. If it is wrong to treat people with disrespect, then the failure or refusal to listen to what girls say, or see things from their point of view, amounts to wrongdoing (to wronging them), and at the heart of that wrongdoing (or wronging) is a failure of empathy. Gilligan herself doesn't stress empathy or the fact of moral wrong-doing in her discussions of dissociation and selflessness. But once one does, one is in a position to answer the frequently heard criticism that care ethics encourages selfless concern for others and so runs counter to the feminist goal of liberating women from the stereotypical behavior and attitudes that have so disadvantaged them in the past.[18] Perhaps some forms of care ethics do encourage selflessness and self-denial in a retrograde fashion. But a care ethics that is centered around the idea of empathy gives us the tools to make *moral criticisms* of the patriarchal (or other) attitudes and behaviors that have caused many women to value and/or exemplify self-denial and selflessness. This is the very opposite of an encourage-ment to self-denial and selflessness and is certainly in keeping with feminist ideals and goals. In chapter 9, I want to return to this theme as it specifically relates to issues of social justice. But at this point, I think we need to go back to our discussion of the nature of autonomy.

16. My sketchy account of the causal origins of autonomy tends to support what Natalie Stoljar calls the "feminist intuition" that "preferences influenced by oppressive norms of femininity cannot be autonomous," that a fully autonomous individual doesn't have such preferences. In the light of my discussion of respect and empathy, the example of the girl who is taught/forced to think she has to become a nurse rather than a doctor in fact illustrates *how* the influence of oppressive social norms of femininity can undermine autonomy. See Stoljar's "Autonomy and the Feminist Intuition," in C. MacKenzie and N. Stoljar, eds., *Relational Autonomy: Feminist Perspectives on Autonomy, Agency, and the Social Self* (New York: Oxford University Press, 2000), esp. 95.

17. See *In a Different Voice*, (Cambridge: Harvard University Press, 1982), chapter 3, and also "Hearing the Difference: Theorizing Connection" in *Anuario de Psicologia* 34 (2003): 155–161.

18. For an example of such criticism, see Martha Nussbaum, *Sex and Social Justice* (New York: Oxford University Press, 1999), 74ff. Gilligan offers her own kind of answer to this criticism in "Hearing the difference . . . ," in "Reply by Carol Gilligan," *Signs* 11 (1986): 324–333, and originally in *In a Different Voice*, chapter 3.

I shall be assuming here that autonomy in the sense of thinking and deciding things for oneself is possible in a causally deterministic universe. Of course, autonomy in this sense is to some extent a matter of degree, but I do hold and think it reasonable to hold that the mere fact that one has been influenced in one's thoughts or decisions does nothing to show a lack or absence of autonomy. Obviously, it can sometimes be reasonable, for example, to take someone's advice, but there is a difference between taking advice and feeling impelled to do or think *whatever* a certain other person or institution tells you to. The former can involve an exercise of autonomy; the latter clearly doesn't. It is very difficult to spell out this distinction in satisfying and complete detail, but this is something philosophers have sought and continue to seek to do, and rather than turn this book into a treatise on the nature of autonomy, I want at this point simply to gesture toward these familiar, though philosophically challenging, distinctions. My purpose here, rather, is to indicate how familiar ideas about autonomy relate to notions like respect, empathy, and caring, and that is what I have just been doing.

Annette Baier tells us that we are all "second persons," that we have to be a "you" for some nurturing other before we can be an "I" for ourselves.[19] This seems obvious once it is stated—though it took a feminist to point it out explicitly for the first time and to point out how that fact seems neglected in traditional liberal/rationalist ("masculine") theories or discussions of autonomy. More significantly, perhaps, the fact that we are originally second persons indicates that autonomy is at the very least *causally* relational. But the present attempt to understand autonomy by reference to respect and caring fills out the idea of relational autonomy in a very specific way. Our account says that such autonomy is just what respect for autonomy—understood as involving empathic care or caring—*tends to produce.*

Now autonomy as the developed and exercised capacity to think and decide things for oneself is pretty clearly good for people. To be sure, it can be difficult and even painful to think and act autonomously, and if we took a very crude (and shortsighted) hedonistic view of how human beings flourish, autonomy might seem problematic. But despite all the problems that can accompany autonomy (and that can lead some people to attempt to "escape from freedom"), it still seems to most of us, intuitively, to be a highly desirable state, and its status as such has been defended by many philosophers, myself included.[20] So I think we should assume here that autonomy is an important human good. In that case, our care ethics treats respectful, empathic caring both as morally incumbent on parents and as the likeliest way to produce the highly desirable state of

19. Annette Baier, "Cartesian Persons," in her *Postures of the Mind: Essays on Mind and Morals* (Minneapolis: University of Minnesota Press, 1985) 84ff.

20. For defense of the personal desirability of autonomy, see, e.g., Brad Hooker's "Is Moral Virtue a Benefit to the Agent?" (in R. Crisp, ed., *How Should One Live?* [Oxford: Clarendon Press, 1996], esp. 145); and my *Morals from Motives*, Ch. 8.

autonomy. But think, too, about what autonomy *involves*. We have argued that autonomy is inconsistent with selflessness, and that means that autonomous people can recognize and aren't afraid of their own desires or aspirations. This, too, is a desirable state for a person to be in,[21] and that means, I think, that we are now in a position to usefully expand on Baier's idea that we are and have to be second persons before we become first persons. What in fact emerges from our previous discussion is the more specifically (or explicitly) ethical conclusion that it is by being initially *treated well as second persons* that we become likely or more likely to *do well as first persons*.

Now the kind of autonomy we have been focusing on involves the realization of the initial human capacity for thinking and deciding things for oneself. I have sometimes slipped in what I hope are harmless ways between references to autonomy as a developed or realized capacity and references to it as the/an exercise of that capacity. And there is also autonomy as a basic human capacity that needs to be developed and that it is desirable to exercise. Still, all these references are to a form of autonomy that is seen as lying within given individuals and as relational only in the sense of having been or needing to be brought about by other individuals (operating in a given society and environment). Feminist relational autonomy is frequently understood in such causal terms, but sometimes autonomy is said (also) to be *constitutively* relational.[22] What does this mean, and how does it fit in with what we have been saying up till this point?

Those who say that autonomy is constitutively relational often cite the fact that our exercise of autonomy requires "cooperating" institutions and social attitudes.[23] Even a woman who is intent on becoming a doctor cannot fulfill her ambition unless some medical school is willing to accept her as a student. So in this case and others, the successful exercise of autonomy would appear to depend on external factors, and those factors can seem more like constitutive conditions than like causes of exercising autonomy. This conclusion may be correct, but what is at work here might also be an ambiguity in the notion of autonomy as between an (exercised) internal capacity for making one's own decisions and the absence of external factors that interfere with one's doing what one wants.

---

21. But the fact that autonomy is desirable or good for individuals in these ways doesn't in any way imply that the autonomous person has to be lacking in empathy. As I explained in chapter 1, the effectiveness of inductive discipline may depend on and is certainly enhanced by the fact that the parent who calls a child's attention to the pain or harm that child has caused, and who does so to prevent the child from causing similar pain or harm in the future, *is exhibiting or modeling empathy*. Really empathic non-sss parents can nurture autonomy and a lack of selflessness—and at the same time instill empathic concern for others—in their children.

22. For various views of the relationality of autonomy, see the essays collected in C. MacKenzie and N. Stoljar, eds., *Relational Autonomy*.

23. See, for example, Jennifer Nedelsky, "Reconceiving Autonomy," and Marina Oshana, "Personal Autonomy and Society," *Journal of Social Philosophy* 29 (1998): 81–102.

When a region in a given country is autonomous, the country (as a matter of law) doesn't interfere in or with various of the region's activities, and religious autonomy is also naturally regarded as an absence of interference (on the part of the state or certain people) with the exercise of religious freedom. But individuals may be free from outside interference at a given time without having the capacity to think or decide things for themselves. The state and its citizens may not interfere with religious liberty, but religious individuals may nonetheless have an entirely submissive or selfless attitude to what their parents or church taught them. In that case, the religious people fail to be autonomous in the sense we have been working with so far, but they do have another kind of autonomy, the kind that involves an absence of outside interference (and that we sometimes attribute, on a larger scale, to regions or provinces in a given country, etc.). This latter kind of autonomy, moreover, appears to be constitutively, and not just causally, relational, because freedom from outside interference seems to just *be* the absence of certain external factors and activities.

We need to say a bit more about this constitutively relational kind of autonomy, and we shall do so in chapter 9. But for the moment, let me point out that interference with an individual's autonomy seems morally at least to require some sort of justification and mention that we will have something substantial to say about when such interference is just or morally acceptable later in this chapter. We have already seen that interference with the free exercise of religion constitutes disrespect and can be condemned as unjust, but chapter 9 will need to expand on this idea and offer a general criterion of when interference with liberty is unjust and when it isn't.

Before we get to chapter 9, however, we still have important work to do on some issues of paternalism. We have spoken of cases where paternalism is morally justified and doesn't show any lack of respect for those in whose lives someone coercively intervenes. But we have described other cases where a patriarchal society denies women their own voice and shows them disrespect—cases, for example, where women are, supposedly for their own good, told that they really don't or shouldn't have the aspirations they say they have. Such treatment of women is disrespectfully and unjustly paternalistic or sexist, and there are a whole host of ways, in fact, in which patriarchy and sexism lead to or embody morally invidious paternalism. But apart from issues of patriarchy and feminism, there are, of course, numerous other cases in which paternalistic treatment of individuals is morally invidious. It can be invidiously paternalistic if a father deprives his son of the money he needs to go to college on the grounds that he (the father) disapproves of the career path the son wants to follow after college, and what is invidious or wrong (and also disrespectful) here can be unpacked in the same sentimentalist terms we have been using all along in this chapter. But not every paternalistic intervention in the life of an adult child or relation (or even a stranger) need be, or is obviously, objectionable, and I would like now to discuss such cases and see how they bear on our general defense of sentimentalist care ethics.

3. When Is Paternalism Justified?

A parent who takes his child to the doctor's over the child's shrieking protests may not lack empathy for how the child feels and will therefore not count, on our sentimentalist care-ethical view of things, as showing disrespect for the child when he makes the child see the doctor. But such coercive behavior is clearly more difficult to justify in moral terms when it concerns an adult, even (or especially?) an adult one cares a great deal about. Still, there are occasions when one adult will be strongly tempted or inclined to act in a coercive paternalistic way toward another adult, and some of these occur between members of the same family.

For example, some motorcyclists say they like the feeling of the wind blowing through their hair and prefer to ride without wearing a helmet, even though they know how dangerous that can be. And one can imagine a case in which a mother or father and an adult son disagree about whether the son needs to, ought to, wear a helmet while riding his motorcycle. In this country, there are differences between various states in regard to passing and enforcing laws requiring cyclists to wear helmets (and there are even differences regarding the wearing of seat belts in automobiles), so it is not surprising that disagreements should exist in individual cases where the state's interests and legislation are not particularly at issue. Imagine, therefore, that someone's adult son absolutely refuses to wear a helmet while riding his motorcycle and his mother, say, disagrees in the strongest terms. Assume further—and this introduces a slightly futuristic element into our imagined example—that the parent knows a way of forcing her son to wear the helmet. Let's say she can pay someone to hook up the helmet to the motorcycle's engine in such a way that the engine won't run unless the helmet registers brainwaves coming from inside it. And she actually does pay someone to do this over the wild and resentful protestations of the son. Has she acted wrongly? Has she shown disrespect for her son's autonomy?

Well, on the more traditional notion of autonomy that liberalism subscribes to, such interference probably does offend or interfere with the son's right to do as he chooses, and the liberal is likely, I think, to say that the parent's interference constitutes an invidious failure to respect the son's autonomy *rights*. But I think the situation isn't quite all that morally clear, and it seems to me that something, indeed a great deal, can be said on the other side. And what can be said can be said from the point of view and in terms of the sentimentalist ideas about respect and autonomy we have defended earlier in this chapter. The mother who forces her adult son to ride with his helmet on might very well (like to parent who forces a child to see the doctor) know how her son feels about her interference. She may empathize fully with his disappointment and anger, but (again, like the parent who forces a child to visit the doctor) she may nonetheless feel that this is something that she has to do, or that at least she ought to do.

Now with young children who are forced to go to the doctor's, one can hope and assume that they will someday appreciate the rightness of what their parent is forcing them to do, but we can imagine that the motorcycle-riding son is wedded, and known to be wedded, to his preference for freedom and certain pleasurable sensations while riding over his own safety and the peace of mind of his mother. The mother can't and doesn't assume he will change his mind about her successful attempt to coerce him into riding with a helmet (even if he has an accident that damages him less because of it). But she may still understand things very well from the standpoint of her son and, despite what she fears may be a permanent disagreement, force him to wear the helmet.

Has she done wrong? The liberal is likely to say she has, but many of us, I think, would intuitively regard her behavior as morally justified or acceptable. That is how I tend to view the matter, and it is also how I think an ethics of empathic care should view it. The woman, in effectively opposing her son's wishes, will not, I believe, have shown him a lack of respect. She will have respected his autonomy not, perhaps, in the sense familiar from liberalism's theory of rights but in the sense, or according to the conception, defended in these pages. And that conception is supported not only by the examples and arguments discussed earlier in this chapter also but by the whole tenor and content of the sentimentalist approach to morality this book has advocated.

But our sentimentalist defense of the mother's intervention is in fact not yet complete. Care ethics places great emphasis on relationships, and that is one reason, for example, it thinks the use of moral principles isn't ideal from a moral standpoint. The husband who has one thought too many shows himself to be less loving than a husband who would think only of his wife and her danger before leaping in to save her. And the relationship he has with his wife seems less good, less intimate, because he consults morality rather than, in this case, acting from intensely caring (and frightened) feelings for his wife. But by the same token (and this is something that Nel Noddings has pointed out to me), the loving mother who forces her son to wear a helmet and who recognizes how her son feels about what she is doing or has done will not drop the matter or evade further discussion after she has succeeded in her purpose.[24] Rather, the concern she has for their relationship and for her son's feelings (not to mention her own) will impel her or at least persuade her to try to continue some sort of dialogue with her son on the subject of what she has done and how he feels about it. No matter if the son is, in the wake of her successful coercion, too angry with her to want to speak further about the matter or to even to want to speak with her at all. She can wait, and if she

---

24. When I wrote ECE, I was unclear in my mind what care ethics, given its emphasis on relationships and connection, should say about paternalistic intervention in the motorcycle helmet case and others like it. However, Noddings's take on such cases has convinced me that the mother's intervention would or could be justified in care-ethical terms. If that is so, then some of the doubts raised in ECE about the general correlation between moral distinctions and distinctions of empathy need no longer trouble us.

loves him, she will wait and bring the matter up if and when he is later willing to discuss it. Their relationship has been damaged even if she has done the right thing in forcing him to wear a helmet, and an empathically caring mother will want to do something to make amends to her son, to try once more to make him understand where she is coming from and, more generally, to reestablish what I am assuming is their previously good relationship. And once one sees that her obligations in this matter aren't just an issue of whether a single act at a single time was morally justified but also concern how, morally and intelligently, to continue on, or reestablish continuity, with her son, then the original decision to make him wear a helmet may seem more justified than it would in the absence of these larger surrounding motivations and future actions on her part.

Now cases where one forces a stranger to do something present somewhat different but not totally different issues, and I shall assume that a stranger might also be justified in forcing someone to wear a helmet while riding on a motorcycle. In fact, the stranger's justification might even seem greater than that we accorded the mother because the stranger as a stranger is in a position rather similar to that of a state or other jurisdiction that passes and enforces a helmet law. Of course, we have voted, most of us, for the officials or legislators who legally coerce cyclists into wearing helmets, though the son of our example might not have been previously old enough to vote. But since most of us think the state may justly and permissibly pass laws coercing the use of helmets, that can only reinforce the view of individual coercive action (by the mother) that we defended earlier. But now that we have so long been interjecting talk of justice into our discussion of respect, autonomy, paternalism, and patriarchy, it is time to say something more explicit or official on that topic.

9

JUSTICE

Although Gilligan's *In a Different Voice* contrasts the voice or ethic of justice with that of caring, many care ethicists have sought to address issues of social justice (and/or of international justice). Rather than discard the notion, they have sought to understand it in terms acceptable to care ethics and to feminism, and to that extent what they have done parallels what has taken place with the notion of autonomy. Gilligan placed autonomy within the putatively masculine voice of justice, but subsequent feminists and care ethicists have sought to give their own (relational and feminist) account of autonomy, rather than simply abandon that seemingly useful and important concept.

Some care ethicists who have discussed justice—most notably, Virginia Held—have argued that our understanding of justice requires us to bring in both elements from care ethics and elements from traditional justice ethics as exemplified, most typically, in Kantian liberal thought.[1] Others have thought that social and international justice could be understood entirely in care-ethical terms, and in recent years Nel Noddings has to some extent moved in this direction.[2] (In her original book, *Caring*, and in other early writings, she held that the sphere of justice was entirely distinct from that of caring.) In this connection, I should also mention the work of Sara Ruddick, whose 1989 book, *Maternal Thinking*, argued that we should see political life in terms of the

---

1. See Held's *The Ethics of Care: Personal, Political, and Global* (New York: Oxford University Press, 2006).

2. See Noddings's *Starting at Home: Caring and Social Policy* (Berkeley: University of California Press, 2002).

mother-child relationship.[3] This wasn't care ethics—it preceded care ethics. But it had an influence on the later-developing ethics of care because it in many ways resembles that ethics. I won't go into details, but the important point here is that Ruddick, like the later Noddings, didn't think we needed to appeal to traditional liberal (or libertarian) views of justice in order to frame a plausible conception of justice. Justice could be conceived entirely in terms appealing to women or to feminism.

I myself have for a long time been pushing a similar idea about and for care ethics. Even before Noddings started writing about justice in terms of caring, I argued in an article (which become part of my later book *Morals from Motives*) that social justice could be conceived entirely in sentimentalist care-ethical terms.[4] But in recent years, there have been two significant developments in my work on justice. First, I have become more interested in questions about international and global justice than I had been previously. Second, I have made use of the notion of empathy in a way that my earlier work did not. Doing so makes it possible to integrate what care ethics has to say or can say about (social, international, global) justice into an overall discussion/picture of moral sentimentalism along the lines of the present book. And that is what I intend to do in the present chapter. Other care ethicists haven't emphasized empathy in their discussions of justice (or, for that matter, in their discussions of autonomy and respect), but I believe empathy is the key to care ethics' greatest potential development and plausibility, both in general and in the sphere of justice.

One caveat or reminder, however, before we launch into our main discussion of justice: liberals (not to mention libertarians) think of rights and justice as independent of and even as *resistant to* considerations of empathy. (On the latter point, see the discussion of free speech and hate speech in *The Ethics of Care and Empathy* [ECE], chapter 5.) But the kind of sentimentalist political philosophy I will be developing here is committed to seeing valid rights and humanly acceptable justice as (having to be) grounded in considerations having to do with our empathic sensitivity to and concern for others. So what such a sentimentalist philosophy has to say about justice and rights involves rethinking those notions in relation to certain liberal views about their provenance and justification that are widespread and influential among philosophers and intellectuals and have trickled down to a certain extent to the (American) public at large. Still, our approach will preserve most commonly accepted *conclusions* about what kinds of social arrangements and processes are or are not just, and that (methodologically speaking) is a good thing.[5]

---

3. See Ruddick's *Maternal Thinking: Toward a Politics of Peace* (Boston: Beacon Press, 1989).

4. See my "The Justice of Caring," *Social Philosophy and Policy* 15 (1998): 171–195.

5. I say "most" because a sentimentalist approach that emphasizes empathy will tend to deny the right to free speech in Skokie-type cases involving hate speech, and liberals want to defend such a right by reference to traditional ideas about autonomy. ECE (chapter 5) argued that however plausible and commonsensical such a liberal view may seem, it is based on or coupled with implausible assumptions about the emotions and about the kind of damage hate speech can sometimes do, and this, I argued, gives us reason to doubt the liberal's assumptions about (rights

But it is now time to be a little more systematic about what sentimentalism along the present lines can or wants to say about justice.

1. The Empathy in Justice

In chapter 8, I attempted to explain respect for autonomy in terms of a sentimentalist ethics of care that sees care as grounded in empathy. I propose now to do the same kind of thing with regard to social, international, and (more briefly) global justice. (I shall not have much to say about rights because a theory of rights can be given in a fairly unproblematic way once a theory of justice has been formulated.) And I would like to begin with social justice and then discuss international and global issues.

I think it is possible to understand the justice of (a given society's) laws, institutions, and social customs *on analogy with* the ethics of individual acts and attitudes of caring. An ethics of empathic caring evaluates the actions of individuals in terms of whether they express, exhibit, or reflect empathically caring motivation, or its opposite, on the part of individuals. But the laws, institutions, and customs of a given society are like the actions of that society, for they reflect or express the motives (and beliefs) of the social group (or subgroups) in something like the way that individual actions reflect or express an agent's motives (and beliefs), though in a more enduring manner that seems appropriate to the way societies typically outlast the individual agents in them. So a sentimentalist ethics of empathic caring can say that institutions and laws, as well as social customs and practices, are just if they reflect empathically caring motivation on the part of (enough of) those responsible for originating and maintaining them. But let me be a bit more specific.

We saw earlier that people are likely to develop more empathy for (groups of) people they know than for those they don't. Still, and as I mentioned, we do have the capacity to develop *some* substantial empathy and concern for distant people we don't know, and in that case, it is perhaps not too much to expect people to develop a *greater degree* of empathic concern *for their compatriots*. We tend to have a lot more in common with compatriots or fellow citizens than with most of the inhabitants of other countries, and even if we don't know, aren't personally acquainted with, many of the citizens of our country, we are part of, and

---

of) autonomy. So unlike the liberal or libertarian, I think we should question the justice or moral necessity of allowing neo-Nazi hate speech in a community like Skokie where there was a large population of Holocaust survivors. (That was the reason why the neo-Nazis targeted Skokie in the first place.)

   I think our sentimentalist approach will also want to defend a narrower view than most liberals and libertarians maintain of the rights of husbands or others who physically or sexually abuse their spouses or women generally. Much more needs to be said about the legal/moral issues here, but I propose to delay that discussion till another occasion.

therefore well acquainted with, the national group, the nation, of which they are all members—and with its common or general culture.

So let us consider the national legislators who originate or pass a given law. And let us simplify matters by assuming that it is only their motivation toward fellow citizens that is relevant to the assessment of the legislation they pass.[6] In that case, we can say, to begin with, that a law is just if it reflects or expresses empathically caring motivation toward their compatriots on the part of the legislative group that is responsible for passing it.[7] But less demandingly, an ethic of empathic care will also want to say that a law is just even if it merely fails to reflect or exhibit a *lack* of appropriate empathic concern on the part of those who promulgate it. Not every action of a malicious person necessarily reflects that maliciousness, and when a malicious person scratches his head, for example, we can say that that action is morally all right because it in no way expresses or reflects that person's malice. And by the same token, morally unsavory national legislators who are largely indifferent to the welfare of their compatriots, to the good of their country, might pass a law that in no way displayed or reflected their greediness or selfishness: for example, a law allowing right turns at red stoplights throughout the nation. That law would be just or at least not unjust, according to the view I am defending here.[8] We now need to see whether we arrive at plausible judgments about what is or is not just when we apply this approach to important social issues.

Some of what is relevant here has already been considered. I argued in chapter 8 that religious intolerance and persecution reflect an absence of empathic concern and respect for fellow citizens (or fellow inhabitants of a given country), and I was already at that point willing to say that this shows religious intolerance and persecution to be unjust. But the present chapter's explicit treatment of the conditions of social justice makes it clearer, I think, why a claim of injustice can be said to follow from facts about the motivational bases of intolerance and persecution, as we historically and at present know them. Chapter 8 also showed us that patriarchal social attitudes can embody a

6. What I am saying about particular laws also applies, mutatis mutandis, to the framing and ratification of a constitution. Note, too, that the motives and beliefs that keep a law in existence may also be relevant to its moral assessment. But I shall leave this complication to one side.

7. I assume that we can assess group motives (to a large extent) on the basis of the motives of the individuals in the group, but there will certainly be cases—e.g., where a group is closely divided in its motives and attitudes—where group attribution is a delicate, or sometimes even a vague, matter. In such instances, according to what I have been saying, it is difficult to morally assess a law, but given care ethics, individual acts whose motivation is ambivalent or murky can also be difficult to evaluate. Since all theories allow for hard cases, this doesn't seem to be a particular problem for a care theory of justice.

8. In *Morals from Motives*, I assumed that national legislation should express equal concern for all citizens, but it is difficult to make sense of this in terms of empathy. However, even if national legislators are *more* concerned with their own constituents (and especially their own families and themselves), they may still be motivated by substantial concern for the good of their country, and in that case, I want to say, the laws they pass will be just in care-ethical terms.

lack of empathic concern and respect for the aspirations of girls and women (e. g., to become doctors), and we can certainly say that all laws, customs, and institutions that reflect such attitudes are as unjust as the attitudes themselves (and the situation or society in which they flourish).⁹

Similarly, women who work outside the home have typically ended up doing more total work than their husbands, and this, too, can be considered a form of injustice (or unfairness). If women have to do an inordinate amount of the work that needs doing in their families, that fact reflects social expectations or attitudes that embody a failure of empathy and concern for women's needs and aspirations: for example, the widespread view that women have to take primary responsibility for child rearing and housekeeping *whatever their role outside the home may be*. It may be convenient for men to go along with such attitudes because it gives them more free (leisure) time than they might other- wise enjoy, but a willingness on the part of husbands to overburden their wives in this way constitutes great selfishness toward those they are supposed to love and, commensurately, a great *lack* of empathic consideration for—or fairness toward—their wives. So the view of justice that we have derived here from the ethics of empathic caring *condemns* any situation in which full-time working wives do a great majority of the work of caring within families—rather than encouraging or colluding in the oppression or injustices that women have traditionally suffered or currently have to endure.¹⁰

The case just mentioned illustrates how public attitudes can have unjust repercussions in the private or family sphere (though the causal influence needn't run just one way). But in fact a comprehensive ethics of empathic caring needn't put much (or any?) moral weight on the whole distinction between the personal/ private and the political/public. Both realms are to be judged in terms of empathic care, and there is no reason, for example, why the unfair or unjust distribution of work within families shouldn't be a subject for political consider- ation and amelioration: perhaps legislatures need to pass laws mandating com- pensation, by their husbands or partners, for women who do a disproportionate

9. Tolerance of various religions doesn't, therefore, mean simply accepting the injustices certain patriarchal religions perpetrate against women: e.g., in denying them equal educational or professional opportunities with men. But there are delicate and difficult practical and theoretical issues about how to deal with and eliminate such injustices in morally acceptable terms. Clitoridectomies are unjust or unfair to women/girls, but that doesn't necessarily mean that it would be right or just to invade a country where this practice occurs in order to eliminate the practice, and those within such a country will also face complicated issues here. But these difficulties are familiar and pose issues/problems to all ethical/political views.

10. Recently available evidence shows that this problem may have existed more in the past than it does today, at least in the United States. In their study *Changing Rhythms of American Family Life* (New York: Russell Sage Foundation, 2006), S. Bianchi, J. Robinson, and M. Milkie report that although wives still do twice as much child care and housework as their husbands, the amount of child care and housework done by fathers has increased sharply since 1965, and the total hours of work done by mothers and fathers are now roughly equal.

amount of housework or caring for children. But this is to raise issues of distributive justice.

2. Distributive Social Justice

A society is just to the degree or extent that its laws, institutions, practices, attitudes, and customs are just, and we have offered a specific criterion for when laws and the rest are just in terms of ideals of empathic caring that apply at the level of social groups. We have been applying that criterion here—I hope successfully—to a large number of issues, but I think that it in fact works well for *all* questions of social justice. The most important issue of justice that we haven't yet considered relates to poverty and equality. Our theory needs to be able to say something plausible about the justice or injustice of serious inequalities of wealth, and this is precisely what I propose to do in the present section of this chapter. However, it may help in doing this if we first say something briefly about the distribution not of wealth, but of political power.

In some societies, a ruling elite denies most people a political voice, a vote, and we consider this a paradigm of injustice. But the injustice can be unpacked in care-ethical terms, because the refusal to grant basic political privileges or rights always—I really think always—expresses and reflects a rather greedy and selfish desire, on the part of the elite, to retain their hegemony of power, privilege, and (typically, though not always) wealth. This constitutes far less empathic concern for (the welfare of) one's compatriots than would be reflected in a fully developed capacity for empathy with others, and so our approach will deem such a situation (politically) unjust.[11]

Now similar criticism can be made of a meritocratic society in which there is no (guaranteed) safety net for the handicapped, the poor, or the unemployed. Even if such a society allows everyone to vote, a power elite may successfully

11. This is less clear in primitive societies where those who don't rule never think to ask for a role in ruling. However, what I am saying does, I think, apply in Asia, despite what is sometimes said about "Asian values." Politicians and others in Asia often claim that Asians are more deferential than people in the West are, and this is sometimes given as a reason why democracy is less applicable or called for in Asia. (On this point, see Daniel Bell's *East Meets West* [Princeton, N.J.: Princeton University Press, 2000].) But remember that nineteenth-century American women were more deferential (to men) than they are nowadays, and if, as I discussed earlier, we follow Carol Gilligan's analysis of why women tend under patriarchy to doubt their own voices and to act and think deferentially (or selflessly), then it is plausible to suppose that something similar lies behind so-called Asian values. Asians may well be deferential because they are used to their voices' not being listened to, and such deference, therefore, far from indicating the irrelevancy of democracy in Asian countries, is actually a sign that people in those countries are being and have been treated disrespectfully and unjustly. This is an argument for, not against, democracy.

Daniel Bell also voices a suspicion that those who invoke "Asian values" to defend their elitist political system and their place within it may be mainly motivated by greed and the desire for power —as well as by contempt for the ruled. Given what I have said in the main text, this, too, supports the idea that democracy is essential to social justice.

oppose all proposals to provide economic help for the handicapped and others, and it is plausible to suppose, once again, that such opposition reflects or exhibits selfishness and greed on the part of the elite that is incompatible with a level of empathic concern for the worst-off members of society that seems well within our human capacities. To be sure, meritocracies have their ideologies, as do monarchies that deny the people all political power: one can refuse people help in the name of what one calls libertarian ideals, just as one can preserve exclusive political power by referring to the divine right of kings. And if this sounds more than slightly Marxian, that is not, I think, a reason to run away from what I am saying here. Marx may have been wrong about many, many things, but what he said about our tendencies to rationalize self-interest or sheer selfishness in the name of ideology rings true to many of us who take a strictly democratic approach to the political realm. And it may ring especially true to feminists (and women) who have, for example, seen scripture cited for the purpose of justifying patriarchal attitudes, practices, and institutions. So I think we need not hesitate to draw the conclusion that a refusal to pass laws instituting a social safety net counts, for reasons having to do with empathy or its absence, as an economic form of injustice.

But of course, it is possible to hold that injustice(s) of an economic kind can exist even when a social safety net is in place, and I would like now to spend some time considering that possibility. A safety net is compatible with enormous differences of wealth and with a considerable amount of poverty, and an ethics of empathic care that turns its attention to issues of (distributive) justice may well want to suggest that justice requires *more* than a safety net, that it requires that the rich and those with high incomes be taxed *more steeply* than those at the lower end of the economic scale. Considerations of marginal utility offer us, in fact, a very good moral reason for preferring and instituting the kind of progressive taxation on the rich and those with high incomes that makes for greater economic equality within society as a whole.

Given decreasing marginal utility, when we tax a rich person's money, we typically do less harm than when we tax a poor person's money. But even more important, when we tax rich or high-income individuals for the benefit of those who are poorer, the latter tend to gain a great deal more than the former lose. This fact gives us some empathic grounds to favor redistributive progressive taxation, and I believe that the justice of progressive tax legislation and the injustice of not instituting such taxation can both be accounted for in care-ethical terms. But we need to be careful here. When we tax rich or high-income individuals (or anyone else), we either take money they already have or actively prevent them from receiving certain moneys, but what we said in chapter 1 entails that we are empathically more sensitive to causing harm (or something bad) than to merely allowing harm (or something bad) to happen. We shy or flinch from maiming or harming a person even if that is the only way we can bring about a greater amount of good for people, and if the acts of a just government express empathic concern for the governed, doesn't that mean that a government should hesitate to cause harm or make things worse for people than they otherwise would be? Isn't this, in turn, then, some sort of reason for governments not to tax the rich for the benefit of the poor? (I take it that it *isn't* a reason for governments to avoid taxation altogether.)

In the empathic care-ethical terms discussed in chapter 1 (and at greater length in ECE), it is indeed such a reason, but that doesn't mean the reason can't be overridden. After all, most deontologists think it can be morally permissible to harm or even kill someone if the benefits of doing so are great enough, and the benefits of progressive taxation clearly are great. Because of diminishing marginal utility, the harm redistributive progressive taxation does to the rich is enormously outweighed by the good it does for those who are poor or not well off, and I think empathic concern for its citizenry would not in fact make legislators "flinch" from instituting various forms of progressive taxation. Quite the contrary. And so our theory can regard such taxation as just, and even as required by justice.[12]

However, nothing we have said indicates that justice requires, or even allows, the progressive tax rate to be as steep as possible, so that society comes progressively closer (excuse the pun!) to complete socioeconomic equality. The highest or steepest rates of taxation and any general insistence on equality, or nearequality, of wealth or income might very well deprive people of incentives to work hard and quite possibly would make society as a whole lose greatly in economic terms. This latter fact is (also) one to which empathic caring is or would be sensitive, so our account of justice needn't insist on the highest rates of progressive taxation and would instead claim that the issue of how steep progressive taxation should be has to depend on empirical considerations.[13] But there is a further, very interesting complication that also needs to be mentioned at this point.

Utilitarians often make use of considerations of marginal utility to argue for progressive taxation, but in addition they hold that the rate of taxation shouldn't be so steep as to diminish overall economic output (or overall social utility). However, the utilitarian also holds that justice requires passing laws that

---

12. Does this, then, mean that where there are no governmental provisions for redistribution and there are enormous disparities in wealth or income, it can be all right and even good for private individuals to forcibly redistribute wealth by stealing from the rich in order to give to the poor or, even, in order to alleviate or mitigate their own miserable circumstances? My answer is a tentative, hesitant yes, that it can be morally all right. But if enough people take matters into their own hands, that can threaten the stability of society, and although threats to the stability of certain societies can be a good thing (as in the case of justified revolutions), a group that threatens social stability can have a lot to answer for. There is no reason, however, that this cannot be unpacked in empathic care-ethical terms.

13. One relevant consideration is how much alienation or solidarity is felt within a given society. Where there is solidarity and/or mutual empathic caring among citizens, hard work may be compatible with mandated economic equality. But this is a complex issue. Cf. G. A. Cohen, "Incentives, Inequality, and Community," reprinted in S. Darwall, ed., *Equal Freedom* (Ann Arbor: University of Michigan Press, 1995), 331–397.

do a great deal (only) for those who are already well-off, when the only alternative is legislation that would do somewhat less good for those who are poorly, or less well, off, and this will seem morally unacceptable to most of us. Rawls's difference principle (in *A Theory of Justice*) is intended precisely to avoid what utilitarianism is counterintuitively committed to here, but I want to argue that the ethics of care can also handle this issue more intuitively than utilitarianism does.

We tend to feel more empathy and empathic concern for those whose situation or condition is bad than for those whose situation or condition is merely not wonderful, and this difference can (therefore) mean that we prefer to help the former, even if we are in a position to do somewhat more good for the latter. But if the sheer or absolute badness of people's situations tends to elicit empathy in such a strong way, our ethics of empathic care ought to take both marginal utility and (what we can very, very roughly call) absolute positionality into account in determining what is moral or just.[14] And since legislators (and framers of constitutions) who are fully empathic will have greater empathy and a special/greater concern for those in their society whose position is bad or terrible (or will be, if nothing is done to help them), our theory of justice mandates a much higher degree of economic equality than utilitarianism provides for.

Put another way, our view requires legislation and institutions that don't reflect a lack of compassion, for compassion is clearly sensitive to (what I would want to call) absolute badness (for individuals).[15] (How hungry one feels and other aspects of what is bad for people may partly depend on the comparisons one makes with how others are doing, but I think the reader can understand, nonetheless, what I mean by talking of absolute badness here.) We feel more empathy for and have more tendency to act on behalf of those who are in bad shape or circumstances, and the term *compassion* takes in that aspect of empathy—we wouldn't call someone compassionate if they wanted to do somewhat

---

14. The idea that one should help those badly off rather than do (somewhat) more good for those not badly off can be found, e.g., in Harry Frankfurt's *The Importance of What We Care About* (Cambridge: Cambridge University Press, 1988), chapter 11; in Joseph Raz's *The Morality of Freedom* (Oxford: Oxford University Press, 1986), chapter 9; in Derek Parfit's Lindley Lecture "Equality or Priority," the University of Kansas, 1991; and in Roger Crisp's "Equality, Priority, and Compassion," *Ethics* 113 (2003), 745–763. Only Crisp stresses empathy as a basis for this moral preference, and these authors disagree among themselves in various ways about whether one should favor worse-off people who are *not* badly off and about other issues relevant to the value of equality. I don't here take sides on these further issues, because I think the relevant deliverances both of empathy and of morality itself are somewhat unclear. This is an important topic, however, for further investigation and elaboration. But let me just add that Rawls's difference principle clearly doesn't focus on sheer badness, but rather on relative position with respect to primary goods. It would be interesting to consider how the view offered here differs from Rawls's in regard to particular social situations, but again, I think this should be left to another occasion. See John Rawls, *A Theory of Justice* (Cambridge: Harvard University Press, 1971).

15. Crisp, "Equality, Priority, and Compassion," makes the same point.

more good for those in acceptable circumstances rather than somewhat less good for those in horrible circumstances.[16]

However, compassion also includes an empathic tendency to respond more to those in immediate danger or misery—where both perceptual and temporal immediacy are meant. For example, those who preferred to install safety devices to help future miners rather than save contemporaneously trapped miners would show themselves to be less than fully compassionate. So what I am now saying is that in addition to being responsive to temporal and also perceptual immediacy, the compassionate person has to be responsive to the sheer badness of someone's (or some group's) situation. But of course, all these are factors we are empathically sensitive to, so we can conclude that compassion marks out a particular subset of the factors empathy is responsive to. We can thus say that a kind of social compassion, or at least laws and institutions that don't manifest a lack of compassion, are a necessary condition of social justice according to an ethics of care.[17]

Now we have for some time been concentrating on the motives of legislators and others toward those who live in their own country. But many will hold that a just society with just laws and institutions will not be indifferent or hostile to the interests of people in other countries, and that seems certainly to be correct. So we need now to begin considering issues of international justice and also, finally, of global justice. As I use terms, international justice includes considerations of how one nation (or its citizens/inhabitants) treats other nations (or their citizens/inhabitants), whereas global justice concerns issues about the possibility and advisability of a having a single global government or about the present system of nation-states as a whole. We shall now begin to focus on these issues.

3. International and Global Justice

Much of what we said in the previous two sections carries over to issues of international and global justice. For example, just as morally decent individuals develop an empathic concern for people (whom they don't personally know) living outside their own country, fully developed empathy on the part of legislators will take in the well-being of people in other countries. Such

---

16. Incidentally, questions about *how many* people are going to be affected can complicate the moral issues we are dealing with here, so I ask the reader to assume, for simplicity's sake, that the same number of people are affected whichever choice one makes in the cases I am discussing.

17. On the moral and political importance of compassion see Martha Nussbaum, "Compassion: The Basic Social Emotion," in Ellen Frankel Paul, Fred Miller Jr., and Jeffrey Paul, eds., *The Communitarian Challenge to Liberalism* (Cambridge: Cambridge University Press, 1996), 27–58. On the role of empathy in understanding political and legal issues, see Jane Mansbridge, "Feminism and Democratic Community," in John Chapman and Ian Shapiro, eds., *Democratic Community: Nomos XXXV* (New York: New York University Press, 1993), 347–361; Diana Meyers, "Social Exclusion, Moral Reflection, and Rights," *Law and Philosophy* 12 (1993): 125f.; and Nussbaum's *Poetic Justice* (Boston: Beacon Press, 1995), 79–121.

legislators will presumably be less concerned with citizens of other countries than with citizens of their own—the ethics of empathic care is not impartialistic like utilitarianism.[18] But the legislation they approve (e.g., the level of humanitarian foreign aid they support) should at least reflect a substantial amount of concern for the welfare of people in other countries (and for the welfare of the countries themselves considered in aggregate terms), and the theory I have offered can explain why, on grounds of justice, this ought to be so.[19]

But notice one implication of my account of (what we can call) international justice. (It is an implication that also holds mutatis mutandis for issues of personal morality, but I shall focus here on the international instance.) On my view, legislation and governmental (or nongovernmental organization [NGO]) action aimed at ameliorating conditions abroad will count as just if it doesn't reflect an absence or deficiency of fully developed empathic caring. But such legislation and action may not succeed in their purpose(s); the good they are intended to achieve may end up failing to materialize, but on our account that won't undercut the justice of what has been done or legislated. Sheer or actual consequences aren't part of the criterion of justice (or, for that matter, of morally right or acceptable action) that I have offered, and quite recently one writer on care ethics has objected to my views on precisely those grounds. In his recent book *The Heart of Justice*, Daniel Engster has claimed that actual good results or consequences are required if genuine and morally acceptable caring is to occur, and he has criticized my own earlier views (in *Morals from Motives*) for emphasizing good intentions/motives over good consequences/results.[20]

I would like now to show you, however, why a more purely consequentialistic treatment of care or caring is morally less attractive or plausible than a sentimentalist care ethics that makes motive and intention its criterion of evaluation in regard to both moral acceptability and justice. Certainly, the road to hell is or could be paved with good intentions. We all have to agree about that. But I think one can emphasize intentions/motives over actual consequences without in any way repudiating—and while in fact actually supporting and helping to make sense of—that old adage.

The road to hell is paved with good intentions because someone can intend to do good but fail to act when the decisive moment arrives or else act but fail to follow through on their original intentions when obstacles arise and/or more effort is required than they had originally anticipated. But a sentimentalist ethics of care can take these facts into moral account. If someone genuinely cares about,

---

18. Given what was said in chapter 8, *respect* for the citizens or inhabitants of other countries doesn't require as much empathy as does respect for fellow citizens or compatriots.

19. I am inclined to say, actually, that a just society and just legislators need to provide substantial humanitarian aid to (the people of) other countries—given circumstances like those that exist in the world today. A concern for international justice may be a condition of a given society's being just.

20. See Engster, *The Heart of Justice: Care Ethics and Political Theory* (New York: Oxford University Press, 2007), esp. 182.

is genuinely concerned to promote, the well-being of another or others, then they try to learn relevant facts that will enhance their ability to help, and they don't give up if and when their initial efforts are unsuccessful. If they give up too easily or don't bother learning facts that are relevant to the success of their efforts, that already, criterially and constitutively, shows that they don't fully or genuinely care about doing the good they say they want to do. So a caring person has to be very concerned about (producing) results and about pursuing, within certain limits, all necessary means to such results. And the field of international justice offers us some fairly clear-cut examples of these conceptual/ethical facts.

For example, there is now a large and growing literature concerning the ways in which foreign aid—either as humanitarian famine relief or as long-term developmental assistance—has gone and therefore can go awry. The government of a country to which food has been sent can confiscate that food from those who need it and use it for nefarious political purposes: for example, to crush resistance to its tyrannical rule.[21] Developmental assistance can turn out and often, in recent decades, has turned out to be ineffective because of local factors that weren't taken into account by those offering the assistance. But morally speaking, there are at least two different kinds of cases here. If the facts or factors that led to failure to substantially help were known in advance or could, with reasonable efforts, have been learned about in advance, then the point made previously applies, and we can criticize those offering help in moral terms because they have (already) shown themselves to be less than genuinely or fully concerned to promote the good they say they want, and perhaps at least *intend*, to promote. To that extent and for such cases, a sentimentalist ethics of care that makes much of motivation can take results/consequences into moral account, and that is because the intentions and motives it emphasizes *are themselves focused on and directed toward producing good results.*

The more difficult or interesting case, as far as I am concerned, is that in which the agency or government that seeks to provide international assistance couldn't really have anticipated the difficulties they end up encountering in trying to do some good. Can their efforts in that case be morally criticized or deemed unfair or unjust because the good consequences being sought didn't actually materialize? That is what Engster seems to think, but my view is that this gives too much importance to actual (as opposed to sought-after)

---

21. Compare Philip Gourevitch, *We Wish to Inform You That Tomorrow We Will Be Killed with Our Families: Stories from Rwanda* (New York: Farrar, Straus, and Giroux, 1998). For discussion of some of the careless and irresponsible (or *negligent*) ways in which agencies, organizations, and/or governments have dispensed food aid, see, e.g., Alex de Waal, *Famine Crimes: Politics and the Disaster Relief Industry in Africa* (Bloomington: Indiana University Press, 1997). On the ways aid can unfairly and unjustly disadvantage women, see, e.g., Jill Steans, *Gender and International Relations* (New Brunswick, N.J.: Rutgers University Press, 1998), chapter 6; and also Eva Feder Kittay (with Bruce Jennings and Angela Wasunna), "Dependency, Difference, and the Global Ethic of Longterm Care," *Journal of Political Philosophy* 13 (2005): 443–469.

consequences. Intuitively, I think that most of us wouldn't blame or even morally criticize a government or agency that ran into unanticipatable factors in its efforts, say, to provide famine relief or developmental assistance and that at least initially, therefore, was unable to produce good results and even perhaps produced unfortunate ones. Most of us, for example, wouldn't see such (initial) failure as an instance or example of *injustice* or *immorality*.

As far as I am concerned, however, the really interesting question concerns what a government or agency *does at that point*. We now know that there are certain kinds of pitfalls that can be encountered in or for our efforts to provide international assistance, but the point about pitfalls is that at least initially they can't be anticipated. If a clever enemy thinks up the idea of digging deep pits and carefully concealing them, and no one has previously heard or thought of such a thing, then if we fall into one of those pits, we can't, at least the first time, be accused of imprudence or carelessness. But if we subsequently don't make efforts to avoid this happening again, if we aren't thereafter circumspect in traversing certain terrain or territory, then we *do* count as imprudent and careless of our welfare. And I think this lesson transposes to moral cases.

We sometimes can't plausibly, and in moral terms, criticize those who initially fail to provide the help they want to provide, but we can criticize them if they don't seek to learn from their mistakes and if they don't redouble their efforts to provide assistance. And that, again for the reasons mentioned earlier, is because genuine caring criterially involves following through on one's original good intentions if and when the going gets tough. Of course, there are limits to this. If it turns out that aid workers and/or medical personnel are likely to be killed if they go into a given country where there is hunger or epidemic disease, then even a genuinely strong empathic concern to help others is likely to yield to prudence and self-interest (i.e., self-concern), and as I have already indicated, sentimentalist care ethics can and should see empathic concern for others as occurring against a persisting background of (normal) self-concern, self-concern that empathy can substantially attenuate but can't be expected to obliterate. Someone who shows concern for her own welfare doesn't automatically exhibit a lack of fully developed empathy, and fully developed or full-blown empathy isn't the same thing as the greatest empathy anyone or a given person could ever develop. However, someone who is willing to make more self-sacrifice than most and who is willing, for example, to risk his life to provide food for those who are starving can be seen as *going beyond* the call of care-ethical duty, that is, as acting *supererogatorily*. (On these points see, ECE, chapter 2.)

In any event, I disagree with Engster about the absolute importance of actual results to an ethics of care and don't believe that the focus the present approach places on motivation leads to unintuitive results. Quite to the contrary, I think the present approach does justice to the somewhat complex and subtle understanding most of us have about the connection between morality, motivation, and consequences.

But let me now take up another issue concerning international justice and its relation to considerations of empathy. As we saw earlier when discussing religious toleration, anger and hatred can lessen or interfere with one's empathy for others, and this can occur in the sphere of international relations almost as easily as it can closer to home. Nowadays (perhaps more than in the recent past) there is great religious intolerance between Christians and Muslims (or Islamists) and a great deal of hatred and anger, too, as a result of occurrences in the international sphere. The West or at least many Americans are angry about 9/11, and that anger has fed Western intolerance toward Islam and its adherents. By the same token, many Muslims are furious about Western actions or interventions in the Middle East, and there is less empathy than one could hope for on both sides. I don't want to cast or apportion blame for this terrible state of affairs, but I do want to mention one implication of our care ethics that bears on issues of morality and (international) justice in present circumstances.

As I mentioned earlier (in a note in chapter 7), some of the studies of empathy that Martin Hoffman mentions in *Empathy and Moral Development* demonstrate that and how empathy can be attenuated or undercut when one is angry with another person. If someone injures me or someone I love or care about, then my anger at them or at what they have done can make me less empathic about them and less concerned to help them, *and this is part and parcel of the way empathy works*. In that case, if someone exhibits less concern for another person because she is angry with the person, that may not show that she lacks a fully developed capacity for (or sense of) empathy or empathic concern for other people. And given our sentimentalist account of morality as based in empathy, that may help to explain why we believe that one's obligations to help another person or persons may be lessened or obliterated if they have injured one (or one's friends or people in general). By the same token, someone who can be empathic and caring about a person who has injured her and/or someone dear to her—for example, the mother whose daughter has been killed and who doesn't want the state to impose the death penalty on the person who killed her—may evince a greater developed capacity for empathy than most people could ever achieve or aspire to. So there is or in some circumstances can be something morally supererogatory about such a mother's request/plea that the state not execute her daughter's killer.

These issues blend into issues of criminal justice at a national, international, or even global level, but I don't want to go into those issues here. Nor do I want to get into questions of tort justice. But I believe it should in any case be fairly clear how the view I have been developing would address questions in these areas, and I in any event think it *would* be useful for me now, and by way of concluding the present chapter, to say just a bit about questions of global justice.

Because of the increasing globalization of today's world, many people are nowadays considering and debating the issue of whether we should try to move toward global government and the related issue of whether, even assuming that we can't from where we are successfully move in that direction, such global governance wouldn't or couldn't in principle be superior, in terms of economic efficiency or overall justice, to what we find in the world at present. Obviously, one worry that people have is that a global government that ran amok might terrorize everyone in the world more effectively than anything feasible under the current system of national governments (and limited supranational or international bodies/organizations). Global governance has the potential to create grave injustices beyond any we already find in the world, but still there are potential advantages in such governance that might be thought and have been said to outweigh, from the standpoint of justice, the potential disadvantages. To mention just one obvious example, world hunger might be more effectively and fairly dealt with if the world were better *organized* and if we had a world government that had at least the modicum of concern for all citizens that democratic countries in the present world show (or have shown or can show) toward *their* citizens.

I guess my own response to these issues is somewhat agnostic. But I don't think that calls into doubt the sort of approach I have been taking to political and other moral issues. If one thinks that a care ethics that features empathy can usefully explain and justify features of justice on the present-day national and international landscape, then one can reasonably hope that it will be useful in explaining or clarifying the issues that surround the question of whether we should move toward global government. If it is difficult to resolve that question at this point, that may be because the issues involved are so complex and subject to so many gaps in our empirical/social scientific knowledge. But if we worry about the tyranny of a global government or aspire to such government because of the advantages it could bring for the elimination of world hunger and/or poverty, then I think the considerations that move us are considerations whose moral significance can be unpacked in the terms and via the kind of arguments that we have already seen an ethics of empathic care rely on. But of course, that also means that such an ethics has its work cut out for it in the future. We can see, therefore, that the ethics of care doesn't have to confine its attention to personal morality and relationships: it can speak of social (including legal and economic or distributive) justice in its own terms, and it can extend its reach to questions of international and global justice as well. And what it has to say in these areas will, I think, seem plausible if the care-ethical approach to personal or individual morality is seen as plausible. If anything, the account of justice sketched in this chapter should make the sentimentalist ethics of individual caring action seem *more* plausible by showing that its basic approach needn't be confined to individual matters but can be extended to cover large-scale moral issues as well. But we now need to discuss an important further issue.

I have been using the idea of empathy as a criterion both of individualistically right action and of just social institutions, laws, attitudes, and customs, and this has meant, more specifically, that actions or institutions count as unjust or wrong (or disrespectful) if and only if they reflect or express a lack of full-blown empathic concern for others on the part of relevant individuals or groups of individuals.[22] The previous discussion has at every point conformed to this now more fully explicit normative/moral criterion, but there is an issue that needs to be raised about how the criterion is to be understood, and it concerns potential differences between men's and women's capacity for empathy. In ECE (chapter 5), I indicated that empathy may in fact come slightly less easily to men than to women because of the higher testosterone levels one finds in males through most periods of their lives. I don't want to rehearse the empirical literature on this question here, but I do want to make a couple of points that are relevant to the present discussion.

Even if testosterone makes some sort of difference, men are capable of great empathy, and moral education that worked in the various ways I have described here and that was directed as intensely at boys as at girls could create a situation in which both men and women demonstrated a great deal more empathy than is typical in the world as we know it. Even if women may invariably be capable, on average, of *greater* empathy and empathic concern for others than men are, men and women *have a great common capacity* for empathy, and it makes sense, I think, to set the standard of what counts as fully empathic or counts as a lack of full-blown empathy by reference to that common capacity, rather than, say, holding men to be acting wrongly when they display a slightly lower degree of empathy than women on average are capable of. In any event, the moral development literature doesn't give us any reason to expect these differences to be very large, and if we move in the direction I have suggested, we can also say that (given a common standard or criterion of right and wrong) women are likely to display *supererogatory* degrees of caring and empathy somewhat more often than men. This may well mean that in a sense women are on average morally more capable or better than men, but it will also mean that men have some sort or degree of excuse when, say, testosterone interferes with (the development of) empathy. As I said, I have discussed these issues further in ECE, but for present purposes, the point has been that what I shall mean and have meant by (fully) empathic concern has reference to the large capacities (for empathy) that are common to men and women, rather than to anything that distinguishes or separates the sexes/genders.[23]

Finally, I want to mention an issue that I have not explicitly spoken of in the present book, the issue of whether it is (inherently) irrational to be immoral or act immorally. I discussed this question at some length in ECE (chapter 7) and

---

22. Remember that one doesn't show oneself to be lacking in empathy, or to be a less than fully empathic individual, if one merely is less empathic than certain (highly empathic) people are. A person isn't lacking in talent just because there are people who are more talented, and one can, for example, be a fully capable driver (of cars) without being the most capable driver there is. For more on this point, see ECE, chapter 2.

23. In a review of ECE (*Notre Dame Philosophical Reviews*, http://ndpr.nd.edu/review.cfm?id=12524), Lawrence Blum raised some of the issues I have just been discussing, and I am indebted to him for getting me to be somewhat clearer about the implications of a care ethics based on empathy.

argued that immoral attitudes and actions show (a certain) heartlessness but aren't as such irrational. (The issue whether we have *reason* to be moral is slightly subtler.) My conclusion was very much in keeping with moral sentimentalism, but I don't propose to repeat the arguments here. On the other hand, sentimentalism about morality doesn't commit one to holding (as apparently Hume held) that there is no such a thing as practical reason or rationality outside the moral sphere, and in ECE (also chapter 7) I sought to account for such rationality in terms of sentiments that differ from those that lie at the heart of morality. But once again, I don't think I should repeat that discussion here. Rather, I propose that we now look at some ways in which the notion of empathy, which *does* lie at the heart of morality, can be applied to philosophical issues that are not specifically ethical.

10

EMPATHY, OBJECTIVITY,

AND RATIONALITY

1. Introduction

We have been using the notion or phenomenon of empathy as a foundational basis for understanding metaethics, normative ethics, and their interrelations. But the notion of empathy also has a surprising use and importance in an area or areas of philosophy that lie outside ethics: in epistemology and the philosophy of science. In this final chapter, therefore, I want to go outside or beyond the ethical to consider the role empathy plays in epistemic/theoretical/intellectual/scientific rationality or reasonableness.[1] If the relevance of empathy to political and individual morality entails the relevance and, in fact, the centrality of feeling and emotion—of sentiment—to morality as a whole, then its relevance to intellectual thought and rationality means that feeling and sentiment are crucial, essential to intellectual thought and rationality. And although one nowadays often sees academic thinkers—especially neuroscientists—arguing for this sort of conclusion, I hope and believe that the more philosophical and conceptual discussion of the present chapter will do a better job of demonstrating the sentimental nature of reason (or, if you will, the indivisibility of reason and emotion) than I have seen done in other discussions. In particular, I shall show that the phenomenon of empathy has an important role to play in helping us understand the epistemological ideal and intellectual virtue of objectivity, and

1. I discuss the relationship between empathy and *practical* rationality and sketch a general account of the latter in ECE, chapter 7.

since objectivity is an important part—though hardly the whole—of intellectual and scientific rationality, empathy and sentiment will turn out to be essential to rationality as well. We normally think of reason and emotion as in some sense separate, but if I am on the right track, it turns out that certain kinds of sentiment or emotion are *part* of rationality, of being rational.

Let's begin by recalling some of the discussion of earlier chapters. It has been argued, for example, that arrogantly dismissive and intolerant attitudes toward other people's ways of life or religions clearly express both a lack of empathy toward them and what we would naturally say was a lack of respect for them. But those who are arrogant and intolerant toward others also typically hate and/ or are angry with those others. Religious persecution has often been said (by those who ought to know better) to be based on a desire for the salvation and well-being of those being persecuted and even tortured, but as John Locke, in the *Second Essay on Government*, wittily and wisely points out, the "dry eyes" of the torturers and persecutors refute the notion that they are motivated by concern for people's well-being. And as I said, it seems as if religious intolerance and worse are typically based on a kind of hatred or anger. This connects with issues of empathy, because anger and hatred drive out empathy, make empathy with those one hates or is angry with either difficult or impossible.

This has a bearing on what we have to say about the connection between empathy and intellectual, epistemic, critical, theoretical, or scientific objectivity. Since anger and hatred toward those one disagrees with intuitively seem incompatible with being objective about their opinions, it would seem that a degree of empathy incompatible with great anger and hatred is a necessary condition of being objective regarding the viewpoints or opinions of others, and that idea gets us part of the way toward a major thesis of this chapter: namely, that objectivity with respect to ideas, facts, and/or arguments is basically and solely a matter of being empathic in certain (as yet here unspecified) ways. But let me not anticipate too much at this point. We have a lot more to consider and argue for before we can be in a position to maintain that general thesis, so let me continue.

As I mentioned in chapter 8, substitute success syndrome (sss) parents tend to create children who doubt themselves and their own ideas and aspirations, children who, to that extent, are lacking in the kind of intellectual and orectic/ volitional autonomy we think is desirable and even necessary to (an) adult (kind of) life. And as we also saw, what sss parents do to their children (of either sex) is what, arguably, is generally done to little girls and women under patriarchy. As Carol Gilligan points out in *In a Different Voice*, patriarchy tends to deprecate women's and girls' opinions and aspirations.[2] Thus, if the nineteenth-century girl says she thinks it is unfair that she can't attend a university, she may be told: "You can't really believe that (you're not the kind of ungrateful girl who thinks things like that); you know that your brother needs to go to a university in order

---

2. *In a Different Voice: Psychological Theory and Women's Development* (Cambridge: Harvard University Press, 1982).

to have a profession but that your place is in the home." Her viewpoint, her idea, her incipient belief in the unfairness of the system gets nipped in the bud through such statements, which are practically as likely to have come from a nineteenth-century mother as from a father. But in crushing the girl's thought, the system also crushes her aspirations, as, for example, when the girl who says she wants to become a doctor is told, not perhaps that she can't attend a university (which might even no longer be true), but that she would *really* (wouldn't she?) rather be a nurse than be a doctor, which is such an unfeminine profession for a woman.

As Gilligan puts it, women and girls under patriarchy learn to distrust or dismiss their own voices, and they consequently lack the autonomy that men more typically have in such conditions. This, too, and as we shall see better in what follows, bears on the issue of how objectivity and empathy connect. Those who doubt their every thought can no more be objective about evidence, arguments, or ideas than those who are so filled with contempt, hatred, or arrogance toward those they are interacting with that they cannot pay serious attention to what those others are saying or arguing. But to demonstrate the crucial role empathy plays in (someone's) being objective, we need to discuss what sorts of entities or mental states can be the focus or subject of empathic reactions.

2. The Focus of Empathy

The kind of objectivity I want to talk about here is not the objectivity *of* matters of fact or things in the world, but objectivity in thinking and arguing *about* matters of fact and, also, of speculation.[3] We have seen that emotions like anger work against and/or undercut both empathy and objectivity, and I have said (though more needs to be and later will be said about this) that the unempathic way in which women and girls are treated under patriarchy (and in which sss parents treat their children) makes them incapable, to a large extent, of objective thinking. I want to eventually defend the idea that the idea of empathy is crucial to and, suitably supplemented, sufficient for understanding what it is to be epistemically or scientifically objective about things. But this major conclusion depends on a proper understanding of what one can be empathic with. I want to claim that an objective person, a person thinking objectively, will be empathic with the point of view of those, for example, whom she disagrees with (and may be engaged in discussions with). However, some readers may wonder whether it is really possible to empathize with a point of view or set of beliefs different from one's own. For them, the idea of empathy with hedonic, orectic, or emotional

---

3. We also sometimes speak of or question the objectivity *of some body of knowledge*, but that, again, isn't the same thing as talking about how objective someone is with respect to such a body of knowledge. I am assuming, by the way, that objective or rationally justified knowledge is possible in certain areas. Regardless of whether that is true, the assumption allows me to more easily make the distinctions I am interested in here.

states or processes makes immediate sense, but they may be less sure about empathy with states or processes that are strictly intellectual and don't (clearly) involve any kind of feeling or conation. We need to address this issue.

As we saw in chapter 1, Martin Hoffman thinks it is possible to empathize with a person's bad situation or condition, even if the person is temporarily enjoying himself or in a good mood—recall his description of empathy with the unwitting victim of terminal cancer. But it could be suggested that such empathy depends on empathizing with the feelings, desires, and misery one knows the person with the cancer will soon or eventually undergo and so is anchored in actual *future* hedonic, emotional, and/or orectic states. However, once one grants the possibility of the kind of case Hoffman talks about, it seems possible to imagine our feeling empathic sadness for someone who doesn't know they are about to die, even supposing that they will *never* know or suffer "what hit them." One has to work a bit to construct such an example, but imagine, for instance, that we somehow learn that a coworker of ours is about to die painlessly from leaked gas in a way that that person doesn't anticipate and that we can do nothing to prevent. Presumably, we can feel empathy for the coworker even though (we may know that) the person we are empathizing with will feel no relevant later pain, frustrated desire, or fearful emotion for us to empathize with. Hoffman says that the ability to feel empathy with other people independently of their present actual feelings is an ability that develops as a child becomes more intellectually or cognitively capable, and perhaps this is also true of the sort of more extreme case I have just described. If so, then one can to a substantial extent empathize with someone's situation or condition independently of what they actually will ever feel (hedonically or emotionally) or desire.

But the person who thinks empathy needs to be anchored in such felt/orectic states might still want to claim that when, for example, we feel empathically sad in thinking about a person who is about to die from leaked gas, we are feeling empathy for the pain or emotion we imagine they *would* feel if they only knew what was about to happen to them (or if the gas only injured rather than killed them). And I don't know really how to argue against this last-ditch refusal to allow (for) empathy with a person's or persons' objective condition or situation. I feel inclined to say that once one allows that there can be empathy with merely hypothetical or potential feelings, empathy has become sufficiently sophisticated to also take on or take in nonhedonic and other situations or conditions *more directly*.[4]

Now the issue or problem that arises for (the possibility of) intellectual empathy—by which I mean empathy with another person's state of (non-

---

4. In "Empathy and Universalizability" (*Ethics* 105 [1995]), John Deigh sees adult empathy as focusing on and sensitive both to general facts about human life and its vicissitudes and to instantiations of those facts in individual lives and circumstances. This seems to allow the focus of empathy to reach out to objective factors that aren't reducible to sheer feelings or hedonic/orectic states.

evaluative) belief or knowledge or with their intellectual/scientific/cognitive point of view—is actually a bit different from the issue we have just been talking about. We have been speaking about the possibility of empathy in cases where the person we are empathizing with will have relevant feelings or desires only *later* or merely *would* have such feelings or desires in imaginable hypothetical circumstances. But the immediate issue for someone who doubts the possibility of intellectual empathy is whether there is enough affective/orectic/hedonic content to (nonevaluative) states of knowledge/belief or (nonevaluative) intellectual points of view to allow there to be empathy with such states or points of view. Nonetheless, what we said about the kinds of cases discussed earlier carries over to some extent to the purely intellectual cases. If (as the discussion at least tentatively concluded) we can relevantly empathize with someone independently of their actual present or future feelings, desires, and so on, it would also seem possible to empathize with someone's present nonaffective, nonhedonic, nonorectic intellectual/cognitive state or processes. And if someone says that the former kind of case depends on empathizing with possible or hypothetic affective and the like reactions to a condition or situation, we can similarly say—and this is a new theme—that empathy with other people's cognitive states can work through empathy with the affective/hedonic/orectic reactions that naturally go with such cognitive states. For example, if I accept a certain scientific hypothesis, I may want to do experiments that test or support it and may feel displeasure when I hear that others right now maintain a contrary view. And one might say that our ability to empathize with states of cognition and purely intellectual points of view depends on such likely or hypothetical affective/hedonic/orectic reactions to what is in itself purely cognitive or intellectual.

In what immediately follows, however, I want to strengthen the case for empathy with what is intellectual or cognitive by pointing out how natural and easy it is to think of people as empathizing with this "side" of another person's life or psychology. And I shall go on to argue additionally that it may not, in fact, be possible (for humans) to hold intellectual positions independently of relevant affect and the like. All of this will help clear the way toward the view it is my purpose to defend here, the view that intellectual/epistemic objectivity can be explained in terms of empathy.

To begin on a personal note, the idea that objectivity might relate to empathy first began to take root in me when it one day occurred to me that I was empathizing with certain people's ignorance or lack of knowledge of the English language. Without thinking about it, I was adjusting my vocabulary in speaking to native Spanish speakers who didn't know a great deal of English. This seemed to me to involve, on my part, a process or state of empathic sensitivity, but it also seemed clear or likely that I wasn't empathizing with my interlocutors' affective states and the like. Of course, it is possible that native Spanish speakers in this country feel embarrassed and fearful speaking with a native English speaker and that I was empathizing with such feelings rather than with their lack of knowledge of the English language. But I don't think this is what was happening. My experience in Miami tells me that native Spanish speakers don't fear conversation with speakers of English, because the lack of knowledge of English isn't much of a disadvantage here and because the city of Miami nowadays belongs at least as much to those who know Spanish as to those who know English. These are facts that native Spanish speakers are as well aware of as I am, so I don't think my empathy with the lack of knowledge of English some of them demonstrate is a function of empathy with their negative feelings (or, for that matter, their positive feelings) about speaking with a native English speaker. Rather, I think what happens when I pretty much unconsciously adjust my speaking vocabulary to someone's lesser knowledge of English is exactly what I was first inclined to think it is, a state or process of empathy with and/or sensitivity to another person's cognitive state(s) or processes.

So apart from our earlier arguments concerning the possibility of empathy with unwitting victims of cancer or poisonous gas, it seems to me commonsensical to suppose that I sometimes (or often) empathize with other people's cognitive states, and I am sure that I and others could find many other commonplace examples of this phenomenon.[5] And if we can empathize with cognitive states independently of other people's emotional/hedonic/orectic states or processes, then it should be possible to empathize with another person's intellectual point of view, assuming that such points of view are also independent of emotional/hedonic/orectic states of processes: in other words, assuming that such points of view are purely or exclusively intellectual or theoretical. But a point of view is different from the kind of cognitive state I was registering when, at different times, I implicitly adjusted my spoken vocabulary to the linguistic knowledge or ignorance of a native Spanish speaker. Linguistic knowledge doesn't in any ordinary or obvious way involve making assumptions or claims about facts or values or anything else, but this is precisely what *is* involved when one adopts or has a certain point of view. A point of view involves making certain assumptions or claims in a way linguistic knowledge and ignorance both seem not to do, and yet many would say that just as linguistic knowledge doesn't have to involve any emotions, desires, or hedonic reactions, neither does an intellectual point of view, and neither do particular intellectual/theoretical assumptions, doubts, or beliefs. But I have doubts about this.

It seems to me possible, even likely, that the making of intellectual assumptions, the having of theoretical beliefs, and more synoptically, the adoption or possession of an intellectual/scientific/philosophical viewpoint all do involve emotional and/or hedonic and/or orectic states or reactions. And by using the term *involve* here, I mean to talk about what is conceptually or constitutively

---

5. The one place I know of where this phenomenon is mentioned is Frans de Waal's *Our Inner Ape* (New York: Riverhead Books, 2005), 6f. But the example he gives is far from commonplace: in an effort to illustrate the great empathic capacities of bonobos, he describes a bonobo, Kanzi, who was on a given occasion empathically sensitive to his sister's (state of) ignorance of various facts and who tried to help her learn more.

involved in a phenomenon rather than (merely) of what is causally involved or involved as a matter of scientific fact when rational beings adopt or possess an intellectual viewpoint or single intellectual belief. So I am asking, or considering, whether there really is such a thing as a purely intellectual viewpoint, belief, assumption, or doubt, and saying that I am to some extent inclined to think not. But to give my reasons, I think I need at this point to bring in some interesting work that Michael Stocker has done in this area.

In "Intellectual Desire, Emotion, and Action," Stocker discusses the ways in which our involvement in intellectual topics and/or disciplines calls upon and requires various emotions, desires, and even actions.[6] If, say, we are scientists, we will *want to know* the answer to certain questions, will in better or worse ways *investigate* certain issues, and will *want to know* how certain experiments we or others do come out. And according to Stocker, our emotions or attitudes are also involved in pursuing science and other supposedly pure intellectual activities, since, when we have no sympathy with a certain area or line of scientific inquiry, we don't get involved in it, and since, when we have *a great deal of* sympathy or respect for what is being said in a given discipline, we don't want, and don't summon the energy, to call its previous findings or present assumptions into question.

All this seems plausible to me, and for present purposes I just want to generalize and/or reconfigure it a bit. Stocker mostly focuses on good or bad intellectual traits like laziness or energy and how they bear on one's devotion to and pursuit of various intellectual/scientific disciplines, and he mentions the emotions involved in accepting a given intellectual position or belief only once or twice. The examples of sympathy and its absence mentioned previously are in fact the only clear examples he gives of emotions tied to particular viewpoints or assumptions, but it is viewpoints or assumptions acquired or maintained in the doing of science (or the pursuit of other intellectual activities), rather than the (mere) fact of energetically or nonenergetically, carefully or carelessly, doing science, that bear most directly on one's objectivity. A lack of energy, or of intelligence, or of ingenuity, or (perhaps even) of carefulness in the pursuit of a discipline doesn't call one's objectivity into question. Rather, objectivity depends on the way one arrives at and defends various assumptions, beliefs, or whole points of view. And emotions and desires are certainly relevant here, both to the objectivity of one's beliefs and the like and to one's actually acquiring or maintaining them. We need to consider the latter point first.

If a person accepts a certain point of view, then we say that the person favors that viewpoint over others. Now outside the area of supposedly pure intellect or science, favoring one thing or person over another involves a *feeling* or *attitude* of greater liking, and unless the defender of pure intellect wants to say that our use of similar language regarding scientific/intellectual viewpoints (sets of beliefs

6. In Amelie Rorty, ed., *Explaining Emotions* (Berkeley: University of California Press, 1980), 323–338.

and assumptions) and regarding particular beliefs/assumptions is strictly meta-phorical, the fact that we say that those who accept certain viewpoints or assumptions *favor* them indicates that there is no such thing as purely intellectual science or purely intellectual work in other disciplines either. But to take refuge in the charge of metaphoricalness seems to me at least to be question-begging. One says such a thing because one wants to maintain that there is such a thing as purely intellectual activity, and what seems more plausible, given the ways we naturally think and speak about these matters, is that both intellectual activities and nonintellectual ones involve emotions, attitudes, or feelings that are in effect unavoidable wherever and whenever human beings are involved in any sort of practical enterprise.

This idea has (at least) two important implications. It means that our worries, to the extent we have had them, about whether one can empathize with purely intellectual states of belief or processes of belief formation are unnecessary because there are, in the human case at least, no such things. (Even total skepticism involves feelings or attitudes toward certain assumptions and the belief some people have in those assumptions, and presumably even Karl Popper *favored* the idea that scientists shouldn't favor/accept hypotheses, but only try to disconfirm them.) And it also permits us, if we want, to think of empathy with states of belief or points of view as latching onto these things through or by means of the affective/orectic states that invariably accompany or help constitute them. We don't *have* to make this claim, but we can or could, and given what we have been saying over the last few paragraphs, we are now in a position to explore and defend the idea that objectivity rests on empathy.[7]

3.   Objectivity Based in Empathy

As I mentioned earlier, intellectual objectivity isn't so much a matter of cognitive states generally but, rather, of how one acquires and, I think, most particularly, of how one maintains certain beliefs. Knowing or not knowing English is certainly a cognitive distinction, but a person's objectivity doesn't at all depend on whether they know English or Spanish—it depends rather on how they maintain beliefs (or doubts). There are, as I shall now argue, more or less

---

7. In chapter 6, we mentioned and discussed Hume's view that one can take in or imbibe the opinions of others via mechanisms of empathy. But this doesn't necessarily support the idea that one can have empathy with purely theoretical/cognitive states because Hume had such a sentimentalist view of what opinions and cognitions generally amount to. However, even if we don't assume a generally sentimentalist view of cognition(s), it does seem as if we can take in or empathize with the opinions of those around us, and I appealed to that fact in chapter 6, in arguing for the usefulness of second-person moral injunctions. It may be unclear whether this empathy has to latch on to some emotion or feeling that is (metaphysically) separate from the injunctions/opinions themselves, but it does increasingly seem clear that we can *somehow* empathize with other people's opinions and points of view.

empathic ways of maintaining beliefs, and *those distinctions*, I shall argue, are the ones that determine whether one is or is being objective with regard to a given intellectual or nonintellectual subject matter. (I hesitate to contrast intellectual subject matters with practical ones, given the naturalness of supposing, as Stocker and I here have in effect argued, that even intellectual subject matters involve us in practical, in the sense of action-oriented, questions and decisions.)

We already anticipated this idea to some extent when we earlier spoke of the ways in which anger with other people's beliefs or viewpoints (and with the other people) can undercut both empathy and objectivity regarding those beliefs or viewpoints. The Spanish Inquisitors obviously lacked both empathy and objectivity with respect to (the viewpoints or beliefs of) those they persecuted, tortured, and tried to convert, and hatred and contempt for those who disagreed with them may have played a major role in producing or constituting that lack of empathy and objectivity. It is perhaps also worth noting that at the present historical juncture, the hatred many Muslims feel toward the West (because of the situation of the Palestinians, because of American interference in Iranian political life decades ago, and for other reasons) and the hatred many Westerners who are not Muslims feel toward Islam (because of 9/11, because of Muslim Holocaust denial, and for other reasons) make it nearly impossible for either side to be empathic with or objective about the other side's point of view. This fact, if it is one, is tragic.

However, there are examples of a lack or absence of objectivity that don't seem to involve emotions as strong as hatred or contempt, and these, too, I think, can be understood in terms of issues of empathy or its absence. In the field of philosophy, for example, there can be disagreements and disputes where it seems (at least to outsiders) that neither side really understands or has tried to understand what the other side is saying (or the other side's intellectual point of view). Such cases, I think, are naturally and plausibly regarded as involving a lack of empathy on both sides for the other side's point of view (alternatively, an empathic inability or failure to see things from the other's side's point of view). For example, neither side may ever actually state the other side's views in an accurate way, a way that the other side would acknowledge as acceptable. And neither side may be *capable* of doing this, in part, presumably, because their strong or rigid commitment to their own point of view makes them not want to see things through the eyes or intellect of someone who totally disagrees with them. Doesn't it seem plausible to say that in such cases neither side is being (completely) objective about the issues that divide them? I think that it *is* plausible to say this, and in that case, we have another instance of how a failure or lack of empathy undercuts objectivity.

But notice what all this entails. Objectivity requires one to be able, and in various situations actually, to empathize with another person's intellectual point of view, and, given what I have been saying, seeing another person's position or argument from that person's point of view means empathically (i.e., through empathy) seeing it in something like the favorable light in which the other person sees it. And that, in turn, means having a certain kind of (possibly mild) favorable emotion toward it. So being intellectually/epistemically/scientifically rational and objective really does require having certain emotions.[8]

It is important to realize, moreover, that a theory that treats empathy as crucial to (and, as we shall see later, sufficient for) being objective doesn't entail that objectivity will eventually lead to agreement. Just as a fully empathic mother may end up taking her protesting child to the dentist's (even while feeling bad about having to do so), so, too, I think, may someone who has fully empathized with the point of view of those who disagree with her still end up disagreeing with them. This often *won't* happen because getting better acquainted with the point of view of those with whom one initially disagrees may lead one to modify one's position or at least (and this is really in a way the same thing) how one defends that position. But it seems plausible to suppose that one might empathize with a different point of view without essentially modifying one's own position, and that possibility means that objectivity, as I am conceiving and describing it, doesn't require or entail eventual agreement among all those who (continue to) think about or discuss a certain issue—a consequence of my position that seems to me to be very desirable.[9]

But to complete our basic picture of the relation between empathy and intellectual objectivity, we have to consider whether empathy is sufficient, not just required, for objectivity. The plausible assumption that objectivity doesn't require eventual agreement is helpful to us here, because empathy clearly isn't sufficient for eventual agreement. But the following kind of example might

---

8. I won't try to say how long the empathy and emotions required by objectivity have to last.

9. Objectivity may require one to modify how one defends one's position in the face of criticisms/ideas deployed from a viewpoint inconsistent with one's own (though I am not talking about anything crazy like the belief that the world is about to end). Now in the *Metaphysics of Morals* (*Doctrine of Virtue*, paragraph 39), Kant says that paying respect to another in conversation means understanding that there is some merit in their ideas. And if we accept this, it would seem that changing how one defends one's views involves acknowledging some sort of merit in another person's ideas and to that extent respecting them. But if objectivity in some sense requires respecting other people's ideas, that in no way works against the idea that objectivity is based in empathy. In an intellectual context, I want to say, empathy with ideas or viewpoints *is* (a form of) respect, and this is very much in keeping with the view of respect for others I defended in chapter 8. What we have been saying also provides something of an answer to Jerome Schneewind's claim (in "The Misfortunes of Virtue," *Ethics* 101 [1990]: 42–63) that virtue theory discourages those who are (presumed) virtuous from according respect to differing points of view: discourages them from really listening to what those who disagree with them on moral questions have to say. The theory of the present book is virtue-ethical in a sentimentalist way, but it clearly doesn't fit Schneewind's picture at all (nor does it particularly encourage people to think of themselves as virtuous).

The present discussion, finally, also suggests a parallel between what I said about justice in chapter 9 and what can be said about justice in intellectual contexts. Being objective in empathic terms is tantamount to doing intellectual justice to other people's points of view, and chapter 9 argued that justice as a moral ideal is also a matter of appropriate forms of *empathic* concern among individuals or governments. Intellectual and moral respect, and intellectual and moral justice, center around our capacity, respectively, for intellectual empathy and for human-welfare-oriented moral empathy.

make one wonder whether empathy was in fact sufficient for objectivity. Imagine that someone is obtuse about accumulating or weighing scientific or other data and ends up with a totally (in intellectual terms) unjustified theory or set of beliefs. Such a person doesn't show or indicate any lack of empathy for anyone else's intellectual viewpoint and, in fact, may not have ever interacted with anyone else in the area where he makes his findings, yet he has shown a great intellectual deficiency in coming to the views he now maintains.

But nothing we have said about this person indicates that his intellectual deficiency or failing is one of objectivity, rather than, say, one of deficient intelligence or imagination. We have to add that the obtuse person who comes to various conclusions doesn't care, for example, that others might or would find his methods or conclusions dubious to make the accusation of nonobjectivity stick, but once we do that, we seem to be ascribing to the person a lack of empathy for the point(s) of view from which others might or would criticize him. He is insouciant or careless about what others may think, and this is a failure of empathy. But when someone *is* empathic with another viewpoint, she won't count as lacking objectivity with respect to that viewpoint, even if she is obtuse or unintelligent with regard to it. Objectivity is not, I am assuming, the only element in being rational and thinking rationally, so when I say that a certain kind of empathy is sufficient for one's being objective, I am not saying that it is sufficient for every other intellectual virtue or (thus) sufficient for full or complete intellectual/scientific rationality.[10]

Given our conclusions about the cases we have discussed, the presence or absence of intellectual, epistemic, or scientific objectivity seems, more generally, to be less a matter of how one actually acquires a given belief or viewpoint than of how one is prepared to defend one's views in the light of others' dissent from (or reluctance to accept) them. In that measure, being objective turns out to be more a *reactive* matter than one might have initially supposed. The old adage "a word to the wise is sufficient" in effect characterizes wisdom in terms of its reactive tendencies, its reactions to(ward) good advice, and though this may or may not be the whole of *wisdom*, I do want to maintain, and in the light of our discussion I don't think it is implausible to maintain, that intellectual/theoretical/epistemic/scientific objectivity *is* essentially a matter of how one empathically reacts or would react to what others think and say. (I shall have more to say about this later.)

But what about those who, because of the depredations of patriarchy or of sss parents, are so intellectually self-doubting and selfless that they can't properly weigh other people's opinions or their own? Well, I don't know what to say

---

10. I am indebted to Seisuke Hayakawa on the subject of the distinction between objectivity and other aspects of rationality. For the opposed view that rationality and objectivity (in science) amount to pretty much the same thing, see Nicholas Rescher, *Objectivity: The Obligations of Impersonal Reason* (Notre Dame, Ind.: University of Notre Dame Press, 1997). But I think treating objectivity, being objective, as just one element in being rational comes closer to ordinary thought and usage. (*Objective* and *unbiased* come closer to being synonyms than *rational* and *unbiased* do.) Furthermore, I assume that both objectivity and being rational come in degrees, and my approach would allow for this.

about the empathic capacities of such people. On the one hand, their selflessness might be thought to make them extremely empathic with, even to the point of always accepting, what other people think, and since this doesn't seem to be a way of being objective about either one's own beliefs or those of others, our account might at this point seem to be in a certain amount of trouble. However, as we saw Hoffman point out earlier, empathy isn't a kind of merging or melting into another, so the intellectually selfless might really seem to lack all empathy and objectivity as well.[11] This would make our theory seem to apply comfortably to such people (though we can't be comfortable with their intellectual or other fate). But there is a further point.

Whatever we say about the empathy or lack of empathy that intellectually selfless people have, we *have* argued that such selflessness is typically produced by a person's being raised by nonempathic sss parents or by a girl or woman's having been raised in a patriarchal environment (including a home) that frequently demonstrates a lack of empathy for girls' or women's desires, ideas, and aspirations. So even if we were to say that the intellectually selfless are (in an extreme and undesirable way) empathic with other people's points of view and yet deficient in intellectual objectivity, we could use the notion of empathy to offer a humanly sufficient condition of someone's being objective by saying that it is both necessary and sufficient for objectivity that one (be able to) empathize fully with other people's points of view and that one have been raised in an empathic way that allows one to be confident, though not rigid or arrogant, about one's own beliefs and aspirations. Since empathy is central to both the (supposedly necessary) conditions just mentioned, we would have made good on the promise to offer an account of objectivity in terms of empathy. But if, for the reasons just mentioned, the second conjunct of this equation turns out to be unnecessary, then the first conjunct may be able to do the job of characterizing objectivity in terms of empathy and do so in a simpler or more unified way than the conjunctive account would allow.

4. Objectivity and Empathic Concern

I have sketched a theory of objectivity, of what is required for someone to count as being objective in some area or areas, in terms of empathy, and along the way I mentioned the problems that arise for us humans when we are incapable of being empathic with one another's viewpoints. The current opposition or enmity that exists between Islam and the West (if that is a proper characterization of the

---

11. In a forthcoming dissertation, Kristin Borgwald says that such people lack *epistemic personhood*, an idea that is modeled on and in some way parallels what people have said about moral personhood. If full empathy requires a full, nonmerged *person* to do the empathizing, then Borgwald's idea supports the notion that the intellectually selfless aren't empathic with the viewpoint of others.

present state of things in the world) is an unfortunate fact for humanity, or so at least I believe (others may disagree). That state prevents or works against intellectual empathy between the two sides, but it also prevents or works against empathic concern for the (nonintellectual) well-being of those on the other side. In other words, and assuming the present theory together with what I argued in earlier chapters, hatred and a lack of empathy make it difficult or impossible for people to be *intellectually/critically objective* about each other's viewpoints or beliefs and also make it difficult or impossible to be *morally concerned* about the others' welfare or happiness. (By the same token, the presence of empathy also makes it possible to live in just and continuing peace with other people even though one doesn't agree with them about important matters.) Thus empathy is necessary to the fulfillment of both intellectual and moral ideals or objectives, and it therefore has an even larger human role to play than anything I said in earlier chapters perhaps indicated.[12]

The idea that empathy plays an important role in overcoming or preventing hatred and conflict between individuals or (very large) groups of individuals is familiar from the literature of psychology and of the specialized field of conflict resolution. And the related idea that empathy makes it easier to overcome disagreements and come to peaceable, constructive, or useful agreements is also a truism of that literature.[13] But unlike philosophy and philosophers, those who write and publish in these fields don't particularly focus on the issue of objectivity, so it is a distinctive feature of the present discussion that it ties empathy not merely to conflict resolution and to overcoming differences or disagreements but to the philosophically and, as we have seen, humanly important notion of objectivity as well.

But note further that if empathy is a key ingredient in objectivity, it will sometimes be difficult to know whether someone is being or has been objective in thinking about a given subject matter. Sometimes we can tell what someone is thinking or feeling, but at other times it is difficult or impossible to do so, and

12. Objectivity probably shouldn't be regarded as an absolute or unconditional human ideal, because there are times when we would rather see people be loving and act lovingly than be objective. In *Morals from Motives* (New York: Oxford University Press, 2001, chapter 5), I argued that a parent, say, who genuinely loves a son or daughter won't and can't, at least initially, be entirely objective about evidence that indicates that that child has done something horrible or criminal. The parent will give the child more benefit of the doubt than an objective observer knowing all the same facts would, and if one can't in general be both completely objective and fully loving, then perhaps it is better not to be completely objective. (This means that the Enlightenment ideal of critical detachment/objectivity about all beliefs and ideas needs at the very least to be qualified.) Note that in a situation where one isn't objective about the issue of what one's son or daughter has actually done, one isn't going to be empathic with the point of view of an objective observer who thinks one's child *has* done something criminal or horrible. In fact, one is likely to be angry with such a person.

13. For two examples of the discussion and defense of these ideas, see R. Lulofs and D. Cahn, *Conflict: From Theory to Action* (Boston: Allyn and Bacon, 2000), chapters 11–12; and J. Zubek, D. Pruitt, R. Peirce, N. McGillicuddy, and H. Syna, "Disputant and Mediator Behaviors Affecting Short-Term Success in Mediation," *Journal of Conflict Resolution* 36 (1992): 546–572.

these differences and difficulties clearly carry over to empathy. Someone might seem to be taking in and seriously considering an intellectual opponent's viewpoint and ideas but actually be deeply resistant to doing so, and so be either deceiving others or taken in himself about how objective he is being about some intellectual issue. And (as Harvey Siegel has pointed out to me) we can even more easily run into epistemological difficulties of this kind in cases of historical knowledge. When Lorentz, whose transformations allowed the difficulties in physics that eventually led to the special theory of relativity to be handled on an ad hoc basis, saw Einstein's theory, he rejected it and gave various arguments for doing so. But (today) we may never know whether he did so for good reasons that had force at the time or whether he was simply too resistant to changing his own ideas (and giving so much credit to Einstein) to give Einstein a fair or objective hearing. (Egotism can interfere with empathic objectivity as easily as it can interfere with proper empathic moral concern for the plight of another individual.) In any event, the assumption that it can be difficult to know how objective someone is being or was in the past is no more implausible than similar assumptions about moral goodness and even rightness.

It is frequently difficult to know a person's motives, and even with regard to a matter as seemingly simple as someone's handing another adult a glass of wine, we may not be sure whether they are trying to poison or trying to revive that other person. On our sentimentalist account of morality, that would make it difficult to know whether the person who hands the glass of wine is acting rightly, but common sense would make a similar judgment about such a case, and more generally, it doesn't go against common sense to suppose that it is often difficult to know whether a particular person is acting rightly (or praiseworthily). The analogous assumption about the frequent difficulty of knowing whether someone is being objective is also entirely commonsensical, and I have raised the issue of our knowledge of objectivity and of moral rightness/goodness, not because it creates difficulties for the present approach that need somehow to be answered, but because it usefully places what we have been saying within a certain kind of epistemological context.[14]

14. Harvey Siegel has pointed out to me one interesting *disanalogy* between the way I am treating morality and the way I am treating intellectual rationality. On my view, empathic caringness is sufficient for someone to count as a morally decent person, but empathicness vis-à-vis other people's ideas and points of view, while sufficient for objectivity, *isn't* sufficient to guarantee that someone is intellectually rational. Once again, though, this seems fairly commonsensical. Aristotle may have regarded a high degree of intelligence and intellectual skillfulness as necessary to ethical virtue, but we nowadays (more democratically and like Kant) hold that such intelligence and skill isn't necessary to moral decency or goodness. We think, rather, that moral goodness and decency are more a matter of the heart and that, therefore, the capacity for being moral isn't widely denied to people because they aren't smart or intellectually agile enough. But we regard intellectual/scientific rationality somewhat differently and as, in particular, depending on an individual's having a degree of intelligence and intellectual agility that may not be all that widespread. (We think people who are taken in by the Monte Carlo fallacy are lacking in rationality, even though most or many people *are* taken in by it.)

5. Relational Objectivity

I would like next to draw out some of the implications of our earlier claim that intellectual/scientific objectivity is a matter of how one reacts or would react to what others say and think. To see or treat objectivity in this way is to regard it as an essentially relational phenomenon and to hold a *relational theory of objectivity*, and of course, this is more than a little reminiscent of the relational theory of autonomy we described and defended in chapter 8. In both cases, empathy plays a crucial role in the relationality, and in both cases the theory being espoused or defended runs counter to a more atomistic or individualistic traditional conception or theory (or set of such).

Autonomy is traditionally conceived as something that exists *within* the autonomous individual and is not essentially tied to other people. But sentimentalist care ethics stresses our connection to others rather than our separateness, and it naturally gives rise to a relational conception of autonomy (though this isn't and hasn't been an easy thing to work out in philosophical terms). Intellectual objectivity has also been traditionally conceived as something lying totally within the individual, and the relational view of objectivity I have defended also emphasizes connection with others over separateness from others. But of course, empathy tends to bind us to other people, so any theory—whether of autonomy or of objectivity—that makes foundational use of empathy will also place more importance on human connection and relationship than atomistic or individualistic theories that don't refer to empathy ever do.

The theory of objectivity I have offered leaves room for the possibility that intellectual objectivity should be understood not only in terms of certain reactive tendencies but also in terms of the conditions of respect (on the part of others) under which a capacity for intellectual and other sorts of objectivity develops or flourishes. This brings or would bring another empathic and relational element into our understanding of objectivity. But in any event, what we have said about objectivity fits in well with and *finds a place within* the new feminist and care-ethical thinking that emphasizes connection and relationality over atomism and individualism. That is one reason that it seemed to me appropriate (and possibly illuminating) to include that discussion in a book that otherwise focuses almost entirely on moral phenomena.

But while we are on the subject of objectivity and feminist thinking, I want to briefly mention some work that comes quite close to and to some degree anticipates what I have been saying in this chapter. In *Whose Science? Whose*

Finally, I have heard it said (though this isn't something I have seen in print) that empathy is so subjective a phenomenon that it couldn't possibly be the basis for (objectively) valid morality. But if empathy is involved in *being objective*, then the point loses all or most of its force. Think, too, about how odd it would be if genuine morality *didn't* involve a crucially important subjective/personal/psychological element. I am indebted here to Kristin Borgwald.

Knowledge? Thinking from Women's Lives, Sandra Harding argues that objectivity about social phenomena (and also about the physical realm) depends on understanding the point of view of those who are or have been typically excluded from doing science or social science, so that biases, for example, in how or what kind of research is done and in how conclusions are formulated, interpreted, and followed up on, can be identified and corrected.[15] I am not sure I entirely agree with everything Harding says in defense of her conclusions, but they are certainly similar to what we have arrived at here. So even if I emphasize empathy and its emotional aspects more specifically than she does, and even if the arguments I give are in fact quite different from hers, it can make sense to think of her discussion and my own as complementing one another.[16]

However, at this point and by way of concluding this chapter, I want to expand the terms of our discussion a bit. We have been focusing on intellectual/scientific objectivity, but objectivity is arguably a necessary condition of being intellectually/scientifically rational, and in recent years, certain scientific discussions have sought to tie such rationality to the emotions. That possibility needs to be considered in relation to what we have previously been saying.

6. Reason, Emotion, and Science

Over the past decade or so, there has been a lot of talk, speculation, and argument about the possibility that reason and emotion (or feeling) may be inextricably linked. People outside philosophy (most famously, Antonio Damasio)[17] have begun to take seriously the idea that (intellectual) reason may contain or involve emotion or feeling, but there has been a great deal of unclarity here about the exact meaning of this last thesis and about the data or facts that have been said to support it. For example (and this is just one example), if parts of the brain that neuroscientists see as responsible for most emotional functioning also turn out to be involved or activated during what are normally regarded as processes of intellectual or scientific reasoning, does this show that such reasoning is essentially or intrinsically also emotional, or does it merely show that what grounds emotion is somehow also causally, or neurologically, required for reasoning processes to occur? Questions of this sort are difficult to answer, but the approach to objectivity and reason taken in the present chapter doesn't

15. Sandra Harding, *Whose Science? Whose Knowledge? Thinking from Women's Lives* (Ithaca, N.Y.: Cornell University Press, 1991).

16. For ideas that are also related (thought not quite so closely related) to what I have been saying, see Alison Jaggar, "Love and Knowledge: Emotion in Feminist Epistemology," reprinted in A. Garry and M. Pearsall, eds., *Women, Knowledge, and Reality: Explorations in Feminist Philosophy* (Boston: Unwin Hyman, 1989), 129–155.

17. See, for example, his *Descartes' Error: Emotion, Reason, and the Human Brain* (New York: Putnam, 1994). For what it is worth, I find Damasio's specific ideas and arguments difficult to pin down in philosophical terms.

require us to answer them. At the beginning of his article, Stocker says that he is going to show that reason involves feeling or emotion, but the argument he gives is a strictly philosophical or conceptual one that doesn't depend, in any way, on the findings of neuroscience. And following Stocker but using the specific concept of empathy in a way that he didn't, I too have, in effect, given an argument connecting reason and emotion in an essential, internal, or a priori way that doesn't depend on any neuroscientific findings. It seems conceptually or necessarily true to say that intellectual reason or rationality entails or includes intellectual objectivity,[18] and I have argued on basically philosophical grounds that the latter essentially involves certain empathic/emotional tendencies. To that extent, what Stocker and I have said may give more philosophically uncontroversial and solid support to the idea that reason essentially involves emotion than anything that can be found in or that derives from the neuroscience literature.[19]

In recent years, there has been a great deal of empirical work done on empathy (or morality) that is clearly in some sense relevant to the present book. I am not just thinking of the various findings from psychology that I have referred to in illustrating and clarifying many points in my argument. Recent work in neuroscience—most particularly, discoveries about the nature and functioning of mirror neurons—also seems relevant to what I have been saying in this book. It turns out, for instance, that when we empathize (or even just see others acting—but I shall leave this to one side), there is activity in our brains that is rather similar to what is going on in those whose emotions or feelings we are empathizing with, and this fascinating scientific discovery therefore pinpoints the physiological or neurological basis for or underpinnings of the psychological phenomenon of contagion and infusion that occurs when we empathize with another person.[20] The contagion of feeling(s) from one person to another may thus causally depend on the activation of mirror neurons, and this tells us something very interesting about empathy.

18. Objectivity about a given subject matter has traditionally been thought to require a certain kind of emotional detachment from it, and if that is so, then someone who held that rationality doesn't require detachment might object to my claim, in the text, that it is a conceptual truth that intellectual rationality requires intellectual objectivity. But if those who hold that rationality doesn't require emotional detachment buy into the ideas espoused in these pages, they can conceive objectivity as actually requiring a certain kind of emotional *engagement*. In that case, both those who think of objectivity in traditional terms and those who think it requires the kind of emotional engagement that empathy involves will (have to) agree that intellectual rationality entails objectivity according to whatever conception of it is actually correct. So there is in fact no reason to question the brief argument given in the main text.

19. However, something (at the very least) close to this idea is also defended in Jaggar, "Love and Knowledge."

20. On mirror neurons in relation to empathy, see M. Schulte-Reuther, H. Markowitsch, G. Fink, and M. Pieske, "Mirror Neuron and Theory of Mind Mechanisms Involved in Face to Face Interactions: A Functional Magnetic Resonance Imaging Approach to Empathy," *Journal of Cognitive Neuroscience* 19 (2007): 1354–1372.

On the other hand, I don't think we needed to know such empirical facts to be able to give a philosophical account of empathy and its role in morality. So the work and results of neuroscience don't seem essential to what we say in moral philosophy, even if they fill out and help illustrate the views that moral philosophy arrives at. And I think similar things might be said about recent work on the evolution of empathy and on the presence (or absence) of empathy in dolphins, elephants, chimpanzees, bonobos, dogs, and other kinds of "lower" animals.[21] Empirical science has at most an ancillary role in normative ethics and metaethics, and if the ideas and arguments of the present book have succeeded or are on the right track, that has to be primarily for philosophical reasons.[22]

21. On evolution and empathy, see, e.g., Frans de Waal, *Primates and Philosophers: How Morality Evolved* (Princeton, N.J.: Princeton University Press, 2006). But the idea that animals are possessed of empathy doesn't mean very much philosophically or ethically if one doesn't, for theoretical reasons, think empathy plays an important role in morality or the moral life. Kantians who don't believe it plays an important role can say that the existence of empathy-altruism in animals simply illustrates the gap there is between what some higher animals do and what is involved in (true) morality, and one sees something like this attitude, e.g., in Christine Korsgaard's reply to de Waal's ideas (see her "Morality and the Distinctiveness of Human Actions" in de Waal, *Primates and Philosophers*, 98–119). Similarly, even though the present book as a whole is an argument for regarding empathy as crucial to (true) morality, it sees facts about animal empathy as illustrating, rather than as important in making the case for, what it says about morality.

22. For similar ideas on why neuroscience or facts about evolution don't have immediate and definitive relevance to questions about or in ethics, see Larry Temkin's untitled contribution to T. Petersen and J. Ryberg, eds., *Normative Ethics: 5 Questions* (Copenhagen: Automatic Press, 2007), 188ff.

CONCLUSION

In this book, I have discussed normative ethics, metaethics, and moral education in (strictly) sentimentalist terms, and the discussion has at almost every point relied on the concept or phenomenon of empathy. My treatment of normative issues concerning individual right and wrong action borrowed, to some extent, from what I had to say about this subject in *The Ethics of Care and Empathy* [ECE]. But what I said here was supposed to stand on its own, and if the reader thinks, for example, that what was said about deontology in chapter 1 was too brief to be really convincing, I urge them to take a look at the earlier book. Perhaps it will be found to be more persuasive on that, or other, normative topics.

Still, what I said about metaethics in chapters 2 through 5 was supposed to give further support to the ideas about normative ethics that were discussed or reported in chapter 1. If I am right that empathy enters into our understanding of normative moral claims (through its role in moral approval and disapproval), then, given what we know about empathy, we should be able to see *why* (we think that) we have stronger moral obligations to people we know or see than to people we don't know or don't see, *why* (we think that) our moral obligations are self-other asymmetric, and even *why* (we think) it is morally worse to cause pain, harm, or death than to (merely) allow it to occur. In any event, the discussion of respect, autonomy, and justice later in the book was in no way truncated or abbreviated, and what that discussion purports to show is that normative political and social morality can be plausibly understood in sentimentalist terms. Our ideals of justice, for example, can be anchored in the normative idea that actions, laws, customs, and institutions are morally objectionable if and only if they exhibit a lack of full-blown empathic concern for others (on the part of individuals or groups). But all of this normative thought and argument is also supported by what we said in earlier chapters about the meaning of moral terminology. Empathy and concern for others are built into the meaning of terms like *right* and *wrong* (and also *just* and *unjust*)—they are part of how the reference of such terms is conventionally, semantically, fixed. And these semantic facts fit in well with, and clearly support, the kinds of claims I was making at the normative level.

The argument here has overall been more constructive than polemical. I have been trying to show that sentimentalism has much more life in it than people, especially ethical rationalists, have thought. It can answer standard objections to its preferred forms of metaethics and to its account of the moral life, but that doesn't, in and of itself, show that Kantian or some other form of rationalism is inadequate as a general approach to ethics. However, in saying what I have had to say in favor of sentimentalist notions, I have at various points indicated, or insinuated, certain criticisms of the way rationalists approach things, and in the book ECE I made some very pointed direct criticisms of (Kantian) rationalist ideas and arguments.

I questioned, for example, whether we really have reason to believe that it is inherently irrational to act immorally or lack morally decent motives (chapter 7), and I also questioned specific aspects of the typical Kantian/liberal view of our autonomy rights (chapter 5). I probably shouldn't rehearse these arguments here, but I do, at least, want to make it clear that my preference for sentimentalism is based not only on what I hope to have shown to be its strengths as a positive account of normative issues and moral meaning (and moral education) but also on what I take to be some very serious defects or weaknesses in rationalist approaches to ethics. Still, I believe it is more important to be positive about sentimentalism than negative about rationalism, because, as Kuhn tells us, it takes a theory to beat a theory. On its own, no amount of criticism of Kantian/liberal views would or could fully undercut such views, even if they do in fact face worrisome, strong criticisms on a number of fronts. So for those who think sentimentalism makes more sense than rationalism in its currently dominant Kantian/liberal embodiment(s), a positive account of metaethics and ethics in sentimentalist terms and an answer to familiar and standard criticisms of sentimentalism are really indispensable. And those are things I have attempted to supply here. Even in an age (primarily) of rationalism, one can hope that a book like the present one may be able to persuade people to take moral sentimentalism more seriously as an intellectual and philosophical option.

INDEX

CPSIA information can be obtained at www.ICGtesting.com
Printed in the USA
BVOW020403011112

304412BV00002B/1/P